The Bible Dates Itself

The Bible Dates Itself

by Arthur Earle

16418

45 Tulip Circle
Southampton, Pa. 18966

CONTENTS

Charts, Tables, and Illustrations

My special thanks to Dr. Anton Glaser, Rev. Michael Gladish, the faculty, students and librarians of the Academy of the New Church, Bryn Athyn, Penn., for their help and encouragement.

Arthur Earle

Chapter I - THE PROBLEM

Though the Old Testament is primarily regarded as a source of spiritual instruction and wisdom the books from Genesis through II Chronicles present in chronological order the story of a family that grew into a nation, then into an empire. That empire, established by David, lasted through the reign of only one successor, David's son Solomon. When Solomon died the kingdom was divided. Its tributaries soon broke away. There remained two small nations, frequently at war with each other, both at times paying tribute to other nations. Eventually, the northern nation, Israel, was devestated by Assyria. Later, the southern nation, Judah, was conquered and destroyed by Babylon. But in time it was reconstituted as a theocracy, tributary to the empire of Cyrus king of Persia.

Nor is this history undated. On the contrary, the passage of time is repeatedly noted. For twenty-two generations the age of the father is given at the time of the birth of his son. Other figures are given that carry the chronology through the long "sojourn" in Egypt, and the still longer period from the Exodus to the fourth year of Solomon when building of the Temple was begun. Thereafter the length of each king's reign is given until the destruction of Jerusalem by Nebuchadnezzar.

The Bible does not tell us in terms that can be directly related to our own calendar when any of these events took place. But Nebuchadnezzar made a record of his conquest of Jerusalem. That record has been found, impressed in cuneiform characters on a clay tablet that has survived the ages. This record not only confirms the biblical account as authentic history, but enables us to date it precisely.

·It would seem, then, that we could date every other event in the Bible by simply adding the numbers in the text, working back from this date. Unfortunately, it is not that easy. Certain other biblical events can be dated from extra-biblical sources, and the simple addition of the figures provided by the Bible does not produce an accurate correlation.

Furthermore, within the Bible itself anomalies appear. A brief review of just one biblical story will serve to illustrate the difficulty.

Abraham and his wife, Sarah, had a son named Isaac. He married his cousin Rebekah who bore twin sons, Esau and Jacob. When the boys were grown, Esau married a Canaanite girl. This made Isaac and Rebekah unhappy. To make certain Jacob would not marry a Canaanite girl he was sent to the home of his mother's brother Laban in Aram (Syria) to take to wife one of Laban's daughters. Jacob did even better; he acquired four wives——Leah and Rachel who were Laban's

1

daughters, and their two servant girls, Zilpah and Bilhah. These bore him one daughter and twelve sons.

Before the twelfth son, Benjamin, was born, Jacob took his whole family back to Canaan. The last of his sons to be born in Syria was Jacob's favorite, Joseph. When Joseph was still quite young he was taken into Egypt by a band of Midianites and sold into slavery. But Joseph found favor in the eyes of the Pharaoh of Egypt who appointed him to a position of authority.

Later, there was great famine in Canaan and Jacob took his family into Egypt. There they were reunited with Joseph who was able to provide them with food and an area in which they could live and raise cattle. Joseph even introduced his father to Pharaoh, whose name, unfortunately, is not given.

The story is told more dramatically in the Bible, but these are the essential events, and each of them is dated in terms of one or another of the principal characters. Here our concern is with Jacob's age, so we need not start with Abraham, or Isaac, but with Esau and Jacob.

When Esau married he was 40 years old (Gen. 26:34). Since Jacob was Esau's twin, Jacob was 40 when he went to Syria to see his uncle Laban. Jacob stayed with Laban for 20 years (Gen. 31:41). Since Joseph was born in Syria, Jacob could not have been more than 60 years old when Joseph was born. And when Pharaoh appointed Joseph to a position of authority, since Joseph was then 30 years old (Gen. 41:46), Jacob could not have been more than 90.

After Joseph's appointment there were seven good years. Then the famine started. After two years of famine Jacob went down to Egypt (Gen. 45:6). He could not have been more than 99 years old. But he told Pharaoh he was 130 (Gen. 47:9).

How are we to explain this discrepancy? Didn't Jacob know how to count? Did he forget his age? Is there a mistake in the text? Or did Jacob lie to impress the Pharaoh? There is no attractive alternative.

This is only a sample. Many more problems arise when the chronological data in the Bible are studied. They not only confuse the stories, they frustrate every attempt to correlate the biblical events with those recorded in the history of other nations, such as Egypt, Babylon, Assyria, and Syria, to place them in historical perspective.

Biblical scholars, following various lines of speculation, arrive at divergent estimates for the dates of important biblical events. Dr. Edwin R. Thiele has published an excellent brief review of these which need not be repeated here.[1] Others adopt varying attitudes. An Anglican prelate of my acquaintance supposes, "The ancient Hebrews were just not very good at arithmetic and were careless as far as chronology is concerned." One writer whose work has been widely read speaks of the "vague Hebraic attitude toward time" and asserts that the events of Hebrew history must not "be understood as in any sense *dated* by them, placed in any secure niches of time," adding that "our innate habit of relating historical figures to definite periods or even to exact years of birth and death (was not) known or even dreamed of by the ancient Hebrews."[1]

Such attitudes I find difficult to share. Writers who were careless about chronology or who had no intention of dating events would not include chronological data. But the Bible contains an abundance of it. Whole chapters, such as Genesis 5, serve no purpose at all if they are not intended to record the passage of a definite interval of time. These numbers must have been significant to the men who wrote them down. Why then are they no longer significant to us?

What of the findings of archeology?

In addition to the records of Nebuchadnezzar and Cyrus of Persia, already mentioned, the archeologists have uncovered many interesting things, but few that provide firm evidence for dating the biblical events. Those that are important so far as chronology is concerned can be reviewed in a few paragraphs.

There are the Amarna Letters, an important and fascinating group of cuneiform documents, written to Pharaoh Amenhotep III and his son, Amenhotep IV (Akhenaton), soon after the latter's accession in -1375. They tell of the invasion of Canaan by the *Khabiri*, associated by Breasted,[2] and others since, with the Hebrew tribes under Joshua.

Pharaoh Merneptah (-1225/-1215) erected in his fifth year a victory stele on which the word "Israel" is found. This word appears in no other Egyptian inscription. The message on Merneptah's stele is translated:

> Devestated is Tehennu; the Hittite land is pacified;
> Plundered is Canaan with every evil;
> Carried off is Askalon; siezed upon is Gezer;
> Yenoam is made a thing of naught;
> Israel is desolated, her seed is not;
> Palestine has become a defenseless widow for Egypt;
> Everyone that is turbulent is bound by king Merneptah...[3]

This inscription is often cited as proof that Pharaoh Merneptah met Israel in battle in Canaan in -1220, which would mean that the Exodus had come at some earlier date and the conquest by Joshua was already accomplished or at least well under way by that time. This is Breasted's opinion[4] and the inference is plausible. But when we put these two ideas together —the battle of Jericho *c.* -1375, and an invasion of Canaan by Merneptah in -1220 —we find ourselves severely at odds with the biblical data.

Merneptah's invasion would have to occur about 155 years after the death of Moses. According to the data in Judges, Jael killed Sisera, and Jabin king of Canaan was defeated (Ju. 4:22-24) about 131 years after the death of Moses, "And the land had rest forty years." (Ju. 5:31). The battle with Merneptah would have to occur during this period of peace. Either the chroniclers omitted a notable event, or the assumptions in regard to the Amarna Letters and the Merneptah stele are wrong.

A list of southern Syrian towns dating from the reign of Thutmose III (*c.* -1501/-1447) contains the names "Jacob-el" and "Joseph-el", "though with regard to the reading of the second there is great uncertainty."[1] On the basis of this tenuous evidence some have argued for an earlier date for the Exodus. Others cite it to prove that there was an "Israel tribe" that never descended into Egypt. Those favoring a later date for the Exodus claim it was this tribe that Merneptah encountered. Elmer Mould has suggested that there was an Israel tribe in Canaan at the same time that the Jacob clans were in Egypt, and "the later historical union of these...tribes gave rise to the tradition of the change in names in Gen. 32:27f."[2]

Such speculations based on scattered bits of evidence are not very helpful. Biblical-sounding names appear in some of the earliest written records and in many locations. There are "Benjamites" and "Dawidum" named on tablets from the kingdom of Mari *c.* -2000. No connection with the biblical narrative can possibly be claimed. If we were to accept Mould's theory we would have to recognize every reference to "Israel" prior to the conquest of Canaan as an anachronism, and seriously alter the text where it tells of the change in Jacob's name on his return to Canaan from Padan-aram. Not only is this without warrant, it solves none of our problems.

On the Merneptah stele all the names are written with the determinative indicating "land", except the name Y S I R A A L (Israel) which is written with the determinative indicating "people". Harrison points this out,[3] noting that the stele contains one or more scribal errors, and suggesting that the determinative used for Israel may be another.[4] Such argument must be used with caution. It could be said with equal justification that the word "Israel" is itself an error. But suppose the determinative for "land" had been intended. Then the rest of the line becomes incongruous, for a *place* does not have *seed*.

Finally, if Israel is a place, the statement need mean only that the place so named was found abandoned, without inhabitants; and, if a people, we learn nothing of their status or their whereabouts. The territory encompassed by the inscription extends from Libya (Tehennu) to the borders of Turkey (the Hittite land). The people called "Israel" could be anywhere in this territory. They could as well be in the Nile delta as in Canaan, and in that case the stele must predate the Exodus.

All of which means that we simply cannot, at this point, determine the significance of this monument.

Shalmaneser III, king of Assyria -858 to -824, mentions Hebrew kings in two inscriptions. One, known as the Monolith Inscription, gives an account of a battle at *Karkar* in which he faced a coalition including "Hadadezer of Aram" and "Ahabbu the Sirilean", taken to be the biblical Ben-hadad king of Syria, and Ahab king of Israel. The battle was fought in -854 or -853.[1]

Just how this fits in is a difficult question. In the Bible there is no mention of such a coalition, or of such a battle, or of Shalmaneser III. Far from being allied with Ben-hadad, Ahab fights against him. In an attempt, with the help of Jehoshaphat of Judah, to take Ramoth-gilead from Ben-hadad, Ahab is mortally wounded (I K. 22).

The second inscription of Shalmaneser III, dated the 18th year of his reign (-841), is known as the Black Obelisk. It pictures a man with his nose to the ground before the conqueror, Shalmaneser. A line of bearers brings tribute. The inscription, as interpreted from the cuneiform, identifies "Jaua bit Humri." This is taken to mean "Jehu of the house of Omri," or even "Jehu son of Omri."[2] But Jehu was certainly not the latter and would have resented any title that associated him with Omri, except "destroyer."

In the Bible only twelve verses (I K. 16:16-28) are devoted to Omri. He was king of Israel for 12 years, during which he moved the capital from Tirzah to Samaria (Heb. *Shomeron*). His son Ahab ruled for 22 years and was succeeded by his son Ahaziah. Ahaziah ben-Ahab[b] died without an heir after 2 years as king. His brother, Jehoram ben-Ahab, then took the throne and ruled for 12 years.

Jehu, encouraged by the prophet Elisha, killed Jehoram ben-Ahab and made himself king. At the same time his men killed Ahaziah king of Judah, who was Ahab's grandson. Jehu demanded the seventy heads of the seventy sons of Ahab.

---

[b] Most translators render *ben* as "son of." Though literally correct, this tends to stress the relationship while weakening the identifying quality of the name. In the present work *ben* is not translated, in conformance with accepted non-biblical standards.

Seventy heads were delivered. He ordered the death of Ahab's wife, the notorious Jezebel. It was his intention to exterminate that family line.

This casts some doubt on the interpretation of the cuneiform, but Shalmaneser's inscription can be of limited help in developing the biblical chronology in any case, for the event it records is not mentioned in the Bible at all. Jehu is not said to pay tribute to anyone, and no Hebrew king is said to pay tribute to Shalmaneser III.

Omri is also named on a carved slab known as the Moabite Stone, so-called because it bears the name "Mesha king of Moab." This king is named in II Kings 3:4. The inscription refers to Omri in the past tense, and mentions but does not name his son. The stone was originally obtained under such suspiciously fortuitous circumstances that some scholars have doubted its authenticity.[1]

The Assyrian annals contain references to the Hebrew kings Menahem, Pekah, Hoshea, Ahaz, Hezekiah and Manasseh. The annals enable us to date precisely at least one important event — the destruction of Samaria and the end of the kingdom of Israel, -722. Unfortunately, there is considerable confusion in the biblical text at this point. But the difficulties are not insurmountable, as we shall discover.

The title "Pharaoh" appears many times in the Bible, but only five men who bore the title are identified by name. The name "Rameses" (Nu. 33:3; rendered "Raamses" in Ex. 1:11) does not count; in the Bible it appears only as the name of a city, though 12 Pharaohs used the name. One Pharaoh is called "So." This name does not appear on any Egyptian king list. One, called "Tirhakah," is said to be "king of Ethiopia" (II K. 19:9). An Ethiopian named Taharka ruled Egypt from -688 to -663. Pharaoh Necho ruled Egypt from -609 to -593. King Josiah of Judah fought Necho at Megiddo in -609 and lost his life in the battle (II K. 23:29). This puts a firm date on the last year of Josiah's reign. The name "Hophra" appears in Jeremiah 44:30. He may be identified as Apries who ruled Egypt from -588 to -569.

Unfortunately, the four Pharaohs named above are concentrated in the short span of 119 years. But the fifth Pharaoh called by name in the Bible belongs to an earlier period.

The Bible calls him "Shishak"; Egyptologists render his name "Sheshonk" or "Shoshenk." He was a usurper, of Libyan ancestry, but a man of wealth and power whose family had lived in Heracleopolis for five generations. His great-grandfather, Musen, had been a priest of the Heracleopolitan temple and commander of the local mercenary troops. Sheshonk married his son to the daughter of Pesibkenno II, last of the Tanite kings

of the Twenty-first Dynasty, thus legitimizing his line.   He
was a "vigorous and able ruler."[1]

Sheshonk left an inscription, commemorating his attack on
the cities of Israel and Judah.   Breasted, with characteristic
caution, dates this inscription "probably about 926 B.C."[2] Because this falls in an era not otherwise datable, and because it
is referred to very precisely in the Bible, this is one of the
most important archeological discoveries related to biblical
chronology.

The biblical reference to Sheshonk reads:

> In the fifth year of king Rehoboam, Shishak king of
> Egypt came up against Jerusalem, and took away
> the treasures of the house of the Lord, and the
> treasures of the king's house. (I K. 14:25, 26)

Thus we know that the 5th year of Rehoboam, son and successor to Solomon, was the year -926.

Four kings of Assyria are named in the Bible.   From
Assyrian records their reigns can be dated.   They are:
    Tiglath-pileser III, -745/-727
    Shalmaneser V, -727/-722
    Sargon II, -722/-705
    Sennacherib, -705/-681
We shall have more to say of them at the proper time.

In 1967 the British School of Archeology in Iraq, excavating
Tell al-Rimah about 50 miles west of ancient Ninevah, uncovered a stele recording an invasion of Syria in -805 by Adadnirari
III.   He conquered Damascus and collected tribute from the
neighboring nations.   Named among the kings who paid tribute
is "Jehoash of Samaria."[3] Jehoash was king for 16 years (II K.
13:10).   No mention is made of his paying tribute to the king of
Assyria.   The name Adadnirari does not appear in the Bible.
The recently-found stele thus helps us to check the chronology
only to a limited extent.   We know that one of the 16 years of
the reign of Jehoash of Israel must be -805, but we do not know
which one.

So far as archeology is concerned nothing else has yet been
found that is a real help in biblical chronology.   What we have
is not much, but we are fortunate to have that.   It is just enough.

While it is true there are no "exact years of birth and death,"
as Chase says, given in the Bible, if this means years with
calendar numbers that are part of a long continuing sequence,
the same can be said of every ancient record.   Later historians
developed the concept of an era beginning with an epoch.   But
such dates were often chosen many years after the event.   Thus

the Era of the Olympiads of the Greeks, reckoned from July 1, -776, was unknown to the people who lived in the early years of that era.   The Roman Era of the Founding of the City, dating from April 22, -753, was established about 700 years later by Marcus Terentius Varro.   And the present Common Era (Christian Era) was not introduced until 533, based on the estimate of Dionysius Exiguus.

Thus it should not surprise us that there is no long, contin-uing sequence of years in the Bible, except for one thing: The Jewish Mundane Era, with the epoch in -3761 of the Gregorian calendar, has been in use, publicly, since the 15th century. *Rosh hashanah*, "beginning the year," number 5,730 of the Hebrew calendar was duly recorded on the 14th of September, 1969, of the Common Era (C.E.).

How was the epoch chosen?   On what basis was the date -3761 established?   Hebrew tradition says their calendar began its count at the time of creation as described in the first chapter of Genesis.   Why then is there no mention of that calendar in Genesis, or in any of the other books that make the Bible literally a book of books?

If the years were not being numbered when the Bible was in the process of being written, how does anyone know what year it is now?   Were the data in the book summed up, or was the figure chosen arbitrarily, perhaps in terms of some little known symbolism?   A study of the chronological data may help toward answering these questions, and perhaps many others.

Before going on it would seem necessary to examine what is currently most generally accepted as valid biblical chronology. I dislike finding fault with the work of others who have sought diligently and sincerely to solve difficult problems.   But what is put forward in this book is, inevitably, in conflict with cur-rently accepted ideas.   In order to make room for new ideas it is necessary to shake older ideas loose.   And this involves much more than simply replacing one set of numbers with another. When the dates are changed historical perspective is alterred. The correlation of ancient Hebrew history with contemporary civilizations is changed.   And in fact, biblical history becomes something quite different from what it had been, or seemed to be, before.

Those who have no firmly fixed ideas regarding biblical his-tory will find no difficulty in accepting the picture that develops later in this book.   The next several pages are not written for them, but for those who have already developed definite ideas on the subject, ideas which in many cases were accepted in the first place without asking for proof, or without careful examination of their basis, because those ideas filled a void and came into conflict with nothing at all.

A great many versions of biblical chronology have been presented over the years. We cannot possibly discuss them all. Since 1945 when it was first published[1] the biblical chronology of William Foxwell Albright has been the most widely accepted. Many books on biblical history have included that chronology in one or another of its several revisions without noting its source. Others have presented essentially the same chronology modified slightly to suit their own ideas.

In its final recension by Albright himself[2] his chronology for the divided kingdom agrees with the biblical data in respect to only 6 of the 29 synchronisms given in the text to correlate the kings of Israel with those of Judah. This might seem reasonable enough if the length-of-reign figures were largely observed, but that is not the case. Albright's chronology disregards 12 of the 39 length-of-reign figures supplied by the text. Eleven are reduced by amounts ranging from 2 to 16 years. (Pekah is allowed only 4 instead of 20 years.) One is increased by 5 years—Ahaz, up from 16 to 21 years.

Albright begins the divided kingdom in -922, thus making the attack by Shishak in the fifth year of Rehoboam fall in -918, contrary to the evidence of the Egyptian record. And, as Thiele points out, "The date 922 is not Biblical, and there is not the slightest evidence that it is historical."[3] Thiele backs this statement with excellent arguments which I shall not repeat here. The nature of this unwarranted adjustment is sufficiently clear when it is noted that Albright also reduces Rehoboam's reign from 17 to 8 years, thus eliminating the effect on later dates for the kings of Judah which would otherwise result from using the date -922 for the first year of Rehoboam. But no corresponding reduction is made in the line of Israel's kings, which is thus extended 9 years relative to the line in Judah.

Admittedly, the problems are perplexing. But this is surely not a valid way of solving them. Nor does it succeed. Albright's dates for Jehoash of Israel (-801/-786) fall from 4 to 20 years later than the date on Adadnirari's stele, which was not available to Albright, and could not be anticipated. But if his chronology was in fact correct, this stele, and any future discovery, would confirm rather than refute it. Albright himself notes, "Individual dates have been revised to agree with subsequent discoveries."[4] Admittedly, then, his chronology is little more than a guess, though he would, presumably, claim that it fairly represents the overall picture. But even this seems doubtful.

An examination of the reasoning on which he bases his date for the birth of Abraham exposes the weakness of the whole structure. In order to avoid any distortion of his arguments they are presented here largely in his own words.[1]

Albright asserts, "*'Apiru - 'Abiru*, later *'Ibri*, 'Hebrew'... meant something like 'donkey-man, donkey driver, huckster, caravaneer.'"— that Harran means "Caravan City,"— that "all the places with which Abraham is connected in Syria and Palestine [were] important caravan stations... in the nineteenth-eighteenth centuries B.C."— that "there was seasonal occupation along the caravan routes of the Negeb of Israel and northern Sinai during the same centuries," but not to any extent in earlier or later times — and that Gerar was occupied as early as the 19th century B.C.

All of the above may be true. It may even be true, as Albright proposes, that "Gen. 20:1 may best be rendered: 'And Abraham departed from there to the Negeb, keeping between Kadesh and the Wall (of Egypt), while he was a resident alien at Gerar."

All of this makes it possible to suppose, as Albright does, that, "his [Abraham's] house and family were at Gerar on the edge of the desert Negeb while he spent his time in northern Sinai leading caravans." But this conclusion is by no means the only possibility. And even if it is accepted, a date in the 19th or 18th century for the birth of Abraham is not thus established.

If Abraham was a caravaneer, the text does not say so. If the places he stopped were busy caravan stations, this is not suggested. If he moved seasonally, this is not confirmed. If he left his family in Gerar, we have no reason to suspect it. In fact, the general impression is that Abraham led a relatively calm, isolated life. His contacts with others seem few and brief.

Albright says, "the nineteenth century B.C. was... the high point of donkey trade in antiquity, [and] there is no evidence for camel caravans or raiding expeditions before the twelfth century B.C." This defeats his position regarding Abraham, for we are told that Abraham's servant took "ten camels, of the camels of his master" (Gen. 24:10) when he went to get a wife for Isaac. Evidently Abraham had more than ten camels. For a donkey caravaneer this is a contradiction in terms and certainly does not suggest that he lived at "the high point of donkey trade," but rather considerably later.

When Joseph was taken to Egypt, only 90 years after Abraham's death, he was taken by "a caravan of Ishmaelites... from Gilead, with their camels..." (Gen. 37:25). It has been said that these and Abraham's camels are anachronistic. This might be a necessary explanation if the dating was firmly established. Since it is not, this becomes a matter of discarding contrary evidence in order to support an unconfirmed hypothesis.

Albright then devotes several paragraphs to the question of the antiquity of chapters 14 and 15 in Genesis. He seems to feel both must have been written well before the 12th century B.C.

Then he says, "the word *dor* did not mean 'generation' in early Hebrew, but 'lifetime' [since] the Arabic cognate *dahrum* often means 'lifetime'... Syriac *dara* is defined as '80 years,' and the word *darum* appears in an inscription of Shamshi-Adad I of Assyria also in the meaning 'lifetime' (seven *daru* elapsed between the climax of the empire of Accad and his own reign, i. e., between *c.* 2250 and *c.* 1750 B.C.)." Which would make *daru* equivalent to about 70 years.

Accordingly, it would seem to follow that in Gen. 15:13 "the equivalent of four lifetimes is explicitly given as '400 years'." Albright then invites us to "allow three lifetimes for the period represented by Abraham, Isaac and Jacob [because] gaps in the genealogies [are] to be expected, since most oral tradition tends to skip over obscure or uninteresting periods [and] archeologists have shown that there are gaps in the genealogical tradition of such regions as the Sudan, Rhodesia, Polynesia and Arabia." Therefore, "it would seem that early Hebrew tradition allowed seven lifetimes or roughly seven centuries for the entire period from Abraham to the Conquest of Canaan. "

If Albright has successfully shown that the chapter containing this "traditional evidence" was written prior to the Conquest of Canaan, as he seems intent upon doing, then he has destroyed its value as historical evidence. Indeed, the 400-year figure is presented as a prediction. The true dating of historical events cannot be proved on the basis of ancient predictions, though the validity of the predictions might be proved by accurate dating of subsequent events.

There is no particular need to prove that the period from the birth of Abraham to the death of Jacob was meant to represent 300 years. We are told that Isaac was born when Abraham was 100, Jacob when Isaac was 60, and that Jacob lived to be 147. This adds up to 307 years, so it seems clear, however we explain it, that this was the period we were intended to understand. But why, if the 400-year period is to follow the death of Jacob, is it written so as to appear to run concurrently with most of the 300-year period? Why, if Hebrew tradition allotted 700 years to the period from Abraham's birth to the Conquest, does *Rabbinic* tradition hold that the 400-year period begins with the birth of Isaac, making the total only 500 years?

If we had clear evidence from extra-biblical sources that Abraham was born *c.* 700 years before the battle of Jericho, Albright's explanation might serve to expand the biblical data to fit the facts. But we have no such evidence. Speculating on some means whereby the data can be made to conform to another speculation regarding the date of Abraham's birth builds a house of cards. No matter how pleasing the result may seem it cannot be regarded as historical fact.

Nor can we arrive at an absolute date for Abraham's birth by adding 700, or any other number of years, to the date of the battle of Jericho, since we have no reliable date for that event.

It was tentatively accepted that Abraham might have been a caravaneer. But there is no evidence. Even if '*ibri* originally referred to that occupation (and this is by no means certain), we cannot judge Abraham's occupation in this way. Moses is said to be recognized by Pharaoh's daughter as a child of the Hebrews (Ex. 2:6), but at that time none of his people could have engaged in such a trade. There is no indication that Jacob or any of his sons followed that profession, nor does Isaac seem to have done so.

Albright equates '*ibri* with '*apiru*. Others concur. Many phonetically similar terms are known from several languages. Many thousands of people known by these names lived over a very broad area for a very long time. Surely they were not all caravaneers. The name must have lost its significance long before Abraham's time, or it meant something else. But further discussion of this point must be deferred.

Thiele's opinion of Albright's date for the division of the monarchy has been mentioned. Albright responds, "E. R. Thiele ... overharmonizes in an effort to save all the numbers of the book of Kings. His system is sometimes in striking disagreement with the data of II Chron. and cannot be squared with the Tyrian chronology of Menander preserved by Josephus."[1]

To the latter point Thiele retorts, "The claim that the date 931 cannot be squared with Tyrian chronology is without foundation in fact."[2] With this, I believe, we must agree. But it is not a telling criticism in any case, for Menander's chronology is not otherwise supported and in view of the numerous errors in Josephus we cannot be sure it is correctly reported.

The broad indictment regarding II Chron. actually refers to one item in 16:1, the only item which Thiele has found himself obliged to take serious exception to, and one of the very few items which Albright happens to accept as correct. The point in question conflicts impossibly with I K. 15:33 and 16:8, and is not essential to the chronology in any case.

As to whether or not Thiele "overharmonizes", that depends upon the validity of the data. If the data are correct they must be harmonized. There may be more than one way of doing it, yet only one that would be correct, but to "overharmonize" would be impossible. However, if an item of data is incorrect any effort to justify it is, inevitably, an attempt to perpetuate error. If that is what Albright's term implies, he has used it

most unjustly. To suggest that Thiele has willfully accommo-
dated faulty data is certainly unwarranted. Yet he may have done
so inadvertently, for his system does not provide safeguards
against the possibility, and in fact, in operation, his methods
increase enormously the chance of doing so.

Thiele begins with a set of rules. If they were rigorously
applied, he would have been unable to complete the task he set
himself. But he allows the data to determine when and how the
rules must change. Thus he starts with the kings of Judah
counting their regnal years according to the accession-year
system and the kings of Israel counting theirs according to the
nonaccession-year system. Then the Judean count is changed
to the nonaccession-year system and, subsequently, both nations
switch to the accession-year system. A certain logic seems to
justify these changes, but they are not really called for by the
text. The logic is in fact *ad hoc*.

The effect of these changes is not great, but other serious
inconsistencies occur. Thiele finds it necessary to allow for
three instances of overlapping reigns among the kings of Israel
and six coregencies among the kings of Judah. These are not
specified by the text; only one is even faintly suggested, except
by the numerical data, particularly the synchronisms. But in
some instances the synchronism is assumed to mark the first
year of coregency and in others the first year of a king's sole
reign. In some instances the length of reign is assumed to
include the period of coregency and in others it is not. Thus we
find in Thiele's scheme that Asa's 41 years include 4 coregent
with his father and 6 coregent with his son Jehoshaphat; Jehoshaphat's 25 years include the 4 coregent with his father and 6
coregent with his son Jehoram, but Jehoram's 8 years do not
include the 6 coregent with his father. In a later sequence we
find Amaziah's 29 years include 24 coregent with his son Azariah
whose 52 years count the 24 coregent with his father and 12
coregent with his son Jotham; Jotham's 16 years include the 12
coregent with his father. But Jotham's 16 years do not include
4 years coregent with his son Ahaz, and Ahaz' 16 years do not
include those 4 years coregent with his father. Where in most
cases both kings count the period of coregency in others only
one king counts it and in this case neither one of them wants it.

Such fine inconsistency is hard to accept. It would seem
most likely that some error in the data or its interpretation has
occurred. But Thiele would have it that this is in fact the way
the original record was written with a few words of clarification
that some later editor left out.[1]

Thiele could not anticipate the discovery of Adadnirari's stele.
His dates for Jehoash of Israel are -798/-782, 1, — from 7 to 23

years too late. This confirms the suspicion that there is some imperfection in his scheme.

So far, the chronology presented in this volume has met the test. Though I have included the Adadnirari stele in this first chapter I did not have knowledge of it until long after the chronology was completed. In fact, I had none of the Assyrian correlations on hand while the chronology was being worked out. Yet, sometimes in surprising ways, they all work.

Dr. Thiele, in his final paragraph, made a statement that expresses so well my own feeling I can do no better than to repeat it: "If these dates are final and absolute, they have nothing to fear from the most careful and exhaustive research — they will stand. If they are not final, and if indisputable evidence can prove them in error, they have no right to stand." Presuming no mistake has been made in dating Adadnirari's stele, Thiele's figures have failed their first test. Hopefully, the chronology presented in this volume will fare better in the years ahead. Time alone will tell.

If I have succeeded where men who have devoted many more years of preparation and professional dedication to the task have not, Jerome foresaw it when he wrote:

> Read all the books of the Old and New Testament,
> and you will find such a discord as to the number
> of years, such a confusion as to the duration of
> the reigns of the kings of Judah and Israel, that to
> attempt to clear up this question will appear rather
> the occupation of a man of leisure than of a scholar.[1]

Good fortune has made me more nearly the man of leisure than most professional scholars, perhaps. But that applies only to the matter of obtaining a livelihood, not at all to the process of preparing this volume.

If, as I believe has been shown, an adequate biblical chronology is lacking, then no real biblical history exists. Our objective is to correct that situation, deriving the chronology directly from the biblical data. This is not a new objective, but the approach is unique. Some time must be spent in explaining the approach itself, and justifying its use. Hopefully, that explanation will satisfy the most exacting without becoming either dull or confusing. But, since this book is intended to be as nearly self-contained as possible the reader may find much that he already knows. Others, I trust, will welcome the information. Chapter 2, therefore, reviews the chronological data from the beginning.

If Adam was born in the year zero, the first subsequent *date* appears in Genesis 5:3 —

> Adam lived one-hundred-thirty years, and begat a
> son named Seth.

Genesis 5 lists ten generations, from Adam to Noah, inclusive, giving the age of paternity for each, and the *terminal age* (age at death) for all but Noah. It ends by reporting the birth of the eleventh generation, the sons of Noah — Shem, Ham and Japheth.

Genesis 11, beginning with verse 10, continues the generations, listing ten more, from Shem through Abram (Abraham). In the books that follow, seven more generations are named — Isaac, Jacob, Levi, Kohath, Amram, Moses, and his sons Gershom and Eliezer.

From Adam to Isaac the age of paternity is given. Jacob's is not given but can be closely estimated, for at least eleven of his sons were born in a seven-year period. But ages are not supplied for most of those sons. For Levi, Kohath and Amram terminal ages are given. But terminal ages cannot be added for chronological purposes, because the lifetimes overlap.

Only one of Jacob's sons is given an age other than a terminal age. That one is Joseph. His age is given when he is sold into slavery, and when he is appointed to an official position by the Pharaoh. But his sons are named without Joseph's age of paternity, and without subsequent mention of their ages.

The genealogy will not carry us beyond the point of Joseph's promotion by the Pharaoh. We must find another thread. It turns up in the statement:

> The sojourning of the children of Israel, who dwelt
> in Egypt, was four-hundred and thirty years. (Ex. 12:40)

(Israel, of course, is an alternate name for Jacob.)

The Bible does not state clearly when the "sojourn" begins. It could begin with the sale of Joseph. It could, conceivably, begin with Joseph's rise to prominence. It could begin when Jacob and the rest join Joseph in Egypt. Rabbinic tradition holds that it begins with the birth of Isaac. Josephus felt it should begin with Abraham's entry into Canaan.

Of these the first seems most logical. It is at this point, very nearly, that the other data runs out. The "sojourn" is considered a period of servitude, and Joseph is not only the first of the sons of Jacob to come into Egypt, he is the only one who came in as a captive. The others came in voluntarily to escape famine in Canaan. Still, we must test each of these possibilities.

This 430-year interval extends the chronology to the Exodus. We could continue with the forty years during which Moses led the people, and follow with Joshua, but only Joshua's terminal age is given (110, according to Jo. 24:25). We are not told how old he was when he became leader nor how long he led.

There are many intervals mentioned in the book of Joshua, the book of Judges, and the two books named for Samuel, last of the judges. But we cannot easily use them. They are no more firmly tied to David at the one end than they are to Moses at the other. In his "Introduction" to *Judges*, Judah J. Slotki, M.A., Ph.D., writes, "There is general agreement that the problem of harmonizing the chronological data presents insurmountable difficulty."[1]   Similarly, Rabbi Dr. S. Goldman, M.A., in his "Introduction" to *Samuel*, writes, "The chronology of *Samuel* is obscure, and reaches firm ground only in a note giving the duration of David's rule (2 Sam. v. 4f.)... For the period of Samuel and Saul, the chronological data in our text are incomplete and vague."[2]   Samuel's age is never given, nor does it tell how long he served.   He anointed Saul to be the first official king over Israel, but Saul's age is not given, nor the length of his reign. The only chronological datum associated with Saul is found in I Sam. 13:1.   A variety of translations have been offered for this verse, none of which is especially edifying.

In the AV we find: "Saul reigned one year: and when he had reigned two years over Israel..."

NAB, NWT, and JPSA versions differ from AV, but only very slightly from each other, reading: "Saul was (?) years old when he began to reign; and two years he reigned over Israel." A statement of identical form is found in II Sam. 5:4 — "David was thirty years old when he began to reign, and he reigned forty years." But we cannot suppose that Saul was king for only two years. Either the number is incomplete, or the line means only that the events which follow took place in Saul's third year, as the AV rendering suggests.   In either case, we are left in the dark regarding the length of Saul's reign.

In his *Dissertation V, Upon the Chronology of Josephus*,[3] William Whiston (1667-1752) wrote:

> Josephus informs us (*Antiquities*, VI, xiii, 5, and xiv, 9) that Saul reigned 18 years during the life of Samuel, and, as the Greek copies add, 22 years after his death; which together make 40 years... the number St. Paul ascribes to him also (Acts 13:21).
> Yet does the old Latin version of Josephus give us here only 2 years, instead of 20; and, in agreement thereto, Josephus gives him, in another place, but 20 years in all, and that expressly (*Antiq*. X, viii, 4).

Styles of writing have changed, but the intervening years have contributed nothing to improve the content of this commentary. Dr. Goldman says essentially the same thing.[1] An abbreviated version is found in the note to I Sam. 13:1 in NAB.

With king David the dating resumes. David was king for forty years (I K. 2:11). From David, through his son Solomon, through 19 more kings and one queen, we can follow the passage of years to the destruction of Jerusalem by Nebuchadnezzar king of Babylon. And this we know took place in -587.

To complete the basic chronology we need only one thing, a bridge across the gap from Moses to David. We find that bridge in I K. 6:1 —

> In the four-hundred-eightieth year after the children of Israel were come out of Egypt, in the fourth year of Solomon's reign over Israel...he began to build the house of the Lord.

The rest should be simple arithmetic.

Beginning with Adam, summing the ages of paternity for the generations up to Noah, as given in Gen. 5, we find that Shem was born in the year of Adam 1556, Noah being 500 years old.

When Noah was 600 years old the flood occurred (Gen. 7:6). Shem was then 100, in the year of Adam 1656.

When Shem was 100 his son Arphaxad was born, "two years after the flood" (Gen. 11:10). But this is contradictory.

Arphaxad cannot be born at *both* times. It must have been one *or* the other. But which? There is really no way to tell. The 2-year difference is certainly not large. Suppose we take Shem's age as correct, temporarily, leaving the question open. The birth of Arphaxad would then be 1656 years after the birth of Adam.

From then until the birth of Abraham we add up another 290 years, from the paternal ages given in Gen. 11. This puts the birth of Abraham in the year of Adam 1946.

Isaac was born, Abraham being 100 (Gen. 21:5), in 2046.

Jacob was born when Isaac was 60 (Gen. 25:26), in 2106.

To establish the year of Joseph's birth we must examine the story more carefully. Remembering that Esau and Jacob are twins, we read:

> Esau was forty years old when he took to wife Judith the daughter of Beeri the Hittite, and Bashemath the daughter of Elon the Hittite, which were a grief of mind to Isaac and to Rebekah (Gen. 26:34, 35).

> And Rebekah said to Isaac, "I am weary of my life because of the daughters of Heth; if Jacob takes a

wife of the daughters of Heth, what good shall my
life do me?" (27:46).

And Isaac called Jacob, and blessed him and said,
"You shall not take a wife of the daughters of Canaan.
Arise, go to Padan-aram, to the house of Bethuel
your mother's father; and take a wife from there of
the daughters of Laban, your mother's brother."(28:1,2).

Jacob obeyed his father. He went to Padan-aram, being then
40 years old, the same as Esau. He served Laban for seven
years, expecting to earn Rachel for his wife. But Laban gave
him Leah instead, and when Jacob complained, Laban said,
"Fulfil her week, and we will give you Rachel also for the
service which you shall serve with me yet seven other years."
(29:27). From this we judge that Jacob was 47 years old when
he married Leah and Rachel, and pledged to work for Laban for
another 7 years, when he would be 54.

The women began a child-bearing contest. Leah was winning
4 to 0, when Rachel gave Jacob her maidservant for a wife.
Leah promptly gave Jacob her maidservant also. The two maid-
servants had two sons apiece. Leah had two more sons and one
daughter, seven children altogether. Rachel managed to have
one son, Joseph.

After Rachel had borne Joseph, Jacob said to Laban, "Send
me away, that I may go to my own place, and to my own
country." (Gen. 30:25). This indicates that Jacob's second
7-year term of service to Laban was completed. Since Joseph
was born before the end of that term, he was born when Jacob
was not more than 54 year old. So Joseph was born not later
than the year of Adam 2160.

(When) Joseph was seventeen years old... his brethren
stripped him of his coat, and cast him in a pit....
There passed by Midianite merchantmen, and they
drew Joseph out of the pit, and sold him....And the
Midianites sold him in Egypt to Potiphar, an officer
of Pharaoh's, and captain of the guard. (Gen. 37:2,
23, 24, 28, 36).

The year would be 2177. If this begins the "sojourn" in Egypt
which lasted for 430 years, the Exodus under the leadership of
Moses must have taken place in the year of Adam 2607. Since
we can identify the 4th year of Solomon's reign with the 480th
year after the Exodus (from I K. 6:1) that must be year 3087.

Solomon ruled for 40 years (I K. 11:42). So his reign continued for 36 years after the temple was begun in his 4th year, and

ended in 3123. He was succeeded by his son Rehoboam.

From Rehoboam through Zedekiah, 19 kings and 1 queen sat on the throne of Judah in Jerusalem for a total of 393 years. Zedekiah's reign ended 3516 years after the birth of Adam when:

> The wrath of the Lord arose against his people (and) he brought upon them the king of the Chaldees, who slew their young men with the sword in the house of their sanctuary, and had no compassion upon young man or maiden, old man, or him that stooped for age; He (the Lord) gave them all into his (Nebuchadnezzar's) hand. (II Chron. 36:16, 17)

> Them that escaped the sword he carried away to Babylon; where they were servants to him and his sons until the reign of the kingdom of Persia. To fulfil the word of the Lord by the mouth of Jeremiah, until the land had enjoyed her sabbaths — for as long as she lay desolate she kept sabbath — to fulfil seventy years. (II Chron. 36:20, 21).

> Now in the first year of Cyrus king of Persia - that the word of the Lord by the mouth of Jeremiah might be accomplished — the Lord stirred up the spirit of Cyrus king of Persia, that he made a proclamation throughout his kingdom, and put it in writing, saying:
> Thus saith Cyrus King of Persia —
> All the Kingdoms of the earth hath the Lord God of Heaven given me; and he hath charged me to build him an house in Jerusalem, which is in Judah. Who is there among you of all his people? The Lord his God be with him, and let him go up.
> (II Chron. 36:22, 23).

Ezra supplies additional documentation concerning Cyrus. Josephus (*Antiq.* XI) adds more. Not all scholars have been willing to accept this documentation as authentic. But there is a clay cylinder known as the Cyrus Cylinder which, though not specific regarding the Jews, establishes beyond question the authenticity of the principle involved. The cuneiform inscription on that cylinder is translated:

> From... to Ashur and Susa, Agade, Ashunnah, Zamban, Nerenu, Deri, with the territory of the land of Gutium, the cities on the other side of the Tigris... the gods who dwelt in them I brought back to their places... all their inhabitants I collected and restored them to their dwelling places...[1]

Adding 70 years to our previous total brings us to 3586. In terms of the Gregorian calendar the year was -537. Adding 537 to 3586 places the birth of Adam in -4123.

In terms of the Hebrew calendar, with its mundane epoch in -3761, this figure is 362 years too large. To conform with this the Hebrew calendar would have to begin, for no discernable reason, in the 37th year of Enos.

We do not have to look far to discover one error. Cyrus issued his proclamation in -537. Nebuchadnezzar conquered and destroyed Jerusalem in -587. The land had lain fallow not for 70 years but for 49. "The word of the Lord by the mouth of Jeremiah" was not fulfilled exactly as stated, it would seem.

This discrepancy is not a modern discovery but was known to Josephus in the 1st century. He wrote (*Antiq*. XI, i, 1) — "The first year of the reign of Cyrus was the seventieth from the day that our people were removed out of their land into Babylon." This, of course, was based on the Bible. Some years later, in *Against Apion* I, 20,[1] he quoted, from the third book of Chaldean History by Berosus:

> Nabuchodonosor...reigned forty-three years...his son Evilmerodach...reigned but two years...Nerig-lissoor...reigned four years...Laborosoarchod... nine months...Nobonnedus, the seventeenth year of his reign, (was beaten by) Cyrus...of Persia.

Josephus concludes, "Nebuchadnezzar, in the nineteenth year of his reign, laid our temple desolate, and so it lay in that state of obscurity for fifty years; but...in the second year of Cyrus, its foundations were laid and it was finished again in the second year of Darius."[2]

Our concern is not with the temple but with the return of the captives in the *first* year of Cyrus as king of Babylon. This was 49 years after the destruction of Jerusalem, not 50.

Subtracting 21 years (the difference between 70 and 49) from 4123, we find the date for the birth of Adam to be -4102. There is still a difference of 341 years between this figure and the Jewish Mundane Epoch.

Had we followed Rabbinic tradition for the beginning of the "sojourn" the results would have been different. Isaac was 60 when Jacob was born; we have calculated that Jacob was 54 when Joseph was born, and dated the "sojourn" from Joseph's 17th year. These three figures add to 131 years. Making allowance for this we would still have a difference of 210 years between the birth of Adam and the beginning of the Hebrew calendar, which would fall in the 80th year of Seth.

Josephus says the Exodus occurred "four hundred thirty years after our forefather Abraham came into Canaan."[3] That would be 25 years before the birth of Isaac. On this basis the Hebrew calendar would start in the year of Adam 185, when Seth was 55 years old. But that is by our calculation. Josephus would not have reached the same conclusion, had he made referrence to the Hebrew calendar, beyond naming the months, for the ages of paternity which Josephus uses from Adam through Nahor, father of Terah, are different from those we have used. Our figures are taken from the Hebrew (Masoretic) text. The data Josephus uses agree, for the most part, with the Septuagint. (*septuaginta* is Latin for "seventy" and the book is often designated by the equivalent Roman numerals, LXX, though formerly LXXII (72) was used. The name derives from the tradition that the book was translated from Hebrew into Greek by seventy-two translators in seventy-two days, a much disputed tradition elaborated by Josephus (*Antiq.* XII, ii).)

It is generally accepted that the Septuagint translation was made c. -285 for Ptolemy II, Philadelphus, then Pharaoh of Egypt. This Macedonian Pharaoh collected a vast number of books for the library of Alexandria from all over the then known world. He also commissioned Manetho, an Egyptian priest, to write in Greek a history of Egypt.

Manetho's work has been lost, except for portions that were copied by others, including Josephus. But the Septuagint must have been available to him, for he included in his work an outrageously satirical version of Moses and the Exodus which, nearly 400 years later, so infuriated Josephus that he copied it in order to refute it. Ironically, in so doing, he preserved it, along with other equally satirical and facetious reports by Cheremon, Lysimachus, and Apion, featuring monstrous interlingual puns.[1] Had Josephus ignored these detractors we would know nothing of them, for their words survive only in his copy.

Both the Septuagint and Josephus' *Antiquities* are extant in several versions differing in minor ways. No attempt will be made here to note these variations. But there are significant differences in the chronological data found in LXX, Josephus, the Masoretic text, and the Samaritan Pentateuch. These are compared in the chart on page 22.

Most of us are familiar with the Masoretic data for this text is followed in all the commonly used English translations. If the advanced ages attributed to the ancients in that text arouse incredulity, the figures in LXX compound the difficulty. The Samaritan figures also run high, but seem more reasonable, for with two explainable exceptions lifespan decreases steadily from Adam to Terah. But this does not prove their accuracy.

The LXX list appears to be a corruption of the Masoretic. Notice that the terminal ages in both lists are generally the

GENEALOGICAL DATA – ADAM to ABRAHAM
From Masoretic, Josephus, Septuagint and Samaritan texts.

	Age of Paternity				Added Yrs.			Terminal Age			
	Mas.	Jos.	LXX	Sam.	Mas.	LXX	Sam.	Mas.	Jos.	LXX	Sam.
Adam	130	230	230	130	800	700	800	930	930	930	930
Seth	105	205	205	105	807	707	807	912	912	912	912
Enos	90	190	190	90	815	715	815	905	905	905	905
Cainan	70	170	170	70	840	740	840	910	910	910	910
Mahalaleel	65	165	165	65	830	730	830	895	895	895	895
Jared	162	162	162	62	800	800	785	962	962	962	847
Enoch	65	165	165	65	300	200	300	365	365	365	365
Methuselah	187	187	187	67	782	782	653	969	969	969	720
Lamech	182	182	188	53	595	565	600	777	777	753	653
Noah	500		500	500							
Shem	100		100	100	500	500	500				600
Deluge when											
Noah was	600	600	600	600	350	350	350	950	950	950	950

(Total from Adam to Deluge
     1656 | 2256 | 2262 | 1307)

Arphaxad was born after the Deluge
     2   12   2   2

	Mas.	Jos.	LXX	Sam.	Mas.	LXX	Sam.	Mas.	Jos.	LXX	Sam.
Arphaxad	35	135	135	135	403	400	303	(438)		(465)	438
Cainanᵇ			130			330				(330)	
Salah	30	130	130	130	403	330	303	(433)		(460)	433
Eber	34	134	134	134	430	270	270	(464)		(404)	404
Peleg	30	130	130	130	209	209	109	(239)		(339)	239
Reu	32	130	132	132	207	207	107	(239)		(339)	239
Serug	30	132	130	130	200	200	100	(230)		(330)	230
Nahor	29	120	179	79	119	125	68	(148)		(304)	148
Terah	70	70	70	70				205	205	205	145

(Total from Deluge to Abraham's birth:
   either   292   993   1172   942
     or   290   1170   940)

Note: Bracketed figures are calculated from the data but do not appear in the texts.

ᵇ Only in *LXX*.

same in the first ten generations. The sole exception is Lamech
But the ages of paternity differ and the added years are made
conformable. This suggests deliberate tampering, but not necessarily by the LXX. The differences may have been introduced
by subsequent editors. Possibly the text translated by the LXX
differed from the surviving Hebrew text.

In the second group — Arphaxad through Terah — the ages of
paternity are 100 years higher in LXX, except Nahor whose
age is 150 years higher, and Terah whose age is the same. The
added years vary and the totals differ. The Samaritan text
agrees, except for Nahor, with the age of paternity in LXX but
agrees with the Masoretic terminal age, except for Eber, and
Terah — where it stands alone against the others.

Josephus omits the added years, except for Noah, and omits
the terminal ages from Shem through Nahor. By omitting the
ages of paternity for Noah and Shem he avoids the amibiguity in
connection with Arphaxad's birth, but delays that event until 12
years after the Deluge.

Josephus' work contains many perplexing discrepancies. It
would take a separate volume to discuss them all. I shall give
only two samples, both touching on a single point.

His list of generations from Terah back to Noah is presented
under the headline: "Abraham was born in the two hundred and
ninety-second year after the Deluge." This sum can be obtained
from the Masoretic data. But the data Josephus presents under
this heading add to 993.[1]

Later he says, "Solomon began to build the temple in the
fourth year of his reign...one thousand and twenty years from
Abraham's coming...into Canaan; and after the Deluge one thousand four hundred and forty years."[2] From this we deduce that
Abraham came into Canaan 420 years after the Deluge. Since he
was then 75, all texts agree, he must have been born 345 years
after the Deluge, not 292, nor yet 993.

Whiston believed that Josephus' work was corrupted by other
hands,[3] but wherever the difficulties originate it would be foolhardy to rely on this work in developing a biblical chronology.

If we accept the figures presented in the Septuagint, we shall
be even further from agreement with the Hebrew calendar. All
in all, the Masoretic text appears to be the most reliable. We
shall work from that. The Septuagint can be appealed to later if
that seems advisable.

We had arrived at a figure of -4102 (Gregorian) for the birth
of Adam. This is close to the date proclaimed for Creation by
James bishop Ussher, Irish archbishop of the Anglican church,
in his two volume *Annales Veteris et Novi Testamenti* (Analysis of Old and New Testaments) published in 1650-54. Bishop

Ussher declared the world was created in 4004 B.C., a date long accepted among Christians as unquestionable fact. Presumably he reached his conclusion by a process similar to the one which we have followed. But he may have chosen a different starting point for the "sojourn", and he may have used a different date for the destruction of Jerusalem. By following Josephus he would, as Whiston does,[1] arrive at a date 36 years too early for the first year of Cyrus. If he began the "sojourn" with the birth of Isaac, thus reducing the total by 131 years, and counted the two years between Arphaxad's birth and the Deluge, all but one year of the difference between our figure of -4102 and his of -4004 would be accounted for. But the point is hardly worth pursuing. Neither date is at all acceptable for the creation of the world, or of the first man. The accumulated knowledge of science ruled out such dates a long time ago. Rather than 4,000 years, we know today the earth was formed more nearly 4-billion years ago, and the first man at least 400,000 years before the epoch of the Common Era.

Our question regarding the determination of the epoch of the Jewish Mundane Era remains unanswered. We know only that the figure cannot be derived by adding the data given in the Bible and the correct date for the conquest of Babylon by Cyrus of Persia, using any of the feasible choices for the beginning of the "sojourn", and applying the common rules of arithmetic.

Perhaps in the 15th century, neither an estimate nor a calculation was made at all. The year number then made public may have been based on a count so old that no one knew how it had been established. Tradition said it began with Creation and that was held whether the biblical data supported it or not.

This, of course, does not constitute an answer to our question.

So far we have taken the years in bunches, making no effort to
determine whether any portion of the data correlates with information from extra-biblical sources. Suppose we work back
from the destruction of Jerusalem by Nebuchadnezzar in -587
toward the destruction of Samaria by Sargon II (or possibly
Shalmaneser V) in -722, and the sacking of Jerusalem by Shishak
(Sheshonk I) in -926.

Nebuchadnezzar first subjugated Jerusalem when he gained
control of the territory in -605, taking it from Pharaoh Necho
of Egypt. Necho had defeated king Josiah in battle at Megiddo
in -609, at which time Josiah was killed. Necho then led his
army in a swing through Syria, meeting no opposition, and re-
claiming to Egypt the territory all the way north to the Euphrates
river. During that time, a matter of three months, Jehoahaz
was king of Judah. But when Necho returned he took that unfortunate king into captivity and put Jehoiakim on the throne.

Three years later Nebuchadnezzar defeated Necho and Jehoiakim became subject to the king of Babylon. For a time he was
a faithful vassal, but then he rebelled, meaning only that he refused to pay the annual tribute.

II Kings and II Chronicles give two different versions of the
events associating Nebuchadnezzar with Jehoiakim. Neither
account is entirely clear. It would seem that Nebuchadnezzar
sent troops to humble the rebellious king of Judah and collect
tribute. But evidently he was not satisfied with the results, for
he came himself and laid siege to the city.

In the interim, Jehoiakim had died. His son Jehoiachin
reigned in his stead. But only for three months. Then:

> Jehoiachin the king of Judah went out to the king
> of Babylon, he, and his mother, and his servants,
> and his princes, and his officers; and the king of
> Babylon took him in the eighth year of his reign.
>
> (II K. 24:12)

Not the eighth year of Jehoiachin's reign, but the eighth year
of the reign of Nebuchadnezzar as king of Babylon, -597. The
biblical chroniclers were not always masters of syntax, but they
did know what was going on in the world around them. The
account is chronologically correct.

Nebuchadnezzar put Zedekiah on the throne of Judah. After
some years as a faithful vassal, he too rebelled.

> And it came to pass in the ninth year of his reign,
> in the tenth month, in the tenth day of the month,
> that Nebuchadnezzar king of Babylon came, he, and
> all his host, against Jerusalem, and pitched against
> it; and they built forts against it round about. (II K. 25:1)

In this case it is the ninth year of Zedekiah that is referred to, not the ninth year of Nebuchadnezzar.

> And the city was besieged unto the eleventh year of king Zedekiah. And on the ninth day of the fourth month the famine prevailed in the city, and there was no bread for the people of the land. And the city was broken up, and all the men of war fled by night by way of the gate between two walls, which is by the king's garden. (II K. 25:2-4)

The siege had lasted for exactly eighteen months. The city fell in the 11th year of king Zedekiah, which was the 19th year of Nebuchadnezzar, as II K. 25:8 correctly informs us. This was the year -587.

There is one more date given in II Kings (25:27) —

> And it came to pass in the 37th year of the captivity of Jehoiachin king of Judah, in the twelfth month, on the 27th day of the month, that Evil-merodach king of Babylon in the year that he began to reign did lift up the head of Jehoiachin king of Judah out of prison.

This works out to the year -561, the first year of the reign of Amel-Marduk son of Nebuchadnezzar. The Bible and the Babylonian records are in perfect agreement. There is no indication here of a "vague Hebraic attitude toward time." There is no lack of dating. Nor is there any suggestion of carelessness in arithmetic. But we have gone back only to -609.

Can we carry the dating farther back? Josiah died in -609, after a reign of 31 years. His reign began in -639. Before him Amon was king for two years, -641 and -640. Amon succeeded his father Manasseh who had been king for 55 years. Manasseh's reign began in -696, following the death of his father Hezekiah who had been king for 29 years.

Hezekiah must have become king in -725, the year in which Shalmaneser V began the siege of Samaria. That siege continued in -724 and -723. Then Sargon II succeeded to the throne of Assyria, and in -722 he completed the destruction of Samaria. This was the 9th and last year of Hoshea king of Israel, and it must also be the 4th year of Hezekiah king of Judah.

This correlation conflicts with II K. 18:1, which says the first year of Hezekiah was the third year of Hoshea. That would make the 9th year of Hoshea match the 7th year of Hezekiah. But this argues with verses 9 and 10 of the same chapter which do not even agree with each other, saying:

> ...in the fourth year of king Hezekiah, which was the seventh year of Hoshea ben-Elah king of Israel,

> Shalmaneser king of Assyria came up against Samaria, and besieged it; And at the end of three years they took it; even in the sixth year of Hezekiah, that is the ninth year of Hoshea... (II K. 18:9, 10)

Adding 3 years to any day in the 4th year would bring us to a corresponding day in the 7th year, not the 6th. But it would be correct, if the city was besieged in the 7th, 8th, and 9th year of Hezekiah, to say the siege lasted three years, and this is evidently the point that is intended. But, was the 9th year of Hoshea the same as the 7th, the 6th, or the 4th year of Hezekiah?

It is at this point that most chronologists frankly abandon the biblical data. Others resort to speculation in an attempt to save the situation. (Thiele correlates 9-Hoshea with 9-Ahaz — Ahaz was Hezekiah's father — while Albright makes 9-Hoshea match 14-Ahaz. For these correlations there is neither biblical nor historical evidence.) But the problem is not beyond solution.

Hezekiah succeeded his father king Ahaz, and, in II K. 16:2, we are told that Ahaz was king for 16 years. Then in II K. 17:1 we read:

> In the 12th year of Ahaz king of Judah began Hoshea ben-Elah to reign in Samaria over Israel 9 years.

A small chart makes the sequence of events easier to follow.

Ahaz	12	is	1	Hoshea
Ahaz	16	is	5	Hoshea
Hezekiah	1	is	6	Hoshea
Hezekiah	4	is	9	Hoshea

This confirms our previous finding. Obtaining the same answer from the biblical data in two separate ways seems quite enough to over-ride the confusion of II K. 18:1, 9, & 10, and conclusive enough to rule out further speculation on the matter.

Our next check—point is the 5th year of Rehoboam, -926. This is also the 5th year of Jeroboam, who became king of Israel the same year that Rehoboam became king of Judah upon the death of Solomon. We should have a great deal of difficulty if we tried to follow both lines of kings, those of Israel and those of Judah, at the same time, under the best of circumstances. The difficulty is compounded by the fact that the two lines do not show the same total number of years when the length-of-reign figures are added up. From the 5th year of Jeroboam to the 9th year of Hoshea the total is 236 years 7 months. From the 5th year of Rehoboam to the 4th year of Hezekiah the total is 253. Neither total agrees with the extra-biblical figure. From -722 to -926 is 204 years. We have a minimum discrepancy of 32 years 7 months, a maximum discrepancy of 49 years, between the biblical totals and the extra-biblical figure, and a difference between the two biblical totals of 16 years 5 months.

There is no obvious solution to this problem. Thiele solves it by introducing coregencies and overlapping reigns, Albright by disregarding the data.

The text supplies its own solution contained in the correlating data. If we set up a chart of the dual line of kings based on the synchronisms given in the text (see pp. 30-31), we discover just how good that solution is.

We find, for one thing, that we cannot use all of the synchronisms. '1 Omri'='31 Asa' is quite impossible, unless several other items are to be judged wrong instead. Jehoram of Israel is given two synchronisms. Both cannot be right. Since it is obviously impossible for '1 Jehoram of Israel' to match '2 Jehoram of Judah' if '1 Jehoram of Judah' matches '5 Jehoram of Israel', we discard that and use the other. '1 Azariah'='27 Jeroboam II' is also impossible without accepting several other errors instead.

If we use '1 Hezekiah'='3 Hoshea' the other correlations given for these two kings are wrong and we must accept a match between '7 Hezekiah' and '9 Hoshea' which adds 3 years to the discrepancy between the two totals, making it 19 years 5 months.

The entire period covered by the dual kingdom is shortened by the use of a nonaccession-year system, in most cases. This results in 12 overlappings in Judah, reducing that line by 6 years. We also find that some of the length-of-reign data does not fit. Jehoshaphat loses 3 full years, Joash 3, and Ahaz 2, a combined loss of 8 years. Altogether there is a total reduction of 14 years (8+6).

In Israel there are 18 overlappings, reducing the total by 9 years. Jeroboam loses 1 full year, Ahab 2, and Jehoahaz 2 for a total of 5. The full reduction here is also 14 years (9+5).

We added 3 and now we have subtracted 14, a net reduction of 11 years. This reduces the 49-year difference between biblical and extra-biblical history to 38 years. We still have a difference between the two lines of kings. The chart on page 31 shows us where that discrepancy occurs.

Between the end of the reign of Jeroboam II in '26 Azariah' and the beginning of Pekahiah's reign in '50 Azariah', a period of 23 years, we are told Zachariah ruled for 6 months, Shallum for 1 month, and Menahem for 10 years. This amounts to only 10 years 7 months. It would seem there were 12 years and 5 months, though not a continuous period, in which there was no king of Israel. At any rate we are not given an account of that time, so it is not in our total. The remaining discrepancy is 7 years. This is found between the 4th and 12th years of Ahaz, shrouded in confusion regarding the reign of Hoshea.

In one case we are told that '1 Hoshea' = '20 Jotham' though Jotham ruled only 16 years. This makes sense only if we say the year of Hoshea's accession would have been '20 Jotham' if Jotham had lived that long; it corresponds to '4 Ahaz'. Then we are told that '1 Hoshea'='12 Ahaz', and we do what we can to make sense of that. Ahaz loses 2 years, at least, Hoshea gains 7. There are other ways it might be worked out, but one is really no more acceptable than another.

Suppose we let this problem rest for the moment and see what happens if we continue on back. With an accumulated error of at least 38 years in a period of 204 it is difficult to have confidence in figures like the 430-year "sojourn" in Egypt, or the 480-year 'bridge' from Exodus to the 4th year of Solomon. But these figures might reflect the accuracy of the records for the later days of the kingdom, from -722 to -587. In that case the discrepancy will at least grow no larger.

> Solomon reigned in Jerusalem over all Israel forty years. (II Chron. 9:30)

From the 5th year of Rehoboam to the 4th year of Solomon would be 41 years. The biblical data would make the 5th year of Rehoboam -975. Then the 4th year of Solomon would be -1016. The 480-year 'bridge' would place the Exodus in -1496.

No other biblical date commands as much attention as that of the Exodus. Despite the fact that nothing relating to it is found in Egyptian records, aside from the deliberate nonsense of Manetho, no one asks, "Did it happen?" — only, "When?"

How likely is the date -1496?

Egyptologists are uncertain who was Pharaoh at that time. Thutmose I was replaced in -1501, either by Thutmose II or Thutmose III. If the latter, then he was subsequently forced to relinquish the throne to Thutmose II, only to regain it some few years later. But in either case, it appears that Egypt's most energetic queen, Hatshepsut, excercised the power during the period. She was daughter to Thutmose I, wife to Thutmose III, half-sister and also wife to Thutmose II. The Exodus might have been accomplished during this contest for control of the throne. But there are many obvious arguments against it.

We have included in this date the extra 49 years obtained by adding the reigns of the kings of Judah. If we took instead the Egyptian date for the 5th year of Rehoboam, the Exodus would occur in -1447. Some scholars have adopted this date for the Exodus. Though it is difficult to see how the term can be just-

Kings – According to Synchronisms Given in Text.

JUDAH Ref. I K.	King "1-r" (JUDAH)	"synchronism" (JUDAH)	Regnal years	BCE	King "1-r" (ISRAEL)	"synchronism" (ISRAEL)	Ref. I K. (ISRAEL)
14:21	Rehoboam "17"		1	968	Jeroboam		
			17	952	"22" (20 + fraction)		14:20
			1				
15:1	Abijah "18 Jeroboam"	"3" (1 fractional)	17	951	Nadab "2 Asa"		15:25
			18		"2" (both fractional)		
15:9	Asa "20 Jeroboam"		3	949			
			1				
			2	948	"21"		
			1		Baasha "3 Asa"		15:28, 33
			2		"2" (both fractional)		
			3	947			
			1				
			24	924	Elah "26 Asa"		16:8
			26		"2" (both fractional)		
			1				
			2		Zimri "7 days; 27 Asa"		16:10, 15
			27	923	Omri "31 Asa"		16:23
			1		"12" (2 fractional)		
			12		Ahab "38 Asa"		16:29
			38	912			
			1				
22:41	"41" (2 fractional) Jehoshaphat "4 Ahab"		41	909			
			4				
			20	893	Ahaziah "17 Jehoshaphat"		22:51
			17		"2" (both fractional)		
			1	892	Jehoram "18 Jehoshaphat" & "2 Jehoram"		II K. 3:1
			18		"12" (1 fractional)		
II K. 8:16	"25" (20 + 2 fractions) Jehoram "5 Joram"	"8" (2 fractional)	22	888			1:17
			5				
8:25	Ahaziah "12 Jehoram" (1 frac.) "1"		8	881			
			12				
11:3	Athaliah "6"		1	880	Jehu		10:36
			6	875			

Judah ref	Judah king (note)	Judah yr	B.C.	Syn.	Israel king (note)	Israel ref
11:4, 12:1	Joash "7 Athaliah; 7 Jehu"	1	874	7	Jehu "28"	
		22	853	28		
		23	852	1	Jehoahaz "23 Joash"	13:1
	"40" (37)	37	838	15	"17" (14 + fraction)	
		1		1	Jehoash "37 Joash"	13:10
14:1	Amaziah "2 Jehoash"	1	837	2		
14:17	"lived 15 years after Jehoash" (14+fraction)	15	823	16	"16" (2 fractional)	
		1		1	Jeroboam II "15 Amaziah"	14:23
	"29"	29	809	15		
15:1	Azariah "27 Jeroboam"	1	808	16		
		26	783	41	"41" (1 fractional)	
		27	782	1	Zachariah (11 yrs. 6 mon. ?)	15:8
		38	771	12	"6 mon. in 38 Azariah"	
				1	Shallum (7 mon. ?)	15:13
		39	770	1	"1 mon. in 39 Azariah"	15:17
				1	Menahem "39 Azariah"	
		49	760	11	"10" (10 yrs. 11 mon.)	
		50	759	1	Pekahiah "50 Azariah"	15:23
		51	758	2	"2"	
		52	757	1	Pekah "52 Azariah"	15:27
	"52"	1	756	2		
15:32, 33	Jotham "2 Pekah" "16" (1 fractional)	16	741	17		
16:1	Ahaz "17 Pekah"	1	738	4	"20"	20
		5	737	1	Hoshea "20 Jotham" (?)	15:30
		11	731	7		
		12	730	1	"12 Ahaz began 9 years"	17:1
	"16" (12 + 2 fractions)	14	728	3		
18:1	Hezekiah "3 Hoshea" (frac,)	1	725	6		
	(text matches 4 to 7 and, after 3 yrs., 6 to 9)	4 … 7	722	9	(9 + 7 = 16 total ?)	

The kingdom of Judah continues·········"Israel disappears from history.

ified, Rabbi Dr. Isidore Epstein refers to -1447 as "the Bibli-
cal date," while pointing out that "Several other dates for the
Exodus have been suggested ranging from 1584 B.C. to 1144
B.C."[1] Archbishop Ussher set it in -1491.

Clearly, none of the suggested dates has met with unanimous
approval. We cannot examine each of them individually, but all
are subject to the same difficulties, and we can examine those.

The biblical data gives just 40 years between the Exodus and
the battle of Jericho which begins the conquest of Canaan. Pharaohs Seti I (-1313/-1292), Rameses II (-1292/-1225), Merneptah (-1225/-1215), and Rameses III (-1198/-1167), conducted
military campaigns in Canaan. The last of these was in connection with the great invasion-migration of the "Peoples of the Sea"
about -1190. The books of Joshua and Judges make no mention
of these events. If the Exodus occurred earlier than -1230,
it would be difficult to explain how such events could be ignored.
The earlier the date of the Exodus the greater this difficulty.

Looking in the other direction, toward the beginning of the
"sojourn", we have an equally difficult problem. It has been
widely accepted that Joseph and Jacob are to be associated with
the Hyksos domination of Egypt. But this idea deserves to be
examined. Josephus asserts that the Hyksos *are* the Hebrews,
while subtly making it seem that Manetho has said it. He writes:

> Now, this Manetho, in the second book of his Egyp-
> tian History, writes concerning us [the Jews] in the
> following manner. I will set down his very words...:
> "There was a king [of Egypt] whose name was Timaus,
> Under him it came to pass, I know not how, that God
> was averse to us [the Egyptians], and there came, in
> a surprising manner, men of ignoble birth out of the
> eastern parts, and had boldness enough to make an
> expedition into our country, and with ease subdued
> if by force, yet without our hazarding a battle with
> them. So when they had gotten those that governed
> us under their power, they afterwards burnt down
> our cities, and demolished the temples of the gods,
> and used all the inhabitants after a most barbarous
> manner: nay, some they slew, and led their children
> and their wives into slavery. At length they made
> one of themselves king, whose name was Salatis;..
> .he found...a city...which lay upon the Bubastic
> channel, but with regard to a certain theologic no-
> tion was called *Avaris*, this he rebuilt, and made
> very strong by the walls he built about it... This
> whole nation was styled HYCSOS, that is *Shepherd —
> kings*; for the first syllable HYC, according to the

sacred dialect denotes *a king*, and SOS, *a shepherd* - but only according to the ordinary dialect; and of these is compounded HYCSOS: but some say that these people were Arabians... (They) kept possession of Egypt five hundred eleven years." After these, he says, "That the kings of Thebais and of other parts of Egypt made an insurrection against the shepherds (who) were driven out of other parts of Egypt, but were shut up...in Avaris. (Then) Thummosis,...upon his despair of taking the place by siege...came to a composition with them, that they should leave Egypt, and go without any harm to be done to them...and (they) took their journey from Egypt, through the wilderness...(and) they built a city in that country which is now called Judea... and called it Jerusalem." Now Manetho, in another book of his, says, "That this nation, thus called Shepherds, was also called Captives, in their sacred books." And this account of his is the truth; for feeding of sheep was the employment of our forefathers in the most ancient ages; and...they were called Shepherds. Nor was it without reason that they were called Captives by the Egyptians, since one of our ancestors, Joseph, told the king of Egypt that he was a captive, and afterwards sent for his brethren into Egypt by the king's permission.[1]

Notice that it is Josephus, more anxious to prove the antiquity of his people than to give them a good character, who claims descent from the Hyksos. Though Manetho gives his version of the Exodus in a separate account, which Josephus quotes elsewhere,[2] Josephus here presumes that the expulsion of the Hyksos is to be indentified with that biblical event. But the stories do not compare. The Bible does not permit us to suppose that the Hebrews ruled Egypt as the Hyksos did. Nor does it permit us to believe that the Hebrews built Jerusalem. That city is to be identified with Salem, ruled by Melchizedek in the time of Abraham (see Gen. 14:18).

If Salem was built by the Hyksos, after they left Egypt, their era precedes that of Abraham and can have nothing to do with Joseph or Jacob.

As for the 511 years, this may be a later scribal error, for Josephus himself seems to know nothing of this number, and it does not tally with Manetho's list of six Hyksos kings, also quoted by Josephus, whose reigns add to 204 years, 8 months. Furthermore, although the Bible would allow the Hebrews to remain in Egypt for as long as 430 years, Josephus states that the actual time in Egypt was only 215 years.[1] So it seems most unlikely that this 511-year figure belongs in his text.

In any event, the figure is too large. Breasted allows 208 years for Dynasties Thirteen through Seventeen, which includes the Hyksos domination, but feels they actually occupy only the last 100 years of this period, ending in -1580. He characterizes the identification of the Hyksos with the Hebrews as "the naive assumption of Josephus,"[2] yet confidently asserts that the Jacob-tribes must have entered Egypt "at about this age," suggesting that they were "but a part of the Beduin allies of the Kadesh or Hyksos empire."[3] But if this were true it would be difficult to explain why, when the Hyksos were driven out, the Hebrews were allowed, even forced, to stay.

Manetho is quoted on the subsequent Egyptian history down to a king Sethosis, who had a brother Armais who opposed him and was therefore banished. Josephus writes, "The country also was called from his name *Egypt*: for Manetho says that Sethosis himself was called Egyptus, as was his brother Armais called Danaus."[4] This identification pleases Josephus, for he feels it establishes the antiquity he claims for his people. He writes:

> This is Manetho's account; and evident it is from the number of years by him set down belonging to this interval, if they be summed up together, that these shepherds, as they are here called, who were no others than our forefathers, were delivered out of Egypt, and came thence, and inhabited this country three hundred and ninety-three years [actual sum 327] before Danaus came to Argos; although the Argives look upon him as their most ancient king.
>
> (Thus proving the Exodus to have) preceded the siege of Troy almost a thousand years.[5]

The actual date is not important to Josephus. He has accomplished his purpose — to show from records other than those of his own people, and therefore unbiased, that the Jews are more ancient than the Greeks. Of course, the historian with such a purpose cannot help but present a distorted view of the past. Had Josephus been less emotionally involved on this particular point he might have been less willing to claim the Hyksos as his ancestors.

Who, exactly, the Hyksos were, is yet to be determined. Breasted objects to Manetho's analysis of their name on the grounds that the monuments left by these rulers do not bear such a title. Instead, he says, they are marked with the Egyptian title *Hk'*, signifying the idea "Ruler," followed by a syllable for "countries" which, "by slight and very common phonetic changes might become 'sos'; so that Hyksos is a not improbable Greek spelling for the Egyptian title 'Ruler of Countries'."[1]

Not mentioned by either Manetho or Breasted is that *sus* is one of the Arabic words for "horse". The Hyksos introduced the horse into Egypt. He may have been calling himself, not in Egyptian but in his own tongue, "Master of the Horse."

Very probably Arabian, and the record shows, as we might therefore expect, the Hyksos was also a herder of sheep — of all the world's creatures the one most deservedly called *dumb*.

The Egyptian, despising his conqueror, would not be expected to humbly accord him the title he gave himself. So, 'by slight phonetic changes' he mispronounced the title, making it signify in Egyptian, "Leader of Sheep."

Even after the Hyksos had learned proper Egyptian this interlingual pun must have escaped him, for the second syllable, as Manetho points out, is Egyptian slang. But -countries, -horses, -sheep, whatever they ruled, the Hyksos were certainly not the biblical Hebrews.

If more assurance is wanted, note that Joseph, when preparing his brothers to meet the Pharaoh, says, "When Pharaoh asks, 'What is your occupation?' you must say, 'Our work and our father's work has always been with cattle.' For every shepherd is an abomination to the Egyptians."(See Gen. 46:33, 34.)

Clearly, the Pharaoh they are about to meet is not of their people; his ideas differ. He is not Hyksos, a leader of sheep. And, since the Egyptian prejudice against shepherds probably starts with the Hyksos domination, a later period is indicated.

The numerical data, on the other hand, would put Joseph in Egypt even earlier. Taking -926 for the 5th year of Rehoboam, we add 41 and get -967 for the 4th year of Solomon. Adding 480 gives us -1447 for the Exodus, and adding another 430 for the "sojourn" puts Joseph in Egypt in -1877, more than 200 years before the arrival of the Hyksos.

To use all of the biblical data we must add 49 years more.

We found a cumulative error of 49 years in a period of 204. Now we find that the 480- and 430-year figures are probably too large.

Can each individual number be too large? Or rather, are we treating these numbers in a way that makes their sum too large? If the ancient Hebrews were using a counting system with a base-number smaller than the one we use, adding their numbers by our rules would produce just such an effect. This possibility deserves to be carefully explored.

Chapter IV - IN PREPARATION

Is there any such thing as *proof*?   Or is there only *belief*?
Every so-called proof is based on a set of axioms, assumptions
which are themselves not proved but so generally regarded as
true that they are accepted without question.   Even in those
areas of thought classified as science, proof is not qualitatively
different from that applied in criminal justice where decisions
are based on the absence of reasonable doubt. It would be foolish to think that the matter put forward in this book is somehow
different from every other.

We must start with the axioms, then, not only to establish
what they are but also to show what they are not.   For a false
assumption may prevent consideration of valid evidence.

First, some thoughts about the origin and development of the
Old Testament.   A vast literature exists on this subject.   It
cannot be summarized in a few pages, and I shall not pretend to
try. I fully intend to emphasize certain pertinent aspects of the
topic.

The Old Testament is a collection of many separate writings,
an anthology of ancient Hebrew literature. It is by no means the
entire body of that literature which at one time existed.   The
text repeatedly refers to the sources from which it has been
drawn, none of which have survived separately.   That these
various sources, of which at least half a dozen are mentioned,
contained additional information cannot be doubted. Repeatedly
the question is asked, with appropriate variations:

> And the rest of the acts of Solomon, and all that he
> did, and his wisdom, are they not written in the
> book of the acts of Solomon? (I K. 11:41)

to cite only one example.

Several times we are referred to the "chronicles" either of
the kings of Judah or of Israel.   One might suppose this meant
one of the books called *Chronicles* in the present text. This is
not the case, for we simply do not find additional information in
most instances in those books, and sometimes no mention at all
of the matter referred to.

The Hebrews did not carve their records in stone as the
Egyptians, or inscribe their writings on tablets of imperishable
clay as the Babylonians and Assyrians did. They wrote with ink
on leather, linen, or papyrus scrolls, subject to wear and tear
and the ravages of time. Fresh copies of important documents
had to be made periodically or the contents would be lost.

Vital records were preserved in the manner of the Dead Sea
Scrolls, and the even older Elephantine Papyri. This ancient
practice is described in Jeremiah 32, which tells how Jeremiah
bought land and —

took the evidence of the purchase, both that which
was sealed according to the law and custom, and
that which was open...and gave the evidence...to
Baruch...in the presence of the witnesses that sub-
scribed the book of the purchase (i.e., signed the
scroll)...and I charged Baruch before them, saying
...'Take these evidences... and put them in an earthen
vessel, that they may continue many days.' (Jer. 32:11-14)

One document, perhaps preserved in this fashion, was found
by Hilkiah the high priest during the reign of Josiah. Two accounts of the discovery are given, one in II Kings 22, one in II
Chronicles 34. The latter says:

And when they brought out the money that was brought
into the house of the Lord, Hilkiah the priest found
the book of the Law of the Lord given by Moses.
(II Ch. 34:14)

suggesting the possibility that the book was somewhere in the
container in which the money had been collected. II Kings omits
this detail. Since the Temple was being repaired at the time it
has been suggested that the book was uncovered in the course of
reconstruction, perhaps in a hidden crypt.

There are other differences in the two accounts of Josiah's
reign. According to II Chronicles, Josiah began to purge the
land of idolaters in the twelfth year of his reign, while the book
was not found until the eighteenth year. In II Kings it was the
contents of the newly discovered book that inspired Josiah to
institute reforms.

The book Hilkiah found is often taken to be the book now known
as Deuteronomy. Some believe it included only a portion of
Deuteronomy. There are differences of opinion as to which
portion. The point need not be debated here. Our interest is in
the fact that a document had been lost, was subsequently found,
and proved to contain important material that had been forgotten.
This latter point is made abundantly clear in both accounts, for
Josiah, on hearing the book read, says:

...great is the wrath of the Lord that is kindled
against us, because our fathers have not hearkened
unto the words of this book... (II K. 22:13; II Ch. 34:21)

This is not the only instance in which lost books were redis-
covered. The entire official library was reconstituted on two
separate occasions. This is stated in II Maccabees, in a letter
to the Jews of Egypt, which reads:

The same things are reported in the records and in
the memoirs of Nehemiah, and also that he founded

> a library and collected the books about the kings and
> prophets, and the writings of David, and letters of
> kings about votive offerings. In the same way Judas
> also collected all the books that had been lost on
> account of the war which had come upon us, and they
> are in our possession. (II Macc. 2:13,14. RSV)

This is confirmed in Nehemiah 8, which tells of the public
reading of "the book of the law of Moses" by Ezra the scribe,
assisted by a number of men who "caused the people to understand the law."

> And they found written in the law...that the children
> of Israel should dwell in booths in the feast of the
> seventh month...And all the congregation out of the
> captivity made booths, and sat under the booths:
> Since the days of Joshua ben-Nun unto that day had
> not the children of Israel done so; and there was
> very great gladness.   (Neh. 8:14-17)

In the present text the only other reference to this custom is
found in Leviticus 23:39-43.

They also learned that "the Ammonite and the Moabite should
not come into the congregation of God forever." (Neh. 13:1)
This is found elsewhere in the present text only in Deut. 23:3.

We may suppose that Ezra read both Leviticus and Deuteronomy to the people, or that "the book of the law of Moses" was
another document, no longer extant.   It could have been either
the source from which the writers of these books drew their
material, or it could have been a compilation of excerpts from
these two books, or all three could be indebted to a common
source.

The book Ezra read to the people may have been the same as
that discovered by Hilkiah many years earlier. After Josiah had
heard that book:

> The king went up to the house of the Lord, and all the
> inhabitants of Jerusalem with him, and the priests,
> both small and great; and he read in their ears all
> the words of the book of the covenant which was found
> in the house of the Lord. And the king stood on the
> platform, and made a covenant before the Lord, to
> walk after the Lord, and to keep his commandments,
> and his testimonies and his statutes, with all his
> heart, and all his soul, to confirm the words of this
> covenant that were written in this book; and all the
> people stood to the covenant. (II K. 23:2,3. JPSA)
>   (Almost identical is II Ch. 34:29-32.)

The reading by Ezra in the days of Nehemia had a similar effect:

> They... entered into a curse, and into an oath, to walk in God's law, which was given by Moses, the servant of God, and to observe all the commandments of the Lord our Lord, and his judgements and his statutes; and that we would not give our daughters unto the people of the land, nor take their daughters for our sons. (Neh. 10:29, 30)

Not only the people, but the priests, and the Levites, also listened to the reading, "to understand the words of the law." (Neh. 8:13). The reading was such a revelation that one must suppose, even though it is not stated, that the book had been lost and was newly found. During the captivity in Babylon surely much had been forgotten.

For Nehemiah and, later, Judas Maccabaeus to reconstitute the library there had to be sources from which the books could be drawn. One may have been hidden archives of preserved scrolls, possibly in the ruins of the Temple. Being of different ages, the scrolls would be in varying stages of decay, as the Dead Sea Scrolls were. But there may well have been more than one such preserved library. In the 48 cities that belonged to the Levites we might reasonably expect that archives were kept, containing copies of the most important books, at least. What was damaged in one copy might be legible in another, making possible more or less complete reconstruction of the text.

In addition, there would be private collections, containing legal documents such as the evidence of sale that Jeremiah tells of, private correspondence, portions of scripture, and perhaps the writings of the so-called minor prophets who seem to have been men of no particular status in their own time and could well have been private individuals. Which assumes a more widespread literacy than is generally acknowledged for the period. There is abundant evidence that this assumption should be made. The vast quantity of cuneiform writings found in shops and homes of Ur and Nippur, written c. -3000/-2000, indicate the ability to read and write could not even then have been limited to a few. The ancient practice of erecting monuments inscribed with long messages in as many as three languages would make no sense if 90 per-cent of those who passed by would be unable to read any one of them. To suppose that those who spent their lives carving hieroglyphs all over the surfaces of Egyptian buildings had no idea of the significance of what they carved, or that only a minor fraction of those who viewed the finished work were able to understand it, is not credible. The content of much of this work is clearly directed to the common man. Many Egyptian paintings include words spoken by the people represented, in the style of our modern cartoons. One craftsman pictured in the act of making a stone dish says, "This is a beautiful bowl." His companion, working on another piece, replies, "It certainly is." It is hard to imagine that such literary gems were spelled out for the sole appreciation of an erudite nobility. And there are graffitti, definite assurance of the literacy of the many.

Thousands of ancient Sumerian tablets have been translated, revealing many interesting facets of Sumerian culture. Pertinent to the point being examined here are the words of a graduate regarding his teacher:

> He guided my hand on the clay, showed me how to behave properly, opened my mouth with words, uttered good counsel, focused my eyes on the rules that guide the man of achievement.[1]

And a conversation between father and son:

> "Where did you go?"
> "I did not go anywhere."
> "If you did not go anywhere, why do you idle about? Go to school...Don't stand about in the public square or wander on the boulevard...Don't look all around. Be humble and show fear before your monitor. When you show terror, the monitor will like you."[2]

The school (in Sumerian, *edubba*, the first sounds of which give the word a familiar ring) turned young men into professionals, capable of running an estate, abitrating disputes, surveying fields, advising a client regarding the law, writing legal documents, and doing complicated mathematical calculations.

Not everyone received such education. But that does not mean that only the trained professionals were able to read and write and figure. The fact that a man employs a secretary, a bookkeeper, and a lawyer, is not now regarded as proof of his ignorance. Many may have lacked formal education, but that is not the only way to learn. Parental help and self-instruction have been known to produce excellent results in recent times. There is no reason to think them non-existant in the past.[3]

To connect this discussion with the Bible, we have in Judges 17, 18, the story of Micah and a certain "young man out of Bethlehem...who was a Levite...departed out of the city... to sojourn where he could find a place." Micah had a graven image, an ephod, a teraphim, and a molten image, and he said to the young Levite, "Dwell with me, and be to me a father and a priest, and I will give you ten shekels a year, and a suit of apparel, and your victuals."

Neither Micah nor the young Levite should be thought exceptional, for the following instructions are given to cover just such a case:

> And if a Levite come from any of your gates out of all Israel, where he sojourned, and come with all desire of his mind unto the place which the Lord shall choose; Then he shall minister in the name of the Lord his God, as all his brethren the Levites do which stand there before the Lord. (Deut. 18:6, 7)

So this Levite served as Micah's personal priest, until a band of Danites stole the images and induced the Levite to go with them to be the priest of their tribe. (Ju. 18:20ff)

Religious beliefs differed, but otherwise the pattern of civilization was probably little changed from that of ancient Sumer. The school attended by the Levite surely taught him to read and write. Much of his time had probably been spent copying those books which would be most important to him in the performance of his duties. Portions, at least, of such copies may have been preserved.

The first five books, the Pentateuch, Chumash, or Torah, were treated as sacred at an early date, and Joshua perhaps not much later, but "it is to be concluded that none of the other books of the Old Testament ranked as canonical prior to about 400 B.C."[1] With all of the copying and recopying there were many opportunities for minor, and even major revisions, insertions, or corrections to be made before the literature was canonized, and circumstances under which changes were of necessity made even after that time.[2] It would be understandable if the chronological data were not usable at all. That they contain some errors is to be expected. Indeed, the remarkable fact, as we shall discover, is that the errors are so few. But even those few have produced what may fairly be called —the world's oldest half-solved puzzle; for ancient 'corrections' have become part of the problem rather than part of the solution.

I find I am by no means the first to present such thoughts. The German biblical scholar, Professor Rudolf Kittel, said essentially the same thing nearly a century ago. He wrote:

> The Israelitish numbers and the parallel numbers referring to Judah do not agree at the points at which we are able to compare them. Besides, the well-established Assyrian dates differ considerably from those deduced from the Old Testament. Both facts show either that the numbers, originally given accurately, of the Book of Kings, were in course of time altered by disturbing influences (errors of scribes,

misapprehensions of the meaning, etc.), or else that
we are no longer in a position to discover the original methods or reckoning according to which the
sums of the several items were bound to agree; or
finally, that both causes have contributed to bring
about the present state of things. *The latter is
most likely the case.* [1]

Emphasis has been added to Professor Kittel's logical conclusion, for it turns out to be perfectly correct, but he himself
seems to have despaired of finding a solution. Others have used
the idea as an excuse for declaring the biblical data unusable.
At least one theorist has assumed numerous changes in the
counting base, thus seemingly justifying his preconceptions.
But an idea that has been rejected, or abused, is not thereby
invalidated. We need not be discouraged from exploring this one.

Had the ancient Hebrews used a counting base other than ten,
they must have changed to base-ten sometime before -722. For
after that date we have no difficulty with the data. Is it plausible
to suppose that after such a change the earlier system, even the
fact that there had been another system, might be forgotten?

Surely this is not impossible if they could twice lose and
twice forget not only the content but the very existence of
"the book of the law of Moses."

Recognizing the possibility that another counting system was
used does not help to determine what that system was or for
what period it was in use. That is what we must try to do. But
first it would be well to consider certain aspects of what is known
of the history of numbers.

We are all familiar with the so-called Arabic numerals. Most
of us know something of the Roman numerals. The much more
ancient systems used in Babylon and Sumeria are less widely
appreciated.

The Arabic numerals did not come into use in the English-
speaking world until nearly 1500. "In Britain the earliest case
is said to be the rent roll of the St. Andrews chapter in 1490,"
Lancelot Hogben reports. [2] Their use had become increasingly
popular in Italy after the publication in 1228 of an arithmetic for
merchants by Leonardo Fibonacci, called *Liber Abaci. Liber*
means "book"; it also means "free"; *abaci* is the plural of
abacus, the counting device which the new numbers made unnecessary. Despite edicts forbidding the use of the 'infidel ciphers'
— in Florence in 1259, in Padua as late as 1348—their use continued. Even the monks favored them, and it was, in fact, two
monks — Adelard of Bath, and Gerard of Cremona — who were
primarily responsible for their introduction into Italy. Dis—

guised as Moslems, both had attended Moorish universities in Spain where they translated from the Arabic the works of Euclid and Ptolemy and a large number of other important texts.

This accounts for the term 'Arabic numerals', sometimes called Gobar numerals, from the Arabic *ghubar*. The word means "dust" and relates to the Arab's version of a writing tablet which consists of a board covered with dust or fine sand in which the student writes with his finger. (In Hebrew "fine sand" is *abakah*. In Greek *abakos* means "board". Compare Latin, *abacus*, the counting frame.)

The *ghubar* writing is still used in the schools of India. And it is in India, in fact, that the numerals originate. They were introduced into the Arab world about 800, when Baghdad was a center of learning. The Hindus had been using them from about the time of Alexander, *c.* -300, and in the next several centuries there was a major development of mathematics in India. By 470 the Hindu, Aryabhata, had written his mathematical treatise, *Lilavati*. "This author discusses the rules of arithmetic, uses the law of signs of Diophantus, gives a table of sines in intervals of 3 3/4°, and evaluates π as 3.1416."[1] He wrote fractions with one number over the other, but without the bar in between. Rules were stated for calculation with zero, called *sunya* "empty, rest."

English "empty" comes from Anglo-Saxon *aemetig* "empty, idle," from *aemetta* "quiet, leisure, rest." (Webster.)

When the Arabs began using the Hindu *sunya*, they translated it into Arabic as *sif'r* "empty," whence English "cipher."

About the same time that the Hindu produced his cursive numerals a change occurred in the Greek numeration. Until that time the Greek numeral *one* was a vertical stroke, but other numerals were acrophonic; i.e., the initial letter of a number-word was used for its symbol. The number "five" was written Γ, an early form of the more familiar Π, for *pente*. The initial letter Δ (delta) of *deka* "ten", the H (eta) of *hekaton* "hundred", and the X (chi) of *xilioi* "thousand", represented those numbers. Their use was like that of the Roman numerals. Calculations were made with the aid of the abacus.

About -300, the acrophonic numerals were replaced with an entirely different system. A complete new set of alphabet characters was introduced. Their names were the same, but their shapes quite different from the earlier Greek letters. The letter *digamma*, which had been dropped from the alphabet because it appeared in no Greek words, was reinstated. The letters *koph* and *sampi*, which had no counterpart in the older Greek alphabet, were borrowed from the Phoenician alphabet. The first nine letters of this augmented alphabet were assigned values 1 to 9,

the next nine letters – values 10 to 90, the remaining nine –
values 100 to 900.   The added letters, *koph* and *sampi*, had
been selected to fit the sequence where values 90 and 900 would
apply.   This would minimize their use and make them easy to
remember.

The same system is used in Hebrew, but the Hebrew alphabet
supplies only enough characters to reach the number 400.   We
do not know when the Hebrews began to use this system.

Surely there was nothing accidental or haphazard about the
Greek innovation.   If it was not a Greek invention, it was at
least a deliberate intellectual choice.   It was to some extent an
unfortunate choice, for it fostered numerology. With letters and
numbers represented by the same symbols every word has a
numerical value, and many numbers can be pronounced as words.
Superstitious numerological byplay distracted even the serious
Greek mathematicians.

The Greek system is ill adapted to the abacus.   It is therefore safe to assume that it was not chosen with that instrument
in mind.   But mental, and thus written arithmetic is extraordinarily difficult with this numeration for there are just too many
combinations to be memorized.   The Greek mathematician was
virtually forced to use multiplication tables and even prepared
tables of sums and differences for most of his calculations.   The
only apparent advantage of the system is brevity, compactness.
Since this would be significant only in the preparation of tables,
it seems probable that this is what its designers had in mind.

The scholars who accompanied Alexander very probably got
the idea of using mathematical tables in Persia, which had been
Babylonia, and before that Sumeria.   The Sumerians had used
multiplication tables, tables of squares and cubes, of square
roots and cube roots, and of inverses, as early as -2000.   At
that early date they were solving quadratic equations and other
equally complex problems.   The Greek's of Alexander's   time
had not yet approached such problems.   They must have been
impressed.   Understandably, they would think to imitate the
Mesopotamian methods.

But, while the methods were attractive, the cuneiform numerals used in Mesopotamia were not, for the Greeks did not
write on clay.   On paper the cuneiform is especially clumsy.
So the Greeks would be very much interested in some more
convenient script.   In India, apparently, they found what they
were looking for.

The chart (page 47) compares the Hindu numerals, the Greek
and the Hebrew numeral-alphabets.   The similarities between
the upper-case Greek and the Old Hebrew alphabets have been
frequently noted.   But the similarities between the lower-case

Greek alphabet and the Hindu numerals have not, to my knowledge, been previously recognized. Yet many of the lower-case
Greek letters are more like the Hindu numerals than they are
like the upper-case Greek.

Beta and gamma seem to reverse the order of the Hindu two
and three. Delta and Hindu four are nearly the same. Zeta and
seven have much in common. Eta and eight are the same sign
differently oriented. Though digamma is quite different from
the Hindu six that sign is duplicated exactly in the lower-case
Greek xi (*see*) whose value is sixty. Alpha (1), iota (10), and
rho (100) all favor the Hindu one, while retaining a likeness to
their upper-case forms. Is it reasonable to pass all this off as
accident or coincidence?

Since both systems originate about the same time, and just
after Alexander's invasion of India, it would seem most likely
that Hindu and Greek scholars collaborated to some extent,
working from a common model, yet following a somewhat different course for reasons of their own.

Why the Greeks, for all their brilliance, failed to invent zero,
has puzzled generations of scholars. But with the Greeks and
Hindus working out their numerals together the puzzle would
seem even more imponderable. It would appear that the Greeks
actually rejected zero.

But Ptolemy, the great Greek astronomer, in his *Almagest*,
written *c.* 150, did in fact use zero. For both linear and angular
measure he employed the Sumerian sexagesimal system, writing
his numerals in the Greek style. He ruled his paper in vertical
columns —for units, sixtieths, and thirtysixhundredths. And he
wrote a neat "0" in any column that contained no other figure.[1]

Ptolemy's symbol for zero and the use of ruled columns may
have been his own ideas, but the concept of zero was bequethed
him by the Babylonians who learned it from the Sumerians
c. -3000. Contrary to many reports, zero was not first invented
by the Hindus, as Professor Edward Chiera made clear:

> In a volume by a great mathematician there is this
> statement: "It needed all of the philosophical insight
> of the Hindu to take nothing and represent that nothing
> with a concrete symbol." I am sorry to disagree
> with a very great scholar, but the philosophical
> insight of the Sumerian was more than sufficient.
> When they wrote down a series of figures, if in one of
> the columns representing, let us say, the hundreds,
> no figure appeared, they would write in its place a
> sign that meant "not"...That "not" corresponds ap-
> proximately to our "naught," which is itself the same
> as the zero...and they wrote down their "not" at
> least two thousand years before the Hindu..."[2]

It has been objected that the Sumerians were inconsistent in their use of zero, omitting it at the end of a number — as if we were to write "1" for *one*, and also "1" for *ten*. But ambiguity was generally avoided by naming the units of measure, as we distinguish between '1 ounce' and '1 pound'. Yet in some cases this distinction is missing. Whether this caused the Sumerian as much trouble as it causes the archeologist seems doubtful, for the Sumerian had the means and surely the wit to eliminate the difficulty if he felt the need.

It has also been said that the Babylonian or Sumerian zero was no more than a punctuation mark, that the Hindus were the first to treat zero as a number. The point has been debated. Not all mathematicians have agreed that zero should be classed as a number. In reality it depends upon how the term "number" is defined. Is it synonymous with "symbol" or with "quantity"? In fact, the term is used very loosely and may be either.

Certainly zero has unique characteristics. Any other numerical symbol may serve as divisor; zero may not. Multiplying by zero has the effect of subtracting a number from itself. Subtracting or adding zero has no effect. The value of every other digit is affected by its position, but zero always retains its absolute value — nothing at all.

Since our concern is with numeration rather than calculation the point need not be settled. In chronology only addition and subtraction are used. One does not divide or multiply one calendar date by another. So, in an age or a date, zero serves only as a place-holder.

Of central importance in the history of numbers is the ancient Sumerian sexagesimal system (base-60). It is still in common use in the division of the hour into 60 minutes and the minute into 60 seconds, and in the division of angular degrees into fractional units, using the same names. When Sir Leonard Woolley writes, "The origin of the system is still in dispute," he refers not to the people who devised it but to the source of their inspiration. "Most authorities," he continues, "agree in attributing it to metrology. Certainly the weights are consistently sexagesimal — 180 grains make a shekel, 60 shekels make a *mina*, 60 *mina* make a talent..."[1]

This suggestion seems to originate with Prof. Neugebauer[2] who merely supposes that a 60 to 1 ratio was first used for the weights employed in measuring silver, that this convention was subsequently applied to other sorts of measure, and finally to numbers in general. He suggests no reason for the application of that ratio to the weighing of silver, so one question replaces another.

Before the Sumerian could develop the sexagesimal system

Hindu numerals, Greek and Old Hebrew numeral-alphabets.

Value	HINDU	NEW	GREEK Name	OLD	OLD HEBREW	Name	Value
1	?	α	alpha	A	✝	aleph	1
2	ν	β	beta	B	9	beth	2
3	ν	γ	gamma	Γ	∧	gimel	3
4	४	δ	delta	Δ	▷	daleth	4
5	५	ε	epsilon	E	∃	he	5
6	६	Ϛ	digamma	(F)	Y	vau	6
7	७	ζ	zeta	Z	Z	zayin	7
8	τ	η	eta	H	⩑	cheth	8
9	ॡ	ϑ	theta	Θ	⊗	teth	9
10	? ०	ι	iota	I	Z	yodh	10
20	ν ०	κ	kappa	K	Y	caph	20
30	ν ०	λ	lambda	Λ	l	lamedh	30
40	४ ०	μ	mu	M	ツ	mem	40
50	५ ०	ν	nu	N	ッ	nun	50
60	६ ०	ξ	xi	Ξ	∓	samekh	60
70	७ ०	o	omicron	O	O	'ayin	70
80	τ ०	π	pi	Π	⅃	pe	80
90	ॡ ०	Ϟ	koph		⋏	sadhe	90
100	? ००	ρ	rho	P	Ϙ	koph	100
200	ν ००	σ	sigma	Σ	◁	resh	200
300	ν ००	τ	tau	T	W	sin	300
400	४ ००	υ	upsilon	Υ	†	tav	400
500	५ ००	φ	phi	Φ			
600	६ ००	χ	chi	X			
700	७ ००	ψ	psi	Ψ			
800	τ ००	ω	omega	Ω			
900	ॡ ००	ϡ	sampi				

(The arrangement is numerical, *not* phonetic.)

he had to learn to count to sixty.   He did not do this by inventing a continuous sequence of that many digits.   Within the sixty
he employed a shorter cycle, as we do.   We must learn more
about that subordinate cycle.

The earliest Sumerian number signs are found on tablets
bearing pictographic writing.   These were produced prior to
-3000, before the cuneiform writing had been devised.   Two
signs —a circle and a larger circle— represent "one" and some
larger number, generally thought to be "ten". On some of these
early tablets the sign for 'one' is a crescent, made with a round
stylus held at an angle, while the larger number is represented
by a full circle, usually of the same diameter as the crescent,
so that both signs could be made with the same tool, but sometimes there is a difference in size.   In some cases the crescent
is the larger and in others the smaller of the two. In any case,
these signs cannot be evaluated directly.   Even a tablet bearing
many such signs supplies no proof of the numerical values unless
the counting sequence is shown, or arithmetical operations are
included.   Such clues are supplied only on later tablets.

When the value of a particular sign has been discovered it
might seem reasonable to attribute the same value to that sign
when it is found on another tablet, even one made at an earlier
time.   But this is not always a safe assumption.   In different
periods the same sign was often given a different value, as is
readily seen from a study of the *Sumero-Babylonian Sign List*
published by Dr. Samuel A.B. Mercer.[1] The list shows the signs
used for different purposes in six periods, as follows:

"Period 1 - Ur Nina to Manistusu," *c.* -3000/-2400.
"Period 2 - Sargon to Gudea," *c.* -2400/-2100.
"Period 3 - Ur III," *c.* -2100/-1900.
"Period 4 - Babylon I to Kassites," *c.* -1900/-1600.
"Period 5 - Kassites, including Pashe," *c.* -1600/-1200.
"Period 6 - Neo-Babylonian," after -1200.

The high risk of error in guessing the value of a sign is clear
when it is observed that in Period 1:
▸— meant 1.
Ϯ meant 1, or 36 *ka* in land measure.
o meant 1, or 3600.
D meant 1, or 60, or 1/18 th.
▸Ϯ in Period 1 meant 6, in Period 2 meant 1/2, in Periods 3 – 4
meant 1/2 or 10, in Periods 5 – 6 meant 6, as in Period 1.

One logical yet ingenious device that was regularly used is
most clearly illustrated in Period 3 where both ⟨ and ⟨ meant
10, and the sign ◇ meant 60 or 3600. Multiples of 3600 were
represented by placing 'tens' inside the square.

Thus: $\diamondsuit$ = 36,000; $\diamondsuit$ = 72,000; and so on, up to

$\diamondsuit$ = 180,000. $\qquad$ ⌈ But $\diamondsuit$ = 216,000 ⌉

This system for forming multiples was already in use in Period 1, as is shown by the following signs for fractions from that period:

$\emptyset$ = 1/72 ; $\smile$ = 1/36 ; $\mathbb{D}$ = 1/18 ; $\emptyset$ = 1/3 .

We see that the sign for one-third has two parts — a crescent and a circle. Its value is the product of these two, and since the crescent represents 1/18 the circle must represent 6.

This suggests that the two circles, one larger than the other, on tablets of this period, have the respective values 6 and 1.

This suggestion finds support in the fact that many tablets of that era, bearing numerous figures, contain none in which more than five 'unit' signs appear. We should expect 4 of every 10 numbers to have 6 or more 'unit' signs if the 'multiple' stands for 10. Since the number of 'unit' signs does not exceed 5 it is probable that the 'multiple' sign represents 6.

The probability is raised to near certainty by two systems of signs – one for capacity measure, the other for land, two of the most important early uses for numbers.

Capacity Measure

Sign	Period 1	Period 2	Sign	Periods 5, 6
	6 ka	10 ka		6 ka
	12 "	20 "		12 "
	18 "	30 "		18 "
	24 "	40 "		24 "
	30 "	50 "		30 "
	36 "	60 "		
	72 "	120 "		
	108 "	180 "		

Land Measure

Sign	Periods 1-2	Periods 3-4	Periods 5-6
	36 ka	60 ka	36 ka
	72 "	120 "	60 "
	108 "	180 "	108 "
	144 "	240 "	144 "
	144 "		

Periods 3&4 are omitted from the chart of capacity measure because Dr. Mercer's list shows only two signs for the periods, matching the signs for 6 and 18 in Period 5 but with values corresponding to Period 2. The absence of a sign for 30 in Period 1, 50 in Period 2, may be accidental, or may mean it did not appear on the tablets from which the lists were derived. In any case, it is easy to see that the sign would simply have 5 horizontal strokes.

The signs for capacity measure are especially significant for two reasons —

First: These signs are only a short step removed from the pictographic.

Initially, in the pictographic stage, three different vessels would have been depicted, each having a capacity six times that of the next smaller size. The drawings would then be simplified into symbols, such as $\mathbb{U}$ o ᴠ , easily impressed with the round stylus. The tall sign, made by holding the stylus at a very low angle, would represent the large clay vessel used anciently for storing wine or oil. The intermediate sign would represent a pitcher, the small sign a dipper, let us say. Notice that the sign logically suggested for the dipper is the sign shown above for the fraction 1/36, which would be the capacity of the dipper relative to the large vessel.

Repeating the sign for 'pitcher' four or five times would take space on the tablet, which could be saved by showing pitchers in terms of the larger vessel filled to an appropriate level —

$\mathbb{U}$ = O (1 pitcher), and $\mathbb{U}$ = OO (2 pitchers).

Having made this substitution, the scribe would quickly see that he need not represent the fill-lines with graphic accuracy so long as their number was clear. The result is the set of signs shown for 6, 12, 18, & 24, in Period 1. The number indicated in each case is the number of pitchers poured into the large vessel. But the value shown is the total number of dippers represented, which is 6 times the number of pitchers.

When the large vessel is full it is shown without any horizontal marks. This is a 'big unit', equivalent to 6 intermediate units (pitchers), or 36 small units (dippers). Two such 'big units' are represented by the sign for 72, and three by the sign for 108. These signs are nearly pictographic, a stylized representation of two or three large urns, one behind the other, in a row.

Second: Because those who deciphered the script did so, quite naturally, in terms of their accustomed base-10 arithmetic, the values shown are the base-10 equivalent values for the signs. The scribe who was making the signs was evidently thinking in other terms. To him, one-more-than-five is a larger unit.

One-more-than-five dippers is one pitcher.

One-more-than-five pitchers is one urn.

In terms of our numerals he would count: 1, 2, 3, 4, 5, 10. That is, he uses a base-6 counting system. (His 10 is equal to our 6.)

Because the capacity signs are so nearly pictographic we are assured of their antiquity, and since they represent figures in a base-6 system we may reasonably conclude that base-6 was used by the Sumerians at an early stage, very possibly preceding the earliest use of base-10.

The signs for land measure also indicate a base-6 system. Land measure is square measure. The smallest unit shown is a square whose side measures one-more-than-five linear units; that is, 36 unit squares (in base-6 this is 100). There are signs for 2, 3, and 4 such squares. This makes a larger square, so we find a unit sign for 144 unit squares (base-6, 400).

Two larger units of land measure, the signs for which are not reproduced here, were counted in the sexagesimal system. Significantly, we have in this earliest period, a sexagesimal system with an underlying base-6 system. We would say, to obtain sixty the Sumerian has counted 6 ten times. He would explain the procedure quite differently. In base-6 terms he has counted 10 *fourteen* times to obtain what the Sumerian called a "big unit".

In Period 3 the sexagesimal system was extended downwards to include the smaller areas of land measure, as we see from the changed value of the signs. But in Period 5 the older system was restored.

Something similar happened in capacity measure. In Period 2 we have a sexagesimal system (with an underlying base-10?) The signs were then modified, and in Period 5 the base-6 system was again in use. The absence of signs for the larger values leaves us in doubt as to whether the system was pure base-6 in this later period, or whether it was sexagesimal. But this is not important to us here, for our interest is in the earlier periods.

In considering the change to the sexagesimal system in Period 2 it is not enough to say that the counting system was changed. Since physical units of measure are involved we must also consider the physical aspect. The full urn now holds 60 dippers, but still only 6 pitchers. Unless all the urns and pitchers were replaced —an impractical idea— the size of the dipper must have changed, so that 10 dippers would be needed to fill a pitcher, rather than only 6. This may well be an important factor determining the change from base-6 to base-10 in the sub-structure, although it does not tell us why the change to the sexagesimal system was made.

As for the system of weights, Dr. Mercer shows one set of signs used from Period 1 through 6. The ratios and signs are:

1 *se* = 1/180 *gin*,

1 *gin* = 180 *se*,

1 *mana* = 60 *gin*,

1 *guru* = 60 *mana*,

While the larger units are sexagesimal the fraction 1/180 is not. There is a distinct possibility that this system began as a base-6 system also.

Archeology has demonstrated at least a trading connection between Sumer and Egypt, which may have continued for a considerable time but terminated c. -3000.[1] It is therefore worth noting in connection with the present discussion that the Egyptian number-words for 1, 2, 3, 4, 5, and 10, are of "African" origin, while their words for 6, 7, 8, and 9, are of Semitic origin,[2] indicating that the earliest Egyptian counting system was also base-6.

Base-10 is thought to be the natural result of man's having ten fingers. But we do not have a zero finger, and we do not have a two-digit finger. So, at best, this would account for a tendency to favor the quantity called ten. But the number of our fingers gives no clue to the system of numeration devised by the Hindus.

Base-6 is a natural system, because man has five fingers on each of two hands. This makes it easy for him to count by sixes in a most effective way. Try the following routine:

Starting with the right hand, match the fingers one by one with the items to be counted. When the right hand is 'full' count one more item, matching it with the thumb of the left hand. Now count five more items, matching the fingers of the right hand again. Count the next item with the forefinger of the left hand. Repeat this procedure until the left hand is 'full'.

Now count five more items with the fingers of the right hand. Since you have no more fingers to use, make a mark as you count the next item. Your mark represents the number we would call (base-10) number 36. But suppose you were devising a counting system, and a method of numeration to go with it. To record the results of this finger-counting routine you would need three marks —a mark to represent one finger of the right hand, which you might make by stabbing one finger into clay, a mark to represent a finger of the left hand, logically a larger mark which you might make by pressing your thumb in the clay, and a mark for the total reached when you have used all your fingers, logically a still larger mark, which you might make by rapping the edge of your hand on the clay. You have two round marks and a tall one.

With a stylus the marks will be neater and take less space. A piece of the tapering stem from the common cattail makes a good stylus. One end makes a small circle, the other a larger circle. A split leaf from the same plant is wedge-shaped in cross-section. That will make your long vertical mark. Your three marks in order of increasing value from right to left, as you have been counting, look like this: ❚ o o .

This is not place-value notation. The zero or "not" of which Chiera spoke comes in a bit later with the sexagesimal system. This notation is of the same character as the Roman's I, X, and C. But the quantities represented are those we call one, six, and thirty-six. But thinking of them in this way gives a false impression. The cycle of repetition in the counting sequence is like that in our cycle of tens.

The Sumerian cycle is shorter, and therefore easier to learn, and it makes much better use of the fingers as a counting tool. The base-6 finger-counting technique makes it possible to reach a much higher total before making a mark. This would be especially helpful in counting things that move, like sheep, cows, or people. It may have served the Sumerians well for many years.

In counting flocks and herds an assistant might be needed. Error might easily result if the man doing the counting had to divert his attention from the animals in order to make a mark. The assistant might be employed as a scribe, but he could perform a more effective function if he simply recorded the total on his own fingers. That is, each time the Counter used up all his fingers he would signal the assistant who would record the signal as one finger on his right hand, each of which would have a base-10 value of 36. The assistant, following the same routine, would register a base-10 value of 216 for each finger of his left hand. When he had used all his fingers and was finally obliged to make a mark the total count would have reached 1,296.

If the quantity of things to be counted warranted, a second assistant might be employed. He would not run out of fingers until the count reached 46,656 (base-10). [In base-6 this is one-million.]

Not often, in the early years, would a second assistant be needed. But later, as population increased, as herds grew, as armies were organized, and larger quantities of goods were traded an even more rapid counting procedure, a more compact system of numeration, and an ability to reach larger totals without assistants would be wanted. A minor modification in the procedure would provide these advantages. The Counter need only realize that he can readily remember that he has run through the complete procedure, to the point where all of the fingers of his left hand have been used, if he then reverses the roles played by his hands, registering units on the left hand and multiples on the right. He can then repeat the procedure until all of the fingers on his right hand have been used. In our terms he will by that time have counted 60 items. In base-6 terms the number is 140. In the system of numeration so far described this could be written, ⌐ 8̃8̃, but this is too clumsy. This figure will be passed on and recorded as one finger by the first assistant. It must be represented by a single mark. This is the "big unit" of the sexagesimal system.

With 60 as his unit the first assistant now counts 360 as his multiple. He reaches a total of 3600.

The second assistant counts 3600 as his unit. His multiple is 21,600. His total is 216,000 (all in base-10 terms).

The system of numeration now requires a sign for each of these units and multiples. Dr. Mercer shows signs for Period 2 with the specific values called for, with the exception of 6 and 360. But we have seen that the circle, usually taken to mean 10, was also used for 6. The crescent has a value of 60. The combination of circle and crescent, shown below in two alternate forms, can mean 6x60=360. (Later it was used for 10x60 =600.)

The sign for 21,600, evidently used only in Period 2, also shows that the circle means 6. This sign consists of two circles. One of these stands for 3600. The other must have a value of 6, for 6x3600=21,600. The four wedges included in this sign distinguish it from a sign that might mean 6x6, or 3600 x 3600.

The sign for 216,000 combines the circle and crescent, here meaning 60x3600. Four wedges distinguish this sign from any of the other possible values for this combination.

Notice that although the Sumerian and Roman numerals are alike in operation the Sumerian signs of higher value are not arbitrary but are related mathematically to the signs of lower value.

Period 2 - Finger-counting Values and Sumerian Signs.

Total	2nd Asst.		1st Asst.		Counter	
216,000	21,600	3600	360	60	6	1

Beginning with Period 3 several changes occur in the signs, indicating a change in the counting procedure which may reflect the changes that occurred earlier in the system of capacity measure. The sign for 21,600 no longer appears. The circle has a value of 10. The circle-crescent combination means 600. The square is introduced for 3600, and multiples of that sign are used.

The change from 6 to 10 dippers per pitcher may have been sufficiently advantageous to affect, finally, the general system of counting. For applications such as counting the dead on the battle field or taking the census of a city it would be impractical for one Counter to record each item himself. Additional teams could be trained and put to work. But the better solution would be to have several boys count 'tens' and report those 'tens' to the Counter. The 'ten-counter' would need no training. He had only to match his fingers to as many items, then report.

The Counter would treat each 'ten' as a unit. His multiple would then be 60. His total, 600, would become the unit of the 1st Assistant, whose multiple would be 3600.

The 1st Assistant would reach a total of 36,000, and this then becomes the unit of the 2nd Assistant. His multiple is 216,000.

There was a sign for 432,000, but none for 2,160,000, so we presume the 2nd Assistant never got his hands full.

Period 3 and later: Finger-counting Values and Signs.

2nd Asst.		1st Asst.		Counter		Unit
216,000	36,000	3600	600	60	10	1

432,000

Although the numerical results now seem to be sexagesimal with a base-10 substructure, the counting proceeds essentially as before. The system is in reality sexagesimal with a base-6 substructure. But the initial count of units into groups of 10 multiplies by 10 every unit and multiple in the system.

Were we to interpret the system in any other way the great advantage of the sexagesimal finger-routine would be lost. And however speculative it is, that routine makes the system and its features coherent. It even explains the remarkable, though limited use of place-value and zero.

The concept of place-value made it possible for the same sign to be used for 1 and for 60, for 6 and for 3600 in Period 2, 10 and 3600 later. No doubt a counting team would line up in front of a scribe to have the number recorded on their fingers transcribed on clay. The position of each sign, each value, is then inherent in the position of the hand that represents it. The scribe's presentation of the number is a stylized representation of the fingers, distinguishing between units and multiples. Zero, however the scribe writes it, represents a pair of 'empty' hands, all fingers at 'rest'.

Learning to count means learning a word sequence. This is the essence of counting. The sequence must be learned so that it can be repeated without omission or variation. This takes time.

Learning to write and read numbers is a matter of learning to associate the words in the counting sequence with symbols.

Though both learning processes are generally combined, being taught at the same time, they are distinct from each other. One could learn to count orally without learning to read or write numbers, just as one can learn to talk without learning to read or write words. And, in fact, most children learn to speak the numbers long before they learn to recognize the symbols.

The finger-counting routine could be taught to children who had not learned any number vocabulary. It is a mechanical drill, and could be learned much more quickly than a word sequence. In fact, it could be invented and used by a people who had not yet devised a complete oral counting sequence in their language. It is not necessary for the finger-counter to think, "1, 2, 3," but only, "sheep, sheep, sheep," or "man, man, man," while registering each item on his fingers.

Even the scribe need not know words for each number, nor have any idea what the quantities are, so long as he knows what symbol to use for each finger. After the teams have reported, and the digits are recorded, an expert can sum them up. Such a procedure would employ semi-skilled personnel to maximum advantage.

The productive use of semi-skilled personnel was a prime feature of the 'industrial revolution' which multiplied the ingenuity and knowledge of the relatively few to the benefit of the many. Just such an explanation is needed to account for the sudden flowering of Sumerian culture from indiscernible roots.

The Calendar Round

Two other features of the Sumerian cultural package have been the subject of a great deal of speculation—the division of the circle into 360 parts, and the calendar of 360 days. It has been frequently repeated that the Sumerians *thought* there were 360 days in the year and *decided* the circle should have that many parts. One writer whose work is otherwise on a high level of excellence goes so far as to say, "The circular track of the sun in the ecliptic belt of the celestial sphere was mapped out in 360 steps, each corresponding with a day and a night. There is little doubt that the degree had its origin in these 360 natural divisions of the sun's journey..." But this could be true only if there were in fact 360 days in the solar year.

The Chinese, at an early date, succeeded in dividing the circle into 365.25 proportionate parts, corresponding very nearly to the natural divisions of the sun's journey, and developed what must have been a difficult trigonometry on that basis. Had the Sumerians attempted to divide the circle into parts corresponding to a day and a night they would have obtained the same result.

The other suggestion, that they thought there were 360 days in the year and divided the circle accordingly, requires that an exceedingly inaccurate observation inspire the accomplishment of an extremely difficult task. To divide the circle into any arbitrarily chosen number of parts is by no means easy.

Neugebauer believes the "division of the circle into 360 parts originated in Babylonian astronomy of the last centuries B.C."[1] This divorces the 360-part circle from the 360-day calendar completely, for the Babylonians used a lunar calendar of 354 days with extra months intercalated to keep it in line with the seasons.

There is no proof that the Sumerian calendar and the division of the circle are associated. But if the division of the circle into 360 parts is to be so late a development, some other system must have been used earlier, for angular measure of some sort is essential to surveying and to other arts which were developed long before the last centuries BCE.

One can readily divide the circle in two different ways. The easier way is to divide it into quarters, and by bisecting angles thereafter produce 8ths, 16ths, and 32nds. This is the way the circle was divided to produce the mariner's 32-point compass. But the list of Sumerian number-signs does not include signs for 1/8, 1/16, or 1/32, indicating they did not use this method.

The other way is to use the radius of the circle to divide it into 6 parts and, by bisecting angles, to divide it further into 12ths, 24ths, 48ths, and 96ths. Evidently the Hindus used this method, for the table of sines in the *Līlavatī* is given in intervals of 3.75°; i.e., in 96ths of a circle ($3.75 \times 96 = 360$). But the list of Sumerian signs does not include these fractions either.

Why suppose the Sumerians made the number of degrees the same as the number of days in the year, incorrectly counted? Because, the theory goes, they never made the division at all, but held it as an ideal, and worked that ideal into their mathematics, and passed it down to later generations, who finally succeeded in making this very difficult division of the circle.

This theory is an apology for the failure of Elizabethan navigators, cartographers, and instrument makers who could not perform the feat accurately.

The trouble with the theory is that the rules of trigonometry could not be developed on the basis of an ideal. Empirical data from measurement of the sides and angles of triangles of all shapes are needed to work out those rules. There can be no doubt that the ancients really measured angles in degrees.

Had I not discovered a remarkably easy means of dividing the circle into Babylonian degrees I should have nothing to add to this topic. As it is, though I cannot prove the Sumerians used my method, several things encourage me to believe they probably did: 1) My discovery was an accident; 2) It was made while working with a material commonly used by the Sumerians; 3) It requires no knowledge of mathematics; 4) It is so easy!   And 5) It seems far more likely that a Sumerian accident repeated after 5000 years than that someone decided to divide the circle; did it the hard way; and happened to choose just that number of parts into which he could have divided it quite accidentally, and without knowing how to bisect an angle — without even drawing a circle.

I first reported my accident in "Tile Pattern —New Math Discovery?" *Popular Science Monthly* (July 1969). It may be recalled by those who follow that periodical, but will probably be new to most readers of this volume.   Assuming that to be the case, I shall describe the method in full.

To Divide the Circle

Instructions are often more difficult to read than the job is to do, especially if the reader only imagines the task.   To appreciate the ease with which the division is accomplished you may wish to do it yourself.   The tools required are extremely simple, yet so unexpected they could hardly be chosen on purpose.   No dividers, no drawing instruments of any kind are needed.   They are not even helpful.   A straightedge might be used; a length of cord would be better; neither is required.   The material used in the construction is itself the only tool needed.

All that is required is a supply of uniform *squares*.   Sixty squares will suffice to give the idea.   Better, have 168 or more.

Those I originally used were 1" square tiles. The size is convenient to work with. The thickness and rigidity of tile is an advantage. But suitable squares may be cut from cardboard. Any size will do, so long as all are of one size.

Tile is a likely material for the Sumerians to have used, for they decorated and paved with it. But that is not why I used it. That is all part of the serendipity. I was thinking of something else at the time. For now, just say I was playing with tiles.

The Sumerian may have intended only to pave a circular area. I like to imagine him preparing a surface on which the shadow of a gnomon could be recorded as he invented the sundial.

In any event, these are the steps:

1) Arrange six tiles more or less in a circle. Bring them together, corner to corner, to enclose a regular hexagon. You need not be too exact; the second step will improve the first.
2) Set one tile corner to corner with each pair of tiles in the first row, thus enclosing six equilateral triangular spaces. Adjusting the twelve tiles now in the pattern to form those triangles perfects the inner hexagon.
3) Complete the second row by placing six more tiles, each with a side parallel to one of the first six, but not touching. A tile-setter always leaves space between tiles. Without it, thermal expansion would crack the tiles or tear them loose from the surface to which they were attached.
4) To begin the third row, add one tile to each of the six radial paths that have begun to form, extending them outward from the sides of the hexagon. Keep the paths straight, and the space between tiles uniform.
5) Fill the space between the radial paths. In the third row each space will hold just two tiles. Distribute the excess space evenly. Keep the angles between tiles in any one row as uniform as possible.
6) Each subsequent row is set in the same manner as the third. You will find room for one additional tile between radials in each succeeding row.
7) Continue until you run out of tiles, area, or patience. Your pattern should then look like the one on page 61.

This 7-row pattern takes 168 tiles. To set a full pattern with 360 tiles in the circumference requires 60 rows.[1] It contains 10,980 tiles.[2] But it is not necessary to complete this pattern in order to get the message. Indeed, you must have a reason for going that far, and not going farther.

The Sumerian probably first noticed the numerical sequence. Each succeeding row has 6 more tiles. If he was already counting by 'sixes' he would be impressed with this multiplication

table of his base number.   If he was not already counting this
way the tile pattern might provide the incentive.

Whatever his counting system,   the Sumerian would learn
something from the tile pattern about the geometry of the circle.
Noting that the number of tiles in the radial (R), multiplied by 6,
always gives the number of tiles in the row, or course (C), he
would know that $C = 6R$; i.e., $C = 2\pi R$, where $\pi = 3$, as it did to
the Babylonian, and the Hebrew of Solomon's day (II Ch. 4:2).

As the paving of rectangular areas with square tiles is said
to have stimulated geometry in Greece, it is easy to see how the
tile pattern would have stimulated the development of mathematics in Sumer — and generated many other ideas.

The 24-hour day is represented in the fourth row.   This row
bears a peculiar relationship to the full pattern.   The first four
rows contain 60 tiles, the full pattern 60 rows.   A bit of mysti-
cism, number magic, may have influenced the choice for the
number of hours in the day.

Other curious items turn up.   There are 43,560 square feet
in an acre. Extending the pattern to 120 rows requires just this
number of tiles.

But why is the full circle considered to have 360 parts?

The pattern divides the circle into six major segments, each
divided into 2, 3, 4, 5, 6, 7, 8,... parts in succeeding rows.
To avoid the use of fractions in representing these divisions a
common denominator must be found; that is, a number evenly
divisible by as many of these figures as possible, yet one that
is not too large.

A little experiment shows that the best number for the purpose is 60, evenly divisible by 2, 3, 4, 5, & 6. All six segments
then total 360 parts, a number which is not only divisible by
the first six digits but by 8, 9, 10, 12, 15, 18,   and the opposite
factors.   No other number of comparable size has so many (24)
factors.

To make 1/7th of a segment a whole number of degrees also,
requires an inconveniently large common denominator.   Skip-
ping 1/7th but including 1/8th doubles the figure. The gain does
not warrant the inconvenience. So the choice is 360 degrees.

The word "degree" is not the Sumerian word, but it probably
means the same. It derives from Latin *de* by + *gradus* steps.
In Arabic the word is *daraga*, while *darag* means "staircase."
Notice the staircase on each side of the pyramid with the curving
base between each pair of radials.   This may have inspired the
first pyramid of Egypt, the Step Pyramid of Zoser, but the idea
must be saved for another volume.

Neugebauer says the 360-degree circle originates in the last
centuries BCE (see p 57). There is no need to dispute this; he

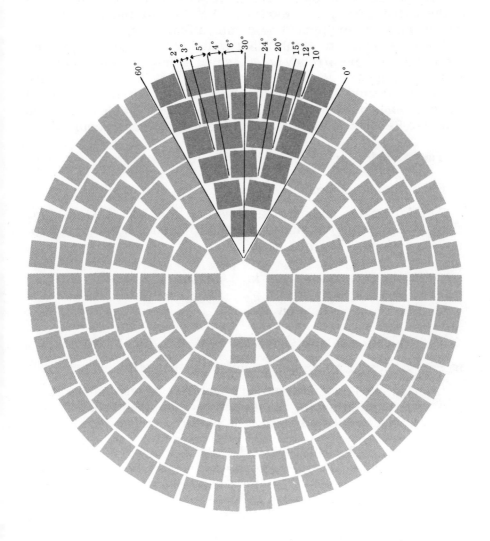

How the Circle Got Its Parts

is probably right. But this refers only to the expression of the circular fractions in sexagesimal terms. It does not say when the tile pattern was laid. That must have occurred some two- to three-thousand years earlier. And for all those centuries the angles were expressed as common fractions.

I had been led to think otherwise, but Mercer's sign list shows, as we have already noted, several fractions represented by simple signs in Period 1. Obviously they knew how to use them. In Period 3, beginning about -2100, the list shows all the fractions needed to express every angle that can be read from the 7-row tile pattern. Surprisingly few are required.

They consist of: $\frac{1}{2}$, $\frac{1}{3}$, $\frac{1}{4}$, $\frac{1}{5}$, $\frac{1}{6}$.

Each major segment is a *sextant*, $\frac{1}{6}$ of a circle.

Smaller angles are expressed as fractions of a sextant, and when necessary as the sum of, or the difference between two or more fractions. For instance,

12° is $\frac{1}{5}$ sextant;   10° is $\frac{1}{6}$ sextant;

2° is $\frac{1}{5}$ - $\frac{1}{6}$ sextant.

The operation is not performed to reduce this to $\frac{1}{30}$ sextant, or $\frac{1}{180}$ circle. This is not so much mathematics as practical instruction. The angle is called "one-fifth minus one-sixth of a sextant." By following the directions contained in that name, the angle can be located on the tile pattern. No more is needed.

The Sumerians had a sign for two-thirds, and one for five- sixths. These are exceptions. Most fractions had a numerator of one. This was true also for the Egyptians, most of the Greeks and other "mathematicians of antiquity" who, Hogben points out, "went to extraordinary pains to split up fractions like 2/43 into a sum of unit fractions, e. g. $\frac{2}{43}$ = $\frac{1}{30}$ + $\frac{1}{86}$ + $\frac{1}{645}$ "[1]

This would seem a perverse preservation of ancient limi- tations, as if they were classical requirements.

The number 360 is not a sexagesimal unit. For a Babylonian in the last centuries BCE to select 360 for the number of parts in the circle is like one of us choosing 600. Men accustomed to the sexagesimal system would choose 60 not 360, just as surely as we would choose 100 if the task had been left to us.

There can be no question that the Babylonian inherited the

divided circle from his cultural forebears, the Sumerians. We need not hesitate to associate the 360 parts of the circle with the 360 days of the Sumerian calendar.

But the association cannot be based on a Sumerian error in counting the days of the year. Any farmer who can count would know in a very few years of observation that 360 days is wrong. Anyone observing the stars with even rudimentary skill would realize the error in one year, or even in six months.

The true nature of the Sumerian 360-day calendar is worth considering.

From very early times man must have noticed that the stars seem to travel from east to west across the sky just a bit faster than the sun. A star that rises just before dawn one day will be seen to set in the west just before dawn six months later. When the same star rises just before dawn for the second time a full year has passed. (Such observation notes the sidereal year which is about twenty minutes longer than the solar year.)

When a star is seen to rise just before dawn and is promptly blotted out by the brightening daylight we speak of its *heliacal* rising, from Greek *helios* "sun". The Egyptians made the heliacal rise of Sirius, the brightest of stars, a major factor in their calendar system. We have no direct knowledge of Sumerian astronomy, but we can safely assume they too were familiar with the behaviour of the stars. Indeed, it is probably from the Sumerians that the Egyptians first learned to observe the heliacal rising of Sirius, for early cultural connection between these two peoples is established, and the Sumerians were the more advanced.

By making it possible to accurately measure angles, the tile pattern would make it possible to measure the change in the separation between a given star and the sun. The daily change amounts to somewhat less than a full degree, averaging about 56' of arc. The Sumerian could not be expected to measure this, and may have found an astronomical observation of 1° or even 2° too difficult. He could measure such an angle on the tile pattern but may have had no sighting device equal to the task. But he would surely have been able to measure a change in the sun's position, relative to a given star, amounting to 10°, or 1/6th sextant. And this change, he would note, took place in about 10 days.

Any term may be defined to suit the user and a group of initiates. If the Sumerian astronomer-priest chose to call the time in which the separation between sun and star increased by 10°, exactly 10 "days", he would be defining a "day" as that period in which the separation between sun and star increased by 1°.

There are exactly 360 such "days" in the year.

This "day" would be approximately 20 minutes longer than the common day from sunrise to sunrise. The beginning of the "day" would therefore circle the clock five times during the year. This would be inconvenient for the practical man, but not the astronomer-priest. With his "day" so defined he could maintain a 360-day calendar that would drift from the seasons, due only to precession,[1] no more than one month in 2000 years.

The exact nature of the priestly calendar would be unknown to the average man, who would measure his days in the usual fashion. But, being told there were 360 days in the year, he would count 360 ordinary days, only to find that the year was not yet officially over. There would follow 5, and sometimes 6 days that did not belong to his calendar at all. (In Egypt these intercalary days were feast days, a sort of annual bonus.) The new year would not start until the astronomer-priest, observing the heliacal rise of the star, announced its beginning. Both the common and the priestly calendar would then count the first day of the new year together. In the priestly calendar there would be no intercalary period.

The Egyptians used a calendar of 12 months, of 30 days each, with 5 intercalary (epagomenal) days at the end. This count of 365 days was kept routinely rather than being annually corrected by the observation of the heliacal rise of Sirius. Instead, the heliacal rise of the star was observed, and the day of its rising noted. Periodically, usually in the fourth year, the date of the observation came one day later in the calendar year. Finally, after many years, the star rose again on the 1st of Thoth, the Egyptian New Year's Day. (The length of this cycle is often given as 1460 years, but this is not precise.)

It would appear that the Egyptians borrowed the Sumerian calendar, with an imperfect understanding of its operation. Had they learned to manage it properly the heliacal rise of Sothis, as they called the star, would not have progressed through the year, and their calendar would not have wandered in respect to the seasons.

What has been said of the Egyptian calendar is established. What has been said of the Sumerian calendar is speculative.

If the Sumerians, despite their achievements in literature, mathematics, and other intellectual pursuits, were unable to tell in the course of centuries that there were more nearly 365 than 360 ordinary days in the year, a fact which the relatively primitive Egyptians of -3000 understood, then no special meaning need attach to the term "day", and they had no need for a tool like the tile pattern.

On the other hand, if they defined "day" in such a way as to make their 360-day calendar reasonably accurate, then they had the tile pattern, or some as yet unimagined device that would serve the same purpose.

Unfortunately, there is no hard evidence. It is all circumstantial. But we have not come to the end of it yet.

There is another factor that would serve to link the tiles and the earliest Sumerian numerals to the square, to the number six, and therefore the six-sided plain figure, the hexagon. That link may even account for the Sumerian discovery of the tile pattern, as it did for my discovery, or rediscovery, 5000 years later.

The link to which I refer is found in the six-sided solid, each face of which is a square. The cube, whose sides have borne spots for thousands of years, is today used only as a gaming device. But the games were devised to suit the dice, not the dice to play the games. Stone dice, spotted like our own, have been found in Egyptian tombs.[1] A game-board found by Woolley in the burial pits of the Sumerian city of Ur bears repeated representations of the dice-number five, and other designs suggesting the ace. Checker-like playing pieces belonging to the game also bear the five. Those numbers are composed of round spots, as the earliest Sumerian numbers were.

A spot is a spot. The similarity may be coincidental. Yet it is logical to suppose that the dice were first used as a counting device.

The cube was held in high regard by the ancients. Perhaps because of its association with salt. Like certain less common minerals, salt crystalizes in the form of a cube. Generally the crystals form in clusters that disguise the cubic shape. From large deposits perfect cubes can be cleaved, but this requires skill. However, simply allowing a saturated salt solution to evaporate will produce some individual crystals large enough to be clearly seen. So the salt-cube relationship would not easily have escaped notice.

How highly men valued salt may be judged from its name — in Hebrew *melach* "salt", *melek* "king", in Arabic *mallach* "salt", *malik* "king", and the names —of the Canaanite deity Molloch, the Ammonite deity Malcam, and Melkarth the patron deity of Tyre.

The importance of the cube is shown by the fact that some primitive cosmologies held the earth to be a cube. The ark of the Babylonian flood legend was a cube, 120 cubits in length, width, and height. Hardly a practical design for a boat, this should probably be considered symbolic, perhaps of the earth itself. Herodotus describes an Egyptian temple, in Buto (Per-Uadjit), dedicated to a goddess identified with Latona (Greek, Leto) the mother of Apollo god of light. This temple, already ancient in -500, was a perfect cube 40 cubits square on the side, hewn from a single block of stone.[2]

In the Bible, regarding "the oracle...the most holy place" in the Temple of Solomon, it is said:

> The oracle he prepared in the house within to set there the ark of the covenant of the Lord.
> And the oracle in the forepart was twenty cubits in length, and twenty cubits in breadth, and twenty cubits in the height thereof; and he overlaid it with pure gold. (I K. 6:19, 20)

The most ancient shrine of the Moslem world, older by far than the religion itself, is the Kaaba, situated in the inner courtyard of the Great Mosque of Mecca. That it was once a perfect cube we are assured by its name, for *ka'b* in Arabic means "cube." But its shape has been changed, as can be clearly seen in an unusual photograph taken by Thomas J. Abercrombie[1] who points out that the shrine was renovated sometime in the late sixth century CE. Mohammad himself is said to have reset the Black Stone, sacred to Islam, now located in the eastern corner of the structure less than five feet from the ground. From this, and the location of the door, close to the same corner, some idea is gained of how extensive the reconstruction was. The Kaaba is now about one-third smaller than originally, when the door was centered in the wall. The structural changes might be evident if the masonry could be seen, but it is regularly sheathed in black silk so that most of the stones are hidden from view.

Of special interest is a statement attributed by Abercrombie to the 'keeper of the Kaaba', Sheik Ameen Abdullah al-Shaibi, "In the 'Days of Ignorance' before Islam, the Kaaba housed 360 stone images. Regularly tribesmen came from all over Arabia to pay homage to the pantheon." Since Mohammad forbade the worship of idols the 360 images were long ago removed.

Did they represent the degrees of the circle, the days of the year, or both? Did the Arabs once use the calendar of Sumer? Was Mecca a Sumerian colony? The answers are not in sight.

They may have had the tile pattern.

Surrounding the reconstructed Kaaba a circular area is paved with large square slabs, clearly set after the building was repaired. Similar stones spot the surrounding area, apparently in more ancient positions. These appear to be remnants of the pattern that divides the circle, with the Kaaba at the center, but as yet I am not able to confirm the suspicion.

Conceivably, the tile pattern originates in Arabia, but the stones of the Kaaba could not serve as proof unless this shrine is much more ancient than is currently supposed.

It would be a coincidence, but perhaps not too remarkable, if each square of the tile pattern represented one face of a cube in the mind of its first designer, as it did in mine when I laid it out. I was, in fact, playing with tiles in lieu of cubes.

The cube is almost as mysterious as the sphere. It has no beginning and no end, until the spots are added. One can imagine a man puzzling over this shape which his hands had formed, perhaps from clay. To master it he marked one side with a spot. On the next side he put one spot and one more. Each side he marked with as many spots as the previous side, and one more. Suddenly he had a device bearing six distinct digits, signs that would help him count.

He could, for instance, mark the passage of time by turning the cube to the next higher number each day. A second cube, distinguished from the first with larger spots, could be used to note the number of times the first die had been cast (i.e. turned or twisted[1]) through all its sides. Each of the larger spots would have the same value as six of the smaller spots. This is the pattern of the earliest Sumerian numerals—a small spot for 1, a larger spot for 6. In the spotted cubes we may have the prime source of their inspiration.

The base-6 finger-counting technique would make the dice unnecessary as an aid to counting. The sexagesimal system would make them obsolete. Their original importance might be forgotten. But while the Sumerians were giving up the dice as a counting device others seem to have found them especially suited to their needs and susceptible of a subtle but important modification.

The riverine, citified Sumerian had plenty of clay and could afford to write and store great quantities of tablets. A nomadic or semi-nomadic people herding sheep and cattle on the arid steppes would have difficulty finding clay, and would not want such heavy, bulky records. To them a counting device able to hold a number as long as it was wanted but capable of instant change would be most attractive. The device would consist of a compartmented case, probably of leather, made to hold two or more dice.

A man might have several hung from his belt, one to count the days of the current year, one to record the years of his life, one to keep count of his sheep, or cattle —new-born to be added, the sold or slaughtered to be subtracted. A woman might want to count the days of gestation, perhaps in the manner of a count-down, as the Romans counted the days of the month. A sheik could keep a running census of his people.

The system described, where six is represented in two ways, as 6 spots on one die or 1 larger spot on another, is redundant.

With the dice firmly fixed in position by the compartments this would be immediately apparent and quite unnecessary. Place-value is an inherent feature of the device. Zero is represented by an empty compartment, one that is resting, idle.

Large and small spots are no longer needed. Instead of substituting the ace on one die for the six on another the six is removed and the ace is put in the next compartment to the left as the next higher number is counted.

This is an entirely new system. The basic rule is $6 + 1 = 10$.

We call this system "base-7", because its 10 has the same value as our 7. (The terminology is relative and subjective. If we were accustomed to the 6+1=10 rule, we would call that system base-10 and our present system would be called base-13.)

The use of our base-7 counting device might be explained:

In the beginning, there was the void.

On the first day,
the sun was made to give light.

On the second day,
the waters were divided into two parts.

On the third day,
the dry land appeared in between.

On the fourth day,
the moon was added.

On the fifth day,
all the animals were made.

On the sixth day, man.

The next day is a day of rest,
for on that day the Creator rested.

If this suggests the first chapter of Genesis, then we may understand that, whatever else it may be, this chapter is also a first lesson in counting in the base-7 system.

The next day is the first day following
the first day of rest.

And so the counting continues to the sixth
day following the first day of rest.

The next day is the second day of rest.

The base-7 [20] *transposes to* ($\backsimeq$) 14 base-10.

The sixth day following
　　the sixth day of rest,

is followed by the 'seventh' day of rest,

　　[100] ≈ 49.

Traditionally an evil number,

this trinity of darkness, in a calendar system based on the dice,

is followed by a Sabbath
　　marked by three signs for rest,

　　[1000] ≈ 343.　　There are three weeks remaining in the year.

The penultimate day is,

　　[1030] ≈ 364.

The final day is a blank day, the void, as it was in the beginning.

　　The year has [103] ≈ 52 weeks.
　　There are [16] ≈ 13 months of 4 weeks each.　　(In base-7
arithmetic, [4]x[16]=[103], but you need not remember this.)
　　Each month has [40] ≈ 28 days.　　(A month is a moon, and
wasn't the moon added on the fourth day?)

　　"And it rained for forty days and forty nights."　Only the
Bible speaks in these terms.　Who would understand such a
period of time?　Someone who thought in base-7 terms would.
He would recognize [40] days as 4 weeks, exactly one month in
a base-7 calendar.

　　"And the water covered the ground for one-hundred-fifty days."
— to us a most unusual period of time.　But it would not seem
strange at all to one who recognized [150] days as [15] (≈ 12)
weeks, exactly 3 months. And anyone familiar with the Tigris-
Euphrates or the Nile valley would know flood seasons of just
such duration, i.e. lasting [40]+[150] days = 4 months.

　　"And Moses was an hundred twenty years old when he died,
and his eye was not dim nor his natural force abated."　At 120
that is difficult to accept.　At [120] ≈ 63 there is no problem.

　　This is a sophisticated counting system, employing place-
value and zero.　Yet it would appear on the basis of these few
points to have been used by the ancient Hebrews hundreds of
years before the appearance of the Hindu numerals and *sunya*.
But, since the Sumerian use of place-value and the concept of
zero predates the Hindu by thousands of years, there is no basis,
per se, for rejecting the Hebrew use of these principles.

The Bible tells nothing of the early Hebrew calendar but some of the month names. The later Hebrews used the Babylonian lunar calendar which in time was modified to become the luni-solar calendar used by the Jews today. In the schism between the Qumran Community and orthodox Judaism an important factor was this highly irregular calendar. The Community considered it "an abomination of the Gentiles and directly counter to the 'certain law from the mouth of God.'"[1] The Community used instead "a solar calendar based on 'the laws of the Great Light of heaven'...in which the year was divided into fifty-two weeks. Each season consisted of three months thirty days long, and a day was added to every season as a link between one season and the next. This solar calendar, which figures also in the Book of Jubilees and in the First Book of Enoch, recommended itself to the sect because of its belief in the unchanging order of God in the universe."[2]

The calendar of Qumran is not the base-7 calendar. Nor can we be certain of the source of the Community's conviction that the calendar should be regular. But the tradition may derive from the perfect regularity of the base-7 calendar, exact knowledge of which had long been lost.

For a moment, let's think again about the Hindu numerals. Before the cursive symbols were devised the Hindu must have had some sort of numerals. The *ghubar* notation was not invented by a man who was just learning to count.

The "matchstick" numerals enjoyed some use in India though they are thought to originate in China. These consist of short vertical or horizontal strokes, actually copied from arrangements of sticks that the arithmetician shuffled as he calculated.

They are written: — ╌ ☰ ☰ ☰ ⊥ Ⅱ Ⅲ Ⅲ

1   2   3   4   5   6   7   8   9

By virtue of repetition it has become very nearly established fact that these provided the basis for the Hindu numerals, because rapid writing might produce ⇃ and ⇒, which look rather like our 2 and 3. But they look much less like the Hindu ل and رل, and that is what counts, for the Hindu form stands between our numerals and any prototype. Furthermore, there is just no model here at all for the digits 4 through 9.

A comparison of the Hindu numerals from 1 to 9 with the dice-numerals from [1] to [12] is much more instructive (p71).

The correspondence is too exact for coincidence. Apparently the Hindu was adapting his accustomed dice-numbers to new writing techniques and, at the same time, converting from one counting system to another —from base-7 to base-10. Perhaps

HINDU NUMERALS over DICE-NUMBERS

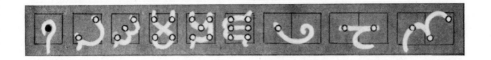

GREEK NUMERALS over DICE-NUMBERS

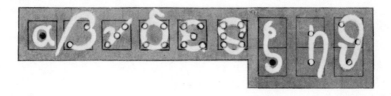

because the scholars with Alexander introduced the abacus, which offered increased speed in calculation, and base-10, which was really incidental. It has no advantage over base-7 except that the numbers are slightly more compact. But this is significant only where very large quantities are involved.

On the dice the Hindu had a separate symbol for each unit increment from [1] to [6], which he now expanded to extend from 1 to 9. The Greeks had an ordered alphabet, providing plenty of signs, but had not thought of using them to represent those unit increments. Probably the Hindu hadn't thought much about it either. The dice-numbers are simple and obvious. It is only the geometric patterns that make them instantly readable. In the same way, I + I = II is obvious, whereas 1 + 1 = 2 is abstract, and arbitrary. Its usefulness is not readily apparent.

We may imagine that a Hindu, in explaining the system of dice-counting, showed how you move the six one place to the left and turn up the one, illustrating the motion with a line in the dust, making the Hindu 'seven' the first *ghubar* numeral.

A Greek reoriented [10], [11], and [12], so they would fit the same width column as the first six digits, then made the same sort of operational sign for 'seven', moving from top to bottom, and reversing the curve to distinguish it from his new 9. (Our modern 9 owes more to the Greek than the Hindu.)

Both Hindu and Greek then devised a new string of symbols. Perhaps they were more alike at first. One or both may have suffered some modification.

It is often stated that zero made the abacus unnecessary. It could not have been apparent either to Greek or Hindu at the time the cursive numbers were designed that this would be so. And, in fact, the statement over simplifies. It ignores other equally important factors that caused written arithmetic to emerge. The package includes easily written, easily recognized numerals, a reasonably regular oral counting cycle that is not too long, so there will be a set of sums, differences, and products that can be memorized without great difficulty.

The Greek numerals are easily written — most with a single stroke. They are easily distinguished from each other. Their oral counting is more regular than the English. One is *ena*; ten is *deka*; eleven (irregular) is *endeka* (regular). But there are too many symbols, and therefore too many sums to learn.

For example: Three is *tria*; thirty is *trianta*; thirty-three is *trianta tria*; all nicely regular. But —

$$
\begin{array}{lll}
 & 33 \text{ in Greek is} & \lambda\gamma \\
\text{Adding} & \underline{22} \text{ which is} & \underline{\kappa\beta} \\
\text{Gives} & 55 \quad \text{and} & \nu\,\epsilon
\end{array}
$$

Knowing how to add the units is no help in adding the tens. And this complexity follows through every operation. What we call simple arithmetic the average Greek finds far from simple.

The dice-numbers present a different difficulty. The system uses zero, and the shorter base-7 cycle has fewer sums, differences, and products to learn than base-10. But transcribing the digits is difficult. If the spots are not set in their customary patterns in tidy frames, they become hard to read.

The writing difficulty was overcome. It could have been done earlier without a change to base-10. But before their contact with the Greeks the Hindus may have been handicapped by their oral counting system.

There are two principal languages spoken by the Hindus — Sanskrit, the language of the scholar, and Hindi, the peasant tongue. Sanskrit would be subject to deliberate scholarly change. Hindi might break down into dialects but could not be manipulated.

In Sanskrit the oral counting is regular with few exceptions, but if oral counting in Hindi is a fair indication of an earlier Sanskrit, as seems quite likely, then written arithmetic was virtually impossible. In Hindi there is no regular pattern, no significant repeat of syllables, from one to one-hundred.

Though primitive is often synonymous with complex, it is not likely that this difficult counting pattern is of peasant origin, for it is not uncommon to hear a peasant make substitutions, such as "two twenties" instead of the Hindi for "forty."

Every ancient system lacked one or more of the essential factors until all were combined, accidentally, by the Hindu scholars of -300. It had to be an accident. The effect could not be anticipated. It could only be realized after the system had been in use for some time that many answers were known at a glance and could be written at once. When these were partial answers to longer problems it was seen that they combined quite readily to give final answers without using the abacus. But this was not a goal; it just happened. The abacus taught them. The Hindu version with horizontal lines numbered shows that $2 + 2 = 4$ every time, and even shows why. A Roman abacus builds the answer but does not teach.

A review of the counting systems in thirty languages finds none that describes the Hindu numerals, not even Sanskrit. All show words for "one" (Sanskrit eg) and "ten" ($desh$) more suited to signs like I and X than 1 and 10. Often the word for 20 has no resemblance to the word for 2, or 30 for 3. In some there is no "ten" in the words for 11 through 19. No one uses his word for "zero" in his names for 10, 20, 30, etc., or even 100.

Unfortunately, these oral systems disclose no other base. Perhaps originally, as in Hindi, there was no cyclical pattern of repetition in any of these languages as high as a man could count. Simplification occurred with adaptation to numerals like the Roman. The Hindu numerals changed the signs, but not the words.

It is true as we see in retrospect that had the Greeks accepted zero their system would have incorporated all the essentials and written arithmetic would almost surely have developed in the west as early as it did in India. But the Greeks had objections which to them, at that time, were perfectly valid and quite inescapable.

1) They wanted a compact script for the tables they planned to use, Mesopotamian style. (For numbers written in tabular form zero is often replaced by notes like [000 omitted].)

2) They despised repetition and zero is decidedly repetitive. (So averse were the Greeks to repetition that when they adopted the Egyptian gods and were told the god of knowledge was called "thoth-thoth-thoth" because he was "three times very very great" they named their counterpart deity Hermes Trismegistus [thrice majestic][1] and made $tauto$- a prefix for words, e.g. tautophonia and tautologia, that deride banal repetition.)

3) Zero stands for that which does not exist. If repetition was objectionable, the repetition of nothing at all was downright repulsive.

How could a Greek write 1000? He chose what seemed more sophisticated means for expressing such a quantity.

Not surprisingly, both Hindu and Greek mathematics flourished in the ensuing centuries after the innovations. Both were required to re-work and re-think the old problems. The exercise was beneficial. Not the specific changes but change per se stimulated growth. But the Hindu, intuitively perhaps, made a better choice of systems and accomplished more as a result.

Of course, it didn't help the west to have the Greek system, vastly superior despite its faults, replaced by that of Rome.

To find that, anciently, Hindu and Hebrew shared a common counting system lends a measure of credence to reports linking these people. Unfortunately, the reports have come to us so indirectly we cannot insist on their validity to support the ideas presented here. But, on the other hand, we have no warrant to discredit these reports entirely, though few scholars have endorsed them with enthusiasm.

One report comes to us through Josephus who takes it from a book *On Sleep* by Clearchus, one of Aristotle's scholars. It claims that Aristotle said, "The Jews are derived from the Indian philosophers; they are named by the Indians *Calami*, and by the Syrians *Judaei*, and took their name from the country they inhabit, which is called Judea." But Aristotle is only repeating what was told him by a Jew, without substantiation of any kind.[1]

Another, from Diogenes Laertius, a 3rd century C.E. Greek writer (proem, 9) again draws upon Clearchus in a work called *On Education* in which he traces the descent of the Indian gymnosophists from the Magi, adding, "Some assert that the Jews also are descended from the Magi."[2]

Megasthenes (Clem. *Strom.* i.15) also associates Jew and Brahman.[3]

However weak the connection there must be some substance to these reports.

If both Hindu and Hebrew used the dice-numbers, we might expect to find this system used elsewhere —in Arabia, for instance, the land between. The history of Arabia is almost as barren as the desert sands, but there is an indication that the dice-numbers were used there. It is found in the title of an ancient collection of Arabian tales, *The Thousand Nights and a Night*, often corruptly called "The Arabian Nights," or more correctly, "The Thousand and One Arabian Nights."

The number of stories should correspond to the number in the title, for the stories are related by Scheherazade to fascinate the Sultan, one story each night. But in no collection are there 1001 stories, as we understand that number. And in view of the framework in which the stories are set, it is hardly likely that an odd period approaching three years is the time-span intended.

There are other ways to divide the base-7 calendar than the way in which it appears the ancient Hebrews did. The year might be given [10] months, each having [10] weeks of [10] days apiece. The month would then have [100] days and [10] months would add

to [1000]days. This would be followed by an intercalary period
of [31] days, recorded separately while the purity and beauty of
the number [1000] was preserved. (Such an intercalary period
would match the sacred month, Ramadan, in the Mohammedan
Calendar.) The first day, or night, of the new year would then
be added to [1000], making "one thousand nights and a night"
correspond to the magic interval mentioned in many of the tales
— a year and a day.

It might be objected that base-7 counting was not in use when
these Arabian tales were written. There is, however, no agreement among Arabists regarding that date. P. H. Newby, who does
not pretend to answer the question, writes, "It is evident that in
the book of *The Thousand and One Nights* we have a collection
of tales not only from many lands, India, Persia, Greece, Syria
and Egypt, but also from different epochs; some of the tales,
especially the Beast fables, are very ancient indeed, others have
been assigned to dates (these vary with the scholar!) between the
tenth and fifteenth centuries A.D. ... The important fact to remember, however, is that... these tales have, in the course of
centuries, passed through the hands of many Arab scribes and
editors, [and] have been transmuted in the process."[1]

As medieval artists painted biblical scenes with European
landscapes, buildings and costumes, story-tellers have ever revised their tales to suit the times and the taste of the audience.
Old jokes are made topical. Attacks on the powerful are back-
dated or wrapped in symbolism. Original ideas are attributed
to sages of the past. Plots of the teller's invention are embel-
lished with famous names. Ancestors are glorified, enemies
made hateful, foreigners foolish, with material from other times
and places. A single tale may contain such a melange of old and
new, of fact and fancy, of there and here, that in itself it spans
ages and continents, blending cultures and customs in a way that
never was.

In each night's story Scheherazade plants the seed of the next
night's tale to hold the Sultan's attention. "The framework of the
book, the story of Scheherazade and the misogynist king, was
Persian in origin (according to an account written in A.D. 987,
while modern scholars trace it to) Indian folklore."[2] The device
is used by the story-teller to draw his own audience back another
night. Weaving the device into the story is part of his art. To
find the tricks of the trade being used in neighboring lands is no
more surprising when the trade is entertainment than when it is
war, or the making of pots or fabrics. Who invented it and when
cannot be told. For an older example may yet be found. At most
it can be said that the earliest use yet discovered is in such a
place and in such an era.

The title may come from India. In that case it tells us nothing of the Arabian counting system. But another example of base-7 counting comes out of Ethiopia, far removed from the Hindu Kush but no distance at all from the land of Sheba whose queen called upon Solomon, and whose name is Hebrew for "seven." The present monarch of Ethiopia, Haile Selasie, claims descent from that famous queen.

The story is told by Herodotus of the Icthyophagi (fisheaters) from Elephantine who went as spies in the service of Cambyses II *c.* -524 to check on the "long-lived Ethiopians." The spies were told by these men "that most of them lived to be a hundred and twenty years old, while some even went beyond that age." The Persians, it was admitted, rarely lived past 80.[1]

We know the Persians were using base-10. It would be difficult indeed to avoid concluding that the Ethiopians used base-7.

Was the use of dice-numbers even more widespread? The English "days" when pronounced in the ancient accent vestigial in the Cockney twang sounds like 'dice', suggesting a connection between the two. And "tally", meaning 'to count', suggests the Latin *tali* "dice". We may have here a foreign word for a familiar object applied to one aspect of that object —in this case, the use to which it was put.

Whether or not the use of dice-numbers proves as common as these tantalizing scraps of evidence suggest, those numbers provide the key to the biblical chronology. To demonstrate this we could simply apply the rules of base-7 arithmetic to the biblical data, and we shall be doing that. But most of us do not think in base-7 terms. To make the numbers more readily understandable it will be best to transpose each one into its base-10 equivalent, then to add by base-10 rules.

Transposing from one system to another does not change the value of a number. In effect, we shall be translating Hebrew numbers into English, just as the words are translated. But with even less danger of distorting the meaning.

To transpose from base-7 to base-10 each digit is multiplied by the value of its position and the results are added. The values are:

$$343, \quad 49, \quad 7, \quad 1;$$

that is— $\quad 7^3, \quad 7^2, \quad 7^1, \quad 7^0,$ for the first four places.

Before proceeding, we must give some thought to the digits 7, 8, and 9. These cannot properly appear in base-7 numbers but we do find them in a few instances prior to the change in the counting base. In some instances it can be shown that they result from the application of base-10 arithmetic to base-7 numbers. When the calculations are corrected the anomalous digits disappear. Other cases require some further explanation.

A change in the counting base would necessitate change in the counting vocabulary. We have no documentary evidence regarding the development of the Hebrew counting sequence, so we cannot come to solid conclusions. But the possibilities are worth thinking about.

There is no reason why the first six numbers should have been affected by the change from base-7 to base-10. In the Hebrew these are:

achath   *shtayim*   *shalosh*   *arba*   *chamesh*   *shesh*

[die:1]   [die:2]   [die:3]   [die:4]   [die:5]   [die:6]

The next dice-number is [die:1 in left box]. The word for 10 is *eser*. It may have meant "big"; cf. *sar*, in Hebrew "officer", in Babylonia "sixty", the 'big unit' of the sexagesimal system. It is clearly related to *ashar*, which in Hebrew means "to become rich", and in Arabic means "ten".

Numerals, like words, are read from right to left in Arabic, though they are written in the same way that we write them. This practice is reflected in our words "thirteen"—"nineteen". It probably also accounts for the word-order in Hebrew:

achad-esreh, shtaim-esreh, shelsh-esreh, arba-esreh,

[die:1+1]   [die:1+2]   [die:1+3]   [die:1+4]

chamesh-esreh, shesh-esreh.

[die:1+5]   [die:1+6]

Next would be *esrim* for [die:2 in left box]. (It is the plural of *eser* and means "twenty".)

The word *shebeth* "rest, inactivity", would seem the root of *shabbath* "day of rest", and *sheba* (now 7) the period from one day of rest to the next, like "week".

Originally, *sheba* and *eser* would have been numerically the same. And it is reasonable to equate *shemona* (now 8) with *achad-esreh*, *tesha* (now 9) with *shtaim-esreh*.

Numerical synonyms are not too unusual. In English "twelve" is "dozen", "twenty" is "score". In Latin *decem et octo* (ten and eight) was also *duodeviginti* (two from twenty), and *decem et novem* was *undeviginti* (one from twenty). The Bible uses "month" as a number, speaking of "a month of years."

Other synonymous expressions may have been used. While [die:2 in left box] was called *esrim* it could also be *sheba-esreh*. And [die:2 with dots] could be either *achad-esrim* or *shemona-esreh*.

Some might feel that a developing language should have fewer synonyms than a mature language, but the opposite is probably true. When there is no word for an idea many may be coined. Some will be dropped, others differentiated. The mature language tends to become more precise and more rigid.

To organize more clearly what has been suggested here the older counting sequence may be written:

| achath, shtayim, shalosh, arba, chamesh, shesh, |

sheba,	shemona,	tesha,
or	or	or
eser,	achad-esreh,	shtaim-esreh,

| shelsh-esreh, arba-esreh, chamesh-esreh, shesh-esreh, |

sheba-esreh,	shemona-esreh,	tesha-esreh,
or	or	or
esrim,	achad-esrim,	shtaim-esrim,

| shelsh-esrim, arba-esrim, chamesh-esrim, shesh-esrim, |

sheba-esrim,	shemona-esrim,	tesha-esrim,
or	or	or
shelshim,	achad-shelshim,	shelsha-shelshim...

The new vocabulary, after the change to base-10, assigns new meanings to the synonyms. The sequence follows every line in the arrangement above, eliminating the word "or". That is, after 'tesha' read 'eser', after 'tesha-esreh' read 'esrim', etc.

To use "sheba-esrim" in the base-7 vocabulary where it would signify [twenty-ten] might seem strange, but in French we find *soixante-dix* "sixty-ten" for 70, and *quatre-vingt-dix* "four-score-ten" for 90, and no alternatives.

One more term must be explained. The word *shibim*, plural of *sheba*, is translated "seventy". This is correct after the change to base-10. In the base-7 sequence it stands for [⋅] —also called *meah* which, in base-10, means 100.

This hypothesis need not be correct in order for the work in the rest of this book to be valid. It is developed here only to discover whether the Hebrew counting vocabulary contains any elements which could be held to invalidate that work. Clearly, it does not.

Each anomalous digit in the text will be examined when it is encountered. To keep the record straight, whenever there is a change in the translated value, as for instance where the word "seven" appears as the translation for *sheba*, the form "7"[10] ⇌ 7 will be used, and this form will be retained thereafter for that item. Where the word "ten" is given as the translation for *eser* the form [10] ⇌ 7 will be used.

Notice that there is no implication in either case of an error in the Hebrew text. The only error is in the present translation of that text, or in the way it is understood. For this the ancient chroniclers cannot be held responsible.

Chapter V - TURNING THE KEY

When we added the data concerning Jacob and Joseph we found that Jacob was not more than 99 when he told the Pharaoh he was "one-hundred-thirty." On closer analysis we reduced this maximum age to 93. In any case, it appeared that Jacob lied, could not count, the biblical data was faulty, or we had misinterpreted the numbers.

Suppose we set the data in tabular form, placing the figures *as given* in one column to be added by base-10 rules. In the next column the appropriate base-7 numerals are written. These are added by the base-7 rule: [6] + [1] = [10]. In the third column the base-10 equivalent for each number is given. This column is added by base-10 rules, like the first.

Event:	As Given	Base seven		Base ten
Jacob goes to Padan-aram at age	"forty"	[40]	≈	28
He marries after serving	"seven"	[10]	≈	7
Joseph is born within the next	"seven"	[10]	≈	7
Joseph is appointed by Pharaoh at age	"thirty"	[30]	≈	21
Food is plentiful for	"seven"	[10]	≈	7
Jacob goes to Egypt after another	"two"	[2]	≈	2
Jacob's age would then be	93	[132]	≈	72

But Jacob claims to be "one-hundred-thirty" [130] ≈ 70 years old.

The numbers *as given* show Jacob's claim to be exaggerated by 37 years. The base-7 sum shows the claim to be understated by 2 years. The transposed figures reflect the understatement.

A 2-year error is more acceptable than a 37-year error, but even that is easily eliminated. We have supposed that Joseph was born at the end of the second "seven"-year term of Jacob's service for Laban. But this is not specifically stated in the text. Evidently he was born at the end of the 5th year of that second term and was two years old when Jacob asked Laban's permission to return to his own country. Jacob would then be [55] ≈ 40 years old when Joseph was born.

This change in understanding reduces all three totals, to 91, [130] and 70, respectively. The first figure is now 39 years away from Jacob's claim. The base-7 sum matches it perfectly. And we can understand Jacob's age on meeting the Pharaoh to be 70, in our terms.

Jacob's intelligence and character are beyond reproach. No error appears in the text. The only error was one of understanding. One could hardly ask for more positive assurance that the key fits the lock.

The text informs us that Jacob took his family back to Canaan after serving Laban for "twenty" years. Some effort is made to account for six extra years, for there was reason to think his total term of service was only fourteen years. Now we know that "seven" plus "seven", (i.e. *sheba* + *sheba*) is "twenty," and there are no extra years to account for. The words:

> I served you fourteen years for your two daughters,
> and six years for your cattle: (Gen. 31:41)

attributed to Jacob, are simply a redactor's attempt to explain why Jacob says he has been with Laban for "twenty" years (v. 38).

Later, such explanations would not be written into the text but would be appended in the form of commentary. Perhaps the first hand to pen these words intended nothing more, but in subsequent copying the commentary became blended with the text, possibly for no reason except that the punctuating devices needed to prevent it had not been developed.

We must now put the key to a major test — the period from the 5th year of Rehoboam to the 4th year of Hezekiah. The data when added by base-10 rules, you recall, resulted in a 49-year discrepancy.

Everything was fine back to -722. The discrepancy develops in the period between -722 and -926. At some point in this period the counting system must have changed, and it must have been nearer -722 than the earlier date for so large a discrepancy to accumulate. To discover just when the change took place it will be helpful to first set the data in tabular form.

| Reference | King | | Length of Reign | |
II Chron.		As Given	Base-7	Base-10
12:13	Rehoboam	"seventeen"	[20]	14
13:1, 2	Abijah	"three"	[3]	3
16:13	Asa	"forty-one"	[41]	29
20:31	Jehoshaphat	"twenty-five"	[25]	19
21:5	Jehoram	"eight"	[11]	8
22:2	Ahaziah	"one"	[1]	1
22:10, 12	Athaliah (queen)	"six"	[6]	6
24:1	Joash	"forty"	[40]	28
25:1	Amaziah	"twenty-nine"	[32]	23
26:3	Uzziah (Azariah)	"fifty-two"	[52]	37
27:1	Jotham	"sixteen"	[16]	13
28:1	Ahaz	"sixteen"	[16]	13
	Hezekiah — first four years			4
			258	198

Our table includes the full reign of Rehoboam. Since his 5th year was -926, his first year must be -930. From -930 to -722, inclusive, is 209 years. The figures *as given*, added by base-10 rules, total 258, 49 years too many. The transposed figures add up to 198, which is 11 years too few.

Transposing has overcompensated. We had every reason to expect that it would. Some of the figures we have transposed were already base-10 numbers. Transposing them as if they were base-7 numbers results in an incorrect reduction in value.

If Ahaz counted with base-10 numbers he would get his full "sixteen" years. This would restore 3 years to the total, making it 201, and reducing the overcompensation to 8 years.

If Jotham also counted with base-10 numbers he too would get "sixteen" years, adding 3 more years to the total which would then be 204. The overcompensation would then amount to only 5 years.

If Uzziah counted with base-10 numbers he would get a full 52 years instead of 37. This would add 15 years to the total, making 219. We would then have a discrepancy of 10 years too many.

We might suppose that Uzziah changed to base-10 during his reign. Suppose he counted [26] years and then switched to base-10. He would reach a total of 52 in another 26 years. The true total would be found by taking [26] $\approx$ 20 and adding 26, giving 46. This is 4 years too many. If he counted [30] and 22 = 52, since [30] $\approx$ 21, the total is 21 + 22 = 43, still one year too many. And this result will be obtained for any count up to [36] $\approx$ 27, plus 16. Going on to [40] $\approx$ 28, plus 12 = 40 leaves us 2 years short. No breakdown gives the right answer. And there is nothing in the text relating to Uzziah to support any assumption of a change to base-10 between years "thirty" and "thirty-six" of his reign. The results obtained by the assumption are not sufficiently accurate to be compelling.

A more careful study of the text is called for. We might look first at the figure given for Amaziah, since it contains the anomalous digit "nine". This may be nothing more than a mistranslation, but such anomalies must always be examined to see if another explanation is warranted.

AMAZIAH

During the latter part of Amaziah's reign we find the king of Israel is named Jeroboam. This is not the same Jeroboam who fought Rehoboam after Solomon's death, but another king of the same name, often referred to as Jeroboam II to avoid confusion, though the Bible never calls him that.

Much more confusing is that the king of Israel during the first part of Amaziah's reign is called Jehoash, and Amaziah's father is also called Jehoash. Both are at times referred to as Joash. The variations are in the Hebrew. The AV reproduces them. Some translations pick one or another spelling and stay with it. Some choose to call the king of Israel Joash consistently, others use this spelling consistently for the king of Judah. The reader who wants to check the information in these pages with one or another translation of the Bible is advised to read with caution.

I have used the name Joash for the king of Judah, and Jehoash for the king of Israel throughout this volume.

Jehoash was king of Israel for "sixteen" years (II K. 13:10). In the second year of Jehoash of Israel Amaziah became king of Judah (II K. 14:1). Jehoash of Israel died and his son Jeroboam ben-Jehoash began to reign in Israel (II K. 14:16).

Amaziah king of Judah lived after the death of Jehoash of Israel for "fifteen" years (II K. 14:17).

Suppose we arrange these figures in tabular form:

Amaziah	1	is	2	Jehoash of Israel
"	[15]≈12		13 ≈ [16]	"
"	[16]≈13		1	Jeroboam ben-
"	[33]≈24		12 ≈ [15]	" Jehoash

Jeroboam ben-Jehoash becomes king of Israel at the end of the year '[15]-Amaziah' on the death of his father Jehoash.

Amaziah lives another [15] years.

In base-7 arithmetic [15] + [15] = [33], and this transposes to 24, which is one year more than we had previously figured for Amaziah.

If Amaziah was said to reign "thirty-three" years the total of the figures *as given* would be increased 4 years and the discrepancy boosted to 53 years. But the total of the transposed figures would be 199. The overcompensation is only 10 years.

But why does the text say "twenty-nine" if it should say "thirty-three"? We must look at it from the point of view of a redactor who is unaware of the base-7 nature of the numbers, supposing the text said "thirty-three." To him this would seem a serious error. The text says Jeroboam ben—Jehoash succeeded his father in the year "15 Amaziah", and Amaziah lived another "15" years. That would add up to 30 at the most. Evidently the redactor equated "15 Amaziah" with "1 Jeroboam" which meant Amaziah had been king for 14 years before that. If he lived another 15 years his total reign must be 29, and that is what the redactor wrote.

We must still account for 10 years. We look now at that portion of the text devoted to Abijah.

ABIJAH

There are few chronological references to the kings of Israel in II Chronicles. There is one relating to Abijah, however, which says he became king the "eighteenth" year of Jeroboam (the first Jeroboam) of Israel.

To find how long Jeroboam was king of Israel we must go to I K. 14:20. When we compare the two accounts of the conflict between Jeroboam and Abijah we find differences, the very least of which is that I Kings renders the name "Abijam." (Some translations regularize the spelling, but the difference is in the Hebrew which also renders the name *Abijahu* in several instances.)

In order to compare the two accounts they are presented here in parallel columns. Where a statement appears in both versions it is spread across both columns with references at either side.

II CHRONICLES	I KINGS

14:20 Jeroboam was king of Israel for twenty-two years.

12:13 Rehoboam was king of Judah for seventeen years. 12:21

13:1,2 In the eighteenth year of Jeroboam Abijah became 15:1,2 king of Judah. Abijah reigned three years.

(13:3-19 describes a battle between Abijah and Jeroboam in which Abijah is the victor.)

13:20-22 Neither did Jeroboam recover strength in the days of Abijah and the Lord struck him and he died. But Abijah waxed mighty, and married fourteen wives, and begat twenty-two sons, and sixteen daughters. And the rest of the acts of Abijah, and his ways, are written in the story of the prophet Iddo.

14:1 And Abijah slept with his fathers, and they buried 15:8 him in the city of David; and Asa his son reigned in his stead.

In his days the land was quiet ten years.

15:9 In the twentieth year of Jeroboam, Asa became king of Judah.

15:25 In the second year of Asa Nadab became king of Israel for two years.

15:28 In the third year of Asa Baasha killed Nadab and reigned in his stead.

In I Kings it is clear that Jeroboam outlived Abijah, for Asa, Abijah's son and successor, is said to become king during the reign of Jeroboam. But according to the account in II Chron. Abijah not only outlived Jeroboam but must have done so for a number of years. After Jeroboam's death Abijah "waxed mighty, and married fourteen wives, and begat twenty-two sons, and sixteen daughters." Yet Abijah is said to be king for only three years. There seems to be confusion on more than one level.

We have some anomalous digits here —in Rehoboam's reign of "17" years, and in Abijam's accession in the "18th" year of Jeroboam's reign. These also require attention.

Since 17 and 18 are base-10 numbers suppose we chart the data on that basis just to see how it works out.

Rehoboam	1	is	1	Jeroboam
"	17		17	"
Abijah	1		18	"
"	3		20	"
Asa	1		21	"
"	2		22	"
"	3		1	Nadab
"	4		2	"
"	5		1	Baasha

It starts out alright. The synchronism of '1-Abijah' with '18-Jeroboam' works, and we can assume that '1-Asa' begins in the last days of '20-Jeroboam' to make that work. Similarly, '1-Nadab' may begin in the last days of '2-Asa'. But Baasha's reign does not begin in '3-Asa'.

According to this chart, Jeroboam outlived Abijah. But the situation changes when we treat the data as base-7.

Rehoboam's reign of *sheba-esreh shanim* is translated as "twenty years" and the chart looks like this:

Rehoboam	[1] ≈ 1	is	1 ≈[1]	Jeroboam
"	"17"[20] ≈14		14 ≈[20]	"
Abijah	[1] 1		15 [21]"18"	"
"	[2] 2		16 [22]	"
"	[3] 3		1 [1]	Nadab
Asa	[1] 1		2 [2]	"
"	[2] 2		1 [1]	Baasha

The synchronisms take an interesting twist. '1-Nadab' now matches '3-Abijah' and '1-Baasha' matches '2-Asa'. But '1-Asa' does not match any year of Jeroboam's reign, because Abijah outlives Jeroboam.

But Abijah outlives Jeroboam by only one year, and that is hardly enough time in which to wax mighty, marry 14 wives and beget 22 sons and 16 daughters, even if these figures are transposed to 11 wives, 16 sons and 13 daughters.

If we explain this as a summary of Abijah's procreative efforts begun even before he became king, one year is too short a time to support the words, "Abijah waxed mighty," or justify the line, "And the rest of the acts of Abijah, and his ways, and his sayings, are written in the story of the prophet Iddo," unless the prophet wrote a very short story.

Abijah should have a longer reign. Re-reading the text with this in mind, we notice three things:

First, II Chron. 14:1 seems to say that in the beginning of Asa's reign "the land was quiet ten years."

Second, we are told that Baasha became king in the third year of Asa's reign.

Third, in I Kings 15:16, and repeated in 15:32, "There was war between Asa and Baasha king of Israel all their days."

Our chart shows Baasha became king of Israel in the second year of Asa, but in either case there cannot be ten years of quiet in Asa's reign.

II Chronicles 14:1 (which, incidentally, is the last verse of chapter 13 in the Hebrew) says:

> Abijah slept with *his* fathers, and they buried *him*
> in the city of David, and Asa *his* son reigned in *his*
> stead; in *his* days the land was quiet ten years.

Of the five third person singular pronouns in this verse (here emphasized) the first four have Abijah as the antecedent. Of this there is no question. The fifth seems to refer to Asa. But garbled syntax is a hallmark of the Bible. The statement, "In his days the land was quiet ten years," may be intended to refer to Abijah. Indeed, since it cannot apply to Asa, it must refer to Abijah.

With "ten" quiet years added to his reign Abijah has time to wax mighty, sire children, perform the acts, follow the ways, and speak the sayings recorded by Iddo.

The effect of this increase in Abijah's reign from [3] to [13] ≏ 10 years on the correlation with the king's of Israel will be considered later. Adding this "ten" years to the *as given* column would extend the discrepancy to 63 years. The sum of the transposed figures, adding these [10] ≏ 7 years and the 1-year increase in Amaziah's reign, becomes 206, just 3 years short of the correct total. Those 3 years are supplied by treating the 16 years of king Ahaz' reign as a base-10 number.

Then it must have been in the first year of the reign of king Ahaz that the counting system was changed. Is there any support for this in the text? — As a matter of fact, there is.

AHAZ

Rezin king of Syria, and Pekah king of Israel came up to Jerusalem to war. They besieged the city. Ahaz sent messengers to Tiglath-pileser III, king of Assyria, saying, "I am your son. Come and save me." Tiglath-pileser responded in a way sufficient to break the siege of Jerusalem. Both Rezin and Pekah withdrew. Ahaz was thus indebted to Tiglath-pileser.

In the biblical account there is a compression of time. Two events are run together. This will be considered in greater detail a bit later.   Here our concern is with the behaviour of Ahaz. When, in the course of events, Rezin was killed and Tiglath-pileser had taken Damascus:

> King Ahaz went to Damascus to meet Tiglath-pileser
> king of Assyria, and saw an altar that was at Damascus. And king Ahaz sent to Urijah the priest the
> fashion of the altar, and the pattern of it, according
> to all the workmanship thereof. And Urijah the priest
> built an altar according to all that king Ahaz had sent
> from Damascus... And when the king was come from
> Damascus, the king saw the altar; and the king approached the altar, and offered thereon. (II K. 16:10-12)

Ahaz had the altar built by Solomon removed from its position before the house of the Lord and placed on the north side of his altar which now held the most honored place. He made other major changes in the design and arrangement of the Temple (II K. 16:17, 18).

There are variations in the interpretation of II K. 16:15, but it is clear that Ahaz told Urijah to make all the sacrifices and offerings on one altar, reserving the other for his own use. It is only reasonable to suppose that the altar Ahaz reserved to himself was the one he had ordered Urijah to build him.   AV quotes Ahaz as saying, "the brazen altar shall be for me to inquire by," implying that it was supposed to be an oracle. And an oracle is expected to speak. The altar's prototype in Damascus must have spoken. What could it have said that would have impressed Ahaz sufficiently to explain his behaviour?

Ahaz had gone to pay tribute, traditionally one part in ten of the annual revenue, or of the king's wealth. Counting 1, 2, 3, 4, 5, 6, 10, and giving one part, would leave six. Counting 1, 2, 3, 4, 5, 6, 7, 8, 9, 10, and giving one part, would leave nine.

When our base-10 counting system is used the part retained is one and one-half times larger than that retained when base-7 counting is used.

If the Syrian oracle taught Ahaz to use the base-10 counting system, it was worth listening to. To Ahaz it may have seemed worth imitating. But the imitation probably disappointed him by refusing to speak. Had Ahaz understood the mechanism by which the oracle spoke he would have wanted the speaker, not just a copy of the box from which the voice issued. Unless Urijah understood and supplied it, the copy could have had no voice.

Whether this interpretation is correct in detail or not makes little difference. Ahaz made drastic changes in Solomon's temple. A man who would break so sharply with tradition in one respect is likely to have done so in another. When the data, as transposed, shows that Ahaz was the man who changed the counting system, we have ample reason for accepting it, none for rejecting it.

By correcting a redactor's error in connection with Amaziah's reign, adding one year to the total, by rescuing [10] years from a syntactical trap and restoring them to Abijah's reign, and by transposing the numbers prior to the reign of Ahaz, we are able to make perfect sense of the data. Each of the kings of Judah can be dated in terms of our own calendar. And there is no discrepancy between these dates and the two events datable from extra-biblical sources which bracket this period of Hebrew history—the attack of Shishak upon Jerusalem in -926, the 5th year of Rehoboam, and the destruction of Samaria in -722, the 4th year of Hezekiah.

Solomon was king for [40]≎28 years (II Chron. 9:30). His reign must begin in -958. The temple was begun in his 4th year, which would be -955.

David was king for [40]≎28 years (I Chron. 29:27). His reign begins in -986.

We cannot readily go farther back along this line for it is not clear how long Saul was king or how this ties in with the data for the period of Judges. We must go back to the fork in the road. The way to the Exodus starts in the 4th year of Solomon. The dates that we have established for the kings of Judah are shown on the chart on the following page. It will not be worthwhile to try to correlate these dates with Assyrian history until we have completed an analysis of the parallel line of kings of Israel. But let us first go to Exodus.

The 4th year of Solomon's reign, the year in which he began to build the temple (-955), was, we are told, the "four-hundred-eightieth" year following the Exodus (I K. 6:1; II Chron. 3:2).

The number "480" contains an anomalous digit. In that form it is not a proper base-7 number. Unless the figure is altogether incorrect, there are two ways in which to explain why it appears in its present form.

One requires that we assume the 4th year of David was an

KINGS of JUDAH, DAVID — HEZEKIAH

Reference	King	Length of reign		Reign began
I Ch. 29:27	David	[40] ≈ 28		-986
II Ch. 9:30	Solomon	[40] 28		958
3:2	Temple begun, 4th year			955
12:13	Rehoboam	"17"[20] 14		930
12:2	Shishak attacked, 5th year			926
13:1, 2	Abijah	[3] 3	) 10	916
14:1	"	[10] 7		
16:13	Asa	[41] 29		906
20:31	Jehoshaphat	[25] 19		877
21:5	Jehoram	"8"[11] 8		858
22:2	Ahaziah	[1] 1		850
22:10, 12	Athaliah (queen)	[6] 6		849
24:1	Joash ben-Ahaziah	[40] 28		843
25:1	Amaziah	"29"[33] 24		815
26:3	Azariah (Uzziah)	[52] 37		791
27:1	Jotham	[16] 13		754
28:1	Ahaz (began base-10 counting)	16		741
29:1	Hezekiah	29		725
	4th year, Sargon conquered Israel			-722

especially significant year which was specified as the "four-hundred-fortieth" year after the Exodus. Since David was king for "forty" years, that would be the time from the 4th year of David to the 4th year of Solomon. A redactor may have added "440" and "40" by base-10 rules to produce the anomalous "480." The base-7 sum of [440] and [40] is [510].

The other explanation assumes an error in translation. In Hebrew the number reads *shemonim v'arba meoth*. The word *meoth* is "hundreds", the *v'* means "and", and *arba* is "four". In this there is no problem. The word *shemonim* is the plural of *shemona* , [11] in base-7, 8 after the change to base-10. It is quite possible that in base-7 this word signified [110]. Then the correct translation would be, "one—hundred—ten and four—hundred"; i.e., "five-hundred ten".

It might be objected, to this interpretation of *shemonim* , that we do not speak of "eleventy" except in jest. On the other hand, we do not hesitate to say "eleven-hundred." I know of no language today that has a special word for 110. But peculiarities no less incongruous are found — the French "sixty-ten" for 70, and "four-score-ten" for 90, for instance. Of course, what is right or wrong in English or French is no proof in regard to Biblical Hebrew. But the fact remains there is nothing imponderable about translating *shemonim* as [110] during the base-7 period.

However it is explained, the number "480"[510] ≈ 252, when added to -955, the 4th year of Solomon, sets the date of the Exodus in -1207.

EXODUS in -1207.

How does this date fit Egyptian history? How likely is it to be correct? A review of the circumstances in Egypt at that time is imperative.

One of Egypt's most notable Pharaohs, Rameses II, has often been considered the Pharaoh of the Exodus. He was one of Egypt's most prolific builders, though he also put his name on many works that he did not build. Many of the temples, statues, and other works which he commissioned are still standing. It is easy to see him as the king who set harsh taskmasters over the descendants of Israel who are said to have "built for Pharaoh treasure cities, Pithom and Raamses." (Ex. 1:11). And this is probably correct. But he is a Pharaoh of the captivity, not the Exodus.

Rameses II died in -1225 after 67 years as king. From the records, and from the condition of his mummy, he is thought to have been nearly 100 years old when he died. He was surely not less than 80. He was succeeded on the throne by his eldest son, Merneptah, already well along in years.

Merneptah successfully repelled a Libyan invasion in the western delta. In his fifth year (-1221) he led an army into the Asiatic portion of the empire. It was after this campaign that he had erected, in -1220, the victory stele on which the name "Israel" appears. As a result of these efforts the empire was effectively maintained until Merneptah died in -1215. Then, for reasons that are not at all clear, the government foundered. There followed a series of usurpations. Breasted names Amenmeses, displaced by Merneptah-Siptah, forced out by Seti II. There may have been one or more other ephemeral Pharaohs in between.

Seti II took the throne in -1209. He held it for 2 years, possibly for 4. "With the disappearance of Seti II those who had overthrown him were unable to gain the coveted power of which they had deprived him," Breasted writes. "Complete anarchy ensued."[1]

The document known as Papyrus Harris, an extraordinary record of the reign of Rameses III (-1198/-1167) completed by his son Rameses IV on his accession, reports on that period of anarchy, "Every man was thrown out of his right; they had no chief for many years formerly until other time. The land of

Egypt was in the hands of nobles and rulers of towns; one slew his neighbor, great and small."[1]

To what extent this situation was caused by Moses and his followers can only be surmised. That they took this opportunity to quit Egypt is certainly not surprising. Papyrus Harris reports a devestating famine at this time. The removal of many farmers and herdsmen from the delta would easily account for that.

Order was not finally restored until the accession of Setnakht in -1200. He was succeeded in -1198 by Rameses III who managed to restore to Egypt some of her former strength and prestige. But his power in Asia was largely nominal. Egypt continued to claim Canaan as part of her empire. In fact, she had no real control there after the great migration of the "Peoples of the Sea."

Rameses III faced the confederation known as "Peoples of the Sea" about -1190. They were Achaeans, Danaans, Sardinians, Sicilians, and others who came both by land and by sea, not just as a military force but as a migrating horde. The Hittite empire fell before them and disappeared from history. The Syrians, Phoenicians, and Canaanites could not resist them. Rameses III met them in battle and succeeded in discouraging them from any idea of moving into the Nile valley.

Many had settled along the way, but their power was finally concentrated in the coastal strip in southern Canaan thereafter called Philistia. These are the Philistines, i.e. "invaders".

Some associate the name Palestine with the Philistines. But Palestine, interpreted "invaded land," may well be the Hebrew designation for the land they occupied themselves. Though the Philistines put the land to tribute they did not set up a strong central government. Theirs was a confederation of cities, not unlike that in Greece.

Whether the Philistines mentioned earlier in the Bible are to be associated with those of this era is debatable. Since any invader might be called that, no racial or cultural connection is implied.

The migration of the "Peoples of the Sea" followed the destruction of Knossus in Crete and the collapse of the Minoan civilization. It is probably to be associated with the Trojan War of which Homer wrote.

From the Exodus in -1207 until shortly before the death of Moses, [40] ≏ 28 years later, -1179, the Hebrews were centered in Kadesh-Barnea. Here they were unaffected by the migration of the "Peoples of the Sea" and the conflict between the invaders and the power of Egypt.

With the death of Moses, Joshua became the leader. The

attack on Jericho followed almost immediately, early in -1178. Had this attack occurred much earlier it would have brought retaliation from Egypt. But after the invasion of the "Peoples of the Sea", though Rameses III maintained considerable influence in Syria, especially in the coastal cities where his sea power was effective and Egyptian trade an important economic factor, the interior of Canaan was beyond his reach. The Philistines effectively blocked the military road from the south. But they did not firmly control the territory to the north and east. So Joshua met no concerted opposition.

This date (-1178) for the battle of Jericho eliminates the problem discussed in chapter 3 (p.32) where it was pointed out that the books of Joshua and Judges knew nothing of any Egyptian military campaigns in Canaan, nor of the migration of the "Peoples of the Sea." But we need not rely entirely on such negative evidence to find support for this date in the biblical text. The Bible is not totally ignorant of that invasion. It is referred to, though rather casually, on four occassions.

In Gen. 10:14 we find, among the descendants of Ham, the Caphtorim (Cretans; Caphtor being the Hebrew name for Crete) "from whom the Philistines sprang." Amos 9:7, and Jeremiah 47:4 make poetic reference to the Philistines from Caphtor.[1] But the important reference is found where Moses says:

> the Avvim, that dwelt in villages as far as Gaza,
> the Caphtorim, that came out of Caphtor, destroyed
> them, and dwelt in their stead. (Deut. 2:23, JPSA)

This assures us that the invasion by the "Peoples of the Sea" or Caphtorim or Philistines, had already occurred prior to the death of Moses. Knowledge of that invasion reached Kadesh— Barnea, though it did not involve the people directly.

With the death of Rameses III in -1167 Egypt declined under a succession of ineffectual rulers. By -1090 the country was divided into two separate kingdoms. No Egyptian army entered Canaan from the time of Rameses III until the time of Solomon, when the Pharaoh of the north took Gezer as a wedding present for his daughter, the bride of the Hebrew king. That would be -958.

From the battle of Jericho, early in -1178, to the accession of David in -986, there is an interval of 193 years, ample time for Saul's short reign and the full period of Judges, which we may yet work out in more detail.

The date -1207 which the base-7 key has induced the data to disclose is by far the most likely date for the Exodus.

The Exodus terminated the "sojourn among strangers" that

began "430" years earlier. [430] ≎ 217. Adding 217 to -1207
takes us back to -1424.   We now have the date, but we do not
know what event in Hebrew history is to be associated with it.
Five possibilities were mentioned earlier: Abraham's entry into
Canaan, suggested by Josephus; Isaac's birth, correct according to Rabbinic tradition; the sale of Joseph; his rise to prominence; Jacob's entry into Egypt. To these we might add —
Jacob's birth, Abraham's death, and Joseph's birth.

These eight possibilities must be considered, but how are
we to choose between them. Unfortunately, there is little data
in the text during the period in Egypt. We are told that Levi had
a son named Kohath, and he a son named Amram, who was the
father of Moses. We are not told the ages of paternity. Only
the terminal ages are given. These do not make a chronology,
but they can be used to check some of the possibilities.

We are told that Moses was "80" years old at the time of the
Exodus (Ex. 7:7). And from this we have the traditional picture
of the octogenarian law-giver with flowing white beard. But
this does not stand up, since we have already found that Moses
was only 63 when he died, i.e. [120] ≎ 63.

In this case, *shemonim* cannot be taken as [110], for that
would leave only [10] years to Moses' death, whereas the text
gives "forty." But it is obvious where the "80" came from, for
120 - 40 = 80 by base-10 rules. When the arithmetic is done by
base-7 rules [120] - [40] = [50], and [50] ≎ 35. The traditional picture gives way to a more believable image of a mature but
physically vigorous leader, a man in his prime.

Since Moses was 35 in -1207 he was born in -1242, the 50th
year of the reign of Rameses II. When Merneptah erected his
stele (-1220) Moses was 21 to 22 years old. These figures are
interesting, but we must consider them later. They do not help
fix the beginning of the "sojourn."

Working back, we can establish a relative chronology for the
events that preceded the "sojourn" and some of those that were
included in it.   With this information in hand we can then compare the consequences of beginning the "sojourn" at one point
or another, taking into account all the available data, the details in the text, and in Egyptian history.

There is no need at this point to concern ourselves with the
patriarchs. Since the earliest date suggested for starting the
"sojourn" is Abraham's entry into Canaan, we can begin with
Abraham's birth.

Terah, Abraham's father, was "seventy" years old when
Abraham was born (Gen. 11:26). The word is *shibim*, an alternate form for [100] ≎ 49.

> Abram was seventy-five years old when he departed
> out of Haran. (Gen. 12:4)

Again the word is *shibim*, this time plus *kamesh* "five." But this time we cannot treat it as the old form of [100] for we are told that Abraham was "100" when Isaac was born, and that was some years later.

Sarah was barren. Abraham wanted children, an heir. So:

> Sarai, Abram's wife took Hagar her maid the Egyptian, after Abram had dwelt ten years in the land of Canaan, and gave her to her husband Abram to be his wife. (Gen. 16:3)

In the following year, Ishmael was born. Abraham is said to have been "eighty-six" (Gen. 16:16).

When Ishmael was "thirteen" and Abraham "ninety-nine" Abraham was told to circumcise himself and all the men of his tribe. He and Ishmael were circumcised on the same day. In the following year Isaac was born, when Abraham was "100."

In these passages all of the arithmetic is base-10: 75+11=86; 86+13=99; 99+1=100. The calculations were evidently made by an editor who did not know of the base-7 counting system. The correct figures must be obtained by base-7 rules.

Abraham took Hagar to wife after [10] ≏ 7 years.
Ishmael was born after [1] 1 year more.
When circumcised, Ishmael was [13] 10 years old.
Isaac was born after [1] 1 year more.

The sums are [25] ≏ 19.

Abraham was [100] ≏ 49 when Isaac was born.
Subtracting [25] ≏ 19
Abraham was [42] ≏ 30 when he went into Canaan.
Adding [10] ≏ 7
Abraham was [52] ≏ 37 when he took Hagar to wife.
Adding [1] 1
Abraham was [53] ≏ 38 when Ishmael was born.
Adding [13] ≏ 10
Abraham was [66] ≏ 48 at the time of circumcision.
Adding [1] 1
Abraham was [100] ≏ 49 when Isaac was born.

Sarah is said to be "ninety" when Isaac was born. From this we deduce that she was [10] ≏ 7 years younger than Abraham. Therefore, Isaac was born when Sarah was [60] ≏ 42.

Since Abraham was 30 when he and Sarah came into Canaan, she must have been 23. The story of Abraham and Sarah in

Egypt, when he asked her to say she was his sister so the Egyptians would not kill him in order to possess her (Gen. 12:10ff), becomes a rather different story. When Abraham is 30 and Sarah is 23 we get an impression that is missing when he is 75 and she is 65.

When Isaac was "forty" he married Rebekah (Gen. 25:20), after Sarah's death at age "one-hundred twenty-seven." Isaac took his bride, and "brought her into his mother Sarah's tent, . .. and he loved her; and Isaac was comforted after his mother's death." (Gen. 24:67)

When we suppose that Sarah was 90 at the time she bore Isaac, her death at age 127 occurs fully 3 years before Isaac's marriage at age 40. The vision of an abnormally dejected middle-aged man morosely mourning his mother for three years while her tent stands haunted and empty finally finding comfort in a wife that his father got for him by sending a servant to Padan-aram has never seemed especially attractive.

When we realize that Sarah was [60] ≈ 42 when Isaac was born and "127"[130] ≈ 70 when she died, we discover that Isaac was [40] ≈ 28 in the year of his mother's death. During his month of mourning, his father's servant was in Padan-aram, arranging the marriage. The youthful Isaac receives his bride with joy, and takes her into a tent that has scarcely had time to gather dust. The connotations of the story are altogether different—sympathetic, warm, and compelling.

When Rebekah bore twin sons, Esau and Jacob, Isaac was [60] ≈ 42 years old (Gen. 25:26). We have already read of Abraham's death (Gen. 25:7), but by any brand of arithmetic it is apparent that the entry is not in its proper chronological place. His terminal age is translated, "one-hundred seventy-five." AV and JPSA render it in archaic Elizabethan style, "an hundred and threescore and fifteen." But this is not faithful to the Hebrew, *math shana v'shibim shana v'kamesh shanim*, literally, "hundred year and seventy year and five years," —when *shibim* is translated "seventy." When *shibim* is recognized as a form of [100] the number is [100]+[100]+[5]=[205], and [205] ≈ 103. Calculation shows Abraham died when Jacob was 12 years old.

Ishmael's death is in the nature of incidental information so far as the chronology is concerned. It too is out of sequence in the text though correctly placed after Abraham's death. He outlived Abraham by only 12 years, living to be "137"[140] ≈ 77 (Gen. 25:17).

Esau married and Jacob went to Padan-aram 16 years after Abraham's death. Seven years later Jacob married and in the next 5 years 11 of his 12 sons were born—all but Benjamin. Two years later he returned to Canaan.

When Jacob returns with his family to Canaan, surprisingly, he does not go at once to see his father Isaac. There is a delay of 60 years, by base-10 calculations, as many scholars have noted and pondered. Some have supposed that the trip from Haran in Padan—aram consumed this time, but that will not work. Jacob left Laban without warning. Three days passed before Laban knew he had gone. Laban then set out in pursuit and overtook Jacob in the mountains of Gilead "7"[10] ≈ 7 days later (Gen. 31:20-23). Jacob had been travelling for only 10 days. He could not have covered more than 20 miles per day, and probably not that much, for he tells Esau the second day following his confrontation with Laban:

> My Lord knoweth that the children are tender, and the flocks and herds with young are with me; and if men should overdrive them one day, all the flock will die. (Gen. 33:13)

Laban could not have travelled more than 30 miles per day, steadily, for 7 days. So the point at which Laban overtook Jacob could be no more than 200 miles from Haran. The mountains of Gilead parallel the Jordan some 20 miles to the east. From Haran to the fords of Jordan must be about 220 miles.

This distance is too short to permit the identification of the biblical Haran with the city of that name located on the Balikh branch of the Euphrates in what is now southern Turkey. This Haran is fully twice as far away as the text would allow.

Another location for Haran must be found.

So far as chronology is concerned, the time spent in traveling from Haran to Canaan is far too short to have any effect.

Jacob settled in Shechem.[1] He seems to have been in no hurry to see his father. He bought a piece of land from Hamor the Hivvite, lord of Shechem, and he must have remained there for several years, for we next read of the rape of Jacob's daughter Dinah, by Shechem, the son of Hamor.

The young man wants to marry Dinah. Jacob requires that all the men of Hamor's tribe be circumcised. This is agreed to, and done. But the wedding does not take place.

While Hamor's men were incapacitated by the circumcision Simeon and Levi "took each man his sword, and came upon the city boldly, and slew all the males," including Shechem and Hamor (Gen. 34).

It is only at this juncture that Jacob leaves the vicinity of Shechem. And this cannot be soon after his arrival in Canaan, for Dinah could not then have been much more than one year old. She must have been twelve, surely, before Jacob would consider giving her in marriage.

Jacob went south to Bethel.   He seems to have stayed there briefly.   As they moved on toward Ephrath (Bethlehem) Rachel gave birth to her second son, Benjamin, but died in childbirth. If this follows the departure from Shechem by only a few weeks or months, and Dinah was then 12 years old, Joseph would have been 13, nearly 14, years old.   When Joseph was "17"[20] $\approx$ 14 he was taken down to Egypt (Gen. 37:2).[1]

These details explain a number of things.   They explain, possibly, why Joseph's jealous brothers did not dispose of him sooner —because his mother was alive and keeping a protective eye on him.   They explain why Benjamin, born in Joseph's fourteenth year, was such a special child to Joseph; why Benjamin is referred to as the child of Jacob's old age, and why the others all refer to him as "the lad" when they take him to Egypt (e.g. Gen. 44:20, 22).   The rest are then in their thirties; Benjamin is about 17.

When Jacob finally visits Mamre, also called Arba ("Four") and Hebron,[2] Isaac is said to be "180" years old.   The Hebrew reads *math ushemonim*, to be interpreted [100]+[110] = [210] $\approx$ 105.   Calculation shows this is 21 years after Jacob returned to Canaan from Padan-aram.

This event is not in its chronological place in the text, as Rashi[3] pointed out a long time ago. We read of the visit to Arba (Gen. 35:27), before reading of the sale of Joseph.   But the figures show that Joseph was sold earlier.   Our calculations place Jacob's visit to Arba (Hebron) 9 years after the sale of Joseph, and just 7 years before Jacob's migration to Egypt.

There are only 6 more items: Jacob's terminal age, given as "147" which we read [150] $\approx$ 84, after he had lived in Egypt "17"[20] $\approx$ 14 years;[4] Joseph's terminal age of [110] $\approx$ 56 years; Levi's terminal age of "137"[140] $\approx$ 77 years; Kohath's terminal age of [133] $\approx$ 73, and Amram's of "137"[140] $\approx$ 77 years.

Since it can be seen that Levi was about 2 years older than Joseph, we can estimate quite accurately the time of his death. This doesn't tell us when Kohath was born, but it does set a limit.

Kohath is named as one of 49 grandsons who came into Egypt with Jacob (Gen. 46:8-26), and it would seem he must have died (A) not later than 73 years after that event, which would set a limit for Amram's birth.   But the list includes the names of five of Jacob's great-grandsons, and it is most unlikely that Judah, for instance, was a grandfather when he came into Egypt at age 31.   Perhaps the list was not completed until the time of Jacob's death.   And it is possible, then, that Kohath was not born until that year.   In which case we would have to say that Kohath died (B) not later than 73 years after Jacob's death.

The following chart shows the chronological consequences of starting the "sojourn" with each of 8 events, considering in each case limits (A) and (B) for Kohath's death.

Event		1	2	3	4	5	6	7	8
Abraham to Canaan	+19								-1424
Isaac born	+42							-1424	1405
Jacob born	+12						-1424	1382	1363
Abraham died	+28					-1424	1412	1370	1351
Joseph born	+14				-1424	1396	1384	1342	1323
Joseph sold	+ 7			-1424	1410	1382	1370	1328	1309
Joseph promoted	+ 9		-1424	1417	1403	1375	1363	1321	1302
Jacob to Egypt	+14	-1424	1415	1408	1394	1366	1354	1312	1293
Jacob died	+12	1410	1401	1394	1380	1352	1340	1298	1279
Joseph died	+19	1398	1389	1382	1368	1340	1328	1286	1267
Levi died	+28	1379	1370	1363	1349	1321	1309	1267	1248
Kohath died (A)	+14	1351	1342	1335	1321	1293	1281		
Kohath died (B)		1337	1328	1321	1307	1279	1267		
(minimum age of paternity for Amram) (A)		+109	+100	+ 93	+ 79	+ 51	+ 39		
(B)		+ 95	+ 86	+ 79	+ 65	+ 37	+ 25		
Moses born	+35	1242	1242	1242	1242	1242	1242	1242	1242
Exodus		-1207	1207	1207	1207	1207	1207		
Kohath died (A)								1239	1220
Kohath died (B)								1225	
Exodus								1207	1207
Kohath died (B)									1206

Suggestions 1, 2, and 3A, must be ruled out at once, for we see that in each case Kohath died more than 77 years before the birth of Moses, but Amram lived only 77 years.

Suggestion 3B and 4A are barely possible. They require that both Amram and Moses be posthumous offspring, conceived in the father's terminal year but born after his death. It would seem unlikely that this would happen in two successive generations, especially with terminal ages of 73 and 77.

Suggestions 7 and 8 are dubious, for it is likely that Amram would have lived past the Exodus, and in 8B Kohath might also. But if this had happened the text would probably have said so.

If there were some compelling reason for accepting one of these disqualified suggestions we should have to weigh the arguments more carefully, but no such reason appears. On the contrary, the more we examine columns 1, 2, 3, 7, and 8, the less attractive they become.

For instance, if Joseph was promoted in -1302, as in column 8, his promotion occurs in the reign of Seti I. But his death in -1267 falls in the 26th year of Rameses II who must have kept him in a position of authority. And the pharaoh who did not remember Joseph and put the people to work building the city of Rameses could not be Rameses II, nor even his son Merneptah.

The same problem arises if Joseph's death occurs in -1286, as in column 7, for Rameses II became pharaoh in -1292. In this case Joseph's promotion comes in the reign of Horemhab, and his career would have to span the reigns of Rameses I and Seti I as well, and continue into the reign of Rameses II. This is unlikely. Successive kings of Egypt were no more inclined to accept the appointees of their predecessors than were the monarchs of other countries, in that or any era.

However, none of the several choices eliminates this difficulty. No matter where we start it, Joseph's career is not confined to the reign of a single pharaoh.

Columns 4, 5, and 6, seem more promising than the others, despite the fact that it would be most logical for the "sojourn" to begin with the sale of Joseph. Of these three, column 5 is best supported by the text.

Presuming Gen. 15 to have historic significance, then verses 15 and 16 of that chapter —

> And you shall go to your fathers in peace; you shall
> be buried in a good old age. But in the fourth gen-
> eration they shall come hither again;

suggest that the "sojourn" is to start with Abraham's death. And the four generations might be counted beginning with the first to be born after his death. That would mean that the sons of Jacob would be the first of those four, and that gives us Levi, Kohath, Amram and Moses.

We are not told that the fourth generation should enter Canaan; only that it should return. Moses returned.

Joseph's promotion in -1375 is interesting. This is the first year of pharaoh Akhenaton, an unusual man who instituted a religious revolution, forbidding the worship of all gods but one — Aton, who was not to be represented by an image either of man or beast. His only sign was the solar disk from which extended rays, terminating in hands, some of which held the *ankh*, symbol of life and breath. Akhenaton wrote poetry in which he addressed Aton, "O thou sole god, beside whom there is no other." One of his hymns to Aton includes several lines virtually identical with lines in Psalm 104.[1]

Akhenaton built a new capital city, Akhetaton, which he vowed never to leave. Here he devoted his energy to his religion, neglecting the affairs of empire. The Hittites pushed south into Syria. The Aramaean *Khabiri*, or *Hapiru*, invaded Canaan from the east. These incursions of the Egyptian provinces prompted the local dynasts to write the pharaoh, calling for assistance. These are the Amarna Letters. They supply a great deal of information regarding this period. Yet scholars have arrived at

remarkably divergent conclusions on the basis of that information. Some have associated the invasion by the Khabiri with the
conquest of Canaan by Joshua. Others[1] have suggested that Abraham entered Canaan at this time.

Khabiri and *Hapiru* resemble phonetically the word *Hebrew*.
This warrants discussion, and it may best be done now.

John Bright has written, "Though important scholars deny
that the two can be identified etymologically, the equation seems
at least possible, if not probable." He points out that the people
variously designated Khabiri, 'Apiru, Habiru, and the like, are
found "all over western Asia from the end of the third milleni-
um to about the eleventh century (BCE)."

"The term 'Khapiru'," Bright adds, "whatever its derivation
(and that is a moot question), seems to have referred originally
not to an ethnic unit but to a stratum of society... Men of any
race might be Khapiru. The term apparently denoted a class
of people without citizenship, without fixed place in the existing
social structure, at times pursuing a seminomadic existence,
living either peacefully or by raiding... In Egypt numbers of
them were impressed as laborers on various royal projects...
While we may not lightly identify the Hebrew ancestors with the
Khapiru (specifically not with those of Amarna), it is legitimate
to think of them as belonging to this class." Some 'Apiru, he
says, are known to have sold themselves into slavery, and "it
is hardly to be doubted, that among the 'Apiru who slaved in
Egypt under Rameses II components of Israel were to be found."[2]

Many scholars, besides Albright whose thoughts on the subject have already been mentioned, have supposed that the word
"Hebrew" derives from "Habiru" or one of its variants, and a
variety of translations have been offered. Josephus, on the
other hand, says, "Sala was the son of Arphaxad; and his son
was Heber, from whom they originally called the Jews, Hebrews."
To this translator Whiston notes, "That the Jews were called
Hebrews from this their progenitor Heber, our author Josephus
here rightly affirms; and not from Abram the Hebrew, or *passenger* over Euphrates, as many moderns suppose... though it
must be confessed that (Gen. xiv. 13) where the original says
they *told Abram the Hebrew*, the Septuagint renders it the
passenger, περάτη ." (Others translate "passer," and "passer-
over.")

The Oxford English Dictionary, after tracing its forms through
French, Latin, and Aramaic, says, "Hebrew lit. 'one from the
other side (of the river)'; f. *'eber* the region on the other or opposite side, f. *'abar* to cross or pass over." Here also, LXX
Gen. xiv. 13 'Abram the passer-over' or 'immigrant' for 'Abram
the Hebrew' is called to the reader's attention.

The word is עברי (*'ibri*). In all but the one instance cited it is rendered in the LXX as *'Ebrai*, with appropriate endings for sex, number, etc., as for instance in Ex. 1:15, "the midwives of the Hebrews," *'Ebraion*. (From this, not the original, the English version derives.) In the one instance the LXX presumably translated *'ibri* as *pĕrátē*, in English "passer-over." So it presently stands, at any rate.

But who applied this term to Abram? Is this what he called himself? What did he call himself before he crossed the river? Was he not already, in his own estimation, *ha'ibri*?

This raises an important question: Does the term *khabiri*, or any of its sound-alike forms, come from the language of the people so designated, or from their neighbors? Since the name appears little changed in several languages, over a broad span both geographically and in time, we must conclude that it originates with the people who bore it. But the meanings attached to it reflect the attitudes of the people who apply it. So in one case it means "slave," and in another "plunderer," and in a third "immigrant." But none of these is likely to be what the Khabiri had in mind to call himself.

Neither is it likely that the LXX intended to call Abraham a "passenger" or a "passer-over." The term *pĕrátē* may be a form of any one of three Greek words, differing slightly in pronunciation but spelled alike. These are:

pératos, "end, goal; accomplishment "
pĕrătos, "last, extreme "
perātós, "to be passed over."

In translating the Septuagint into English the meaning has been drawn from the third form. But in the context of Gen. 14 this seems hardly appropriate. Abraham is called upon to recover the spoil and rescue the captives taken by Chederlaomer and his allies. There is no reason to call upon Abraham the "passer-over" except that his nephew Lot is among the captives. Great deeds, however, might be expected from Abraham the "accomplisher." It seems most likely that this is the meaning the Greek was intended to convey.

But we must not hastily conclude that this was the meaning of *'ibri* as understood by the LXX. There is a distinct possibility that they never wrote *pĕrátē* in the first place.

The meaning of *'ibri*, or הָעִבְרִי (*ha'ibri*) may well be derived from בָּעַר (*ba'ar*) "to burn," for we find curiously divergent meanings for the related terms:

בְּעִיר (*be'ir*) "cattle "
בַּעִיר (*ba'ir*) "combustible "
הִבְעִיר (*hibe'ir*) "to set on fire; to cause to be grazed over."

The biblical Hebrews were herdsmen. Of this there can be
no doubt. Like plainsmen all over the world they must have
maintained the grass by burning. Whether they understood it
in theory or not we cannot say, but there is a sound scientific
basis for this practice. "In open country fire favors grass over
shrubs...A grass fire removes only one year's growth, and
usually much of this is dried and dead...When (the living tissue
of shrubs) is burned, the growth of several years is destroyed."[1]

To the herdsman accidental grassfire, an act of God, is a
serious hazard, easily destroying an entire herd. The prime
feature of ancient Hebrew ritual, the holocaust, may originate
as an offering, made when the grass was deliberately burned,
as a substitute for the wholesale taking that would otherwise
occur. And Khabiri, or *ha'ibri*, called themselves proudly,
"the burners," which the LXX must have rendered *pyratē*, from
the Greek *pyr*, "fire." But some later editor found this an un-
attractive term.

According to Phoenician legend the *Cabeiri* perfected navigation.[2] This art probably developed on the open plains, at
relatively low risk, rather than on the sea. These Cabeiri too
were no doubt herdsmen before they became sailors. It would
be natural for these "burners" to use fire as a naval weapon,
and to them must belong the distinction of inventing so-called
"Greek fire" used effectively by Greek seamen at an early date.
A Greek editor, relating *pyratē* to the naval Cabeiri, must have
read into the term the same meanings we associate with the
word "pirate."[3] Assuming an error had been made he 'corrected' one letter, writing, *pĕrátē* "accomplisher."

During the Amarna period the Khabiri, true to their name,
made fire their principal weapon. In Canaan they burned the
towns, the fields, the stored and the standing grain. The people
fled the fire, but more important, they were forced to turn
elsewhere for food. Many sought refuge in Egypt. One Egyptian officer reported, of a group of these refugees, "They have
been destroyed and their town laid waste, and fire has been
thrown (into their grain?)...Their countries are starving, they
live like goats of the mountain...A few of the Asiatics, who
knew not how they should live, have come (begging a home in
the domain?) of Pharaoh."[4] One such group may well have been
led by Jacob.

Those who suggest the Amarna period for the time of Joshua's
invasion of Canaan, and those who suppose it marks Abraham's
entry into that country, base their speculations on the recorded
invasion by the Khabiri. Focusing attention on that equally important aspect of the period —the flood of refugees from Canaan
into Egypt— we are able to identify the cause of the famine that

plays such an important part in the story of Joseph and his brothers, and Jacob's migration into Goshen, the Nile delta.

The Amarna Letters cry out against the depredations of the Khabiri. They were written over a period of several years, for this was a persistent guerrilla war designed to drive out the settled population and make the land available for pasture. Not all parts of the country were affected at the same time. When Jacob migrated the famine had already affected him for 2 years.

Column 4 of the chart on page 97 gives a date for Jacob's entry into Egypt which is too early. The date in column 6 is too late. The date –1366 in column 5 is in excellent accord with the dating of the letters, in the first several years of the reign of Akhenaton.

Does this mean that it was Pharaoh Akhenaton to whom Joseph introduced his father? It is not likely that Akhenaton would be in the Delta greeting refugees, or that Jacob would be taken 200 miles south to Akhetaton for the meeting. But Akhenaton had chosen one of his young officers to be in charge of the northern province to deal with the refugee problem. His name was Horemhab, and we know a great deal about him, for his biography is preserved on the walls of his tomb, and there are other inscriptions that record the manner in which he rose in the kings's service, became governor of the Delta with its capital at On, then commander-in-chief of the army, and finally, by virtue of a royal marriage, with approval of the resurgent priests of Amen, and confirmed by the oracle of the god, he acceded to the throne as Pharaoh.[1]

Horemhab's name does not appear in the Bible. But he may be identified.

> Joseph was brought down to Egypt; and Potiphar an officer of Pharaoh's, the captain of the guard, an Egyptian, bought him of the hand of the Ishmaelites that had brought him down thither. (Gen. 39:1, JPSA)

> Pharaoh called Joseph's name Zaphenath-paneah; and gave him to wife Asenath, the daughter of Potiphera priest of On. (Gen. 41:45, JPSA)

The title given Joseph has escaped translation, yet *zaphan* means "to hoard, to preserve" and *pinnah*, whose spelling in Hebrew differs but slightly from *paneah*, means "chief, prince." "Preservation Prince" or "Conservation Chief" would be appropriate, considering Joseph's activities.

More important is the identification of Potiphar and Potiphera, seemingly two different men with remarkably similar names. But are they, in fact, two different men. The LXX supplies "Petephre" once, and once "Petephres," where the Masoretic text gives "Potiphar." And, where the Masoretic text gives "Poti phera" the LXX again renders "Petephre."

Rashi took them to be the same man. Whiston notes, "They are also affirmed to be one and the same person in the Testament of Joseph...(and by) Josephus, the Septuagint interpreters, and...other learned Jews of old time." (*Antiq*. II, vi, 1)

The Masoretic text is not necessarily in error. Both terms could apply to the same man at different times if they were titles or epithets rather than proper names.

Such terms seem often to be compounded of several elements, defying direct translation, but with some imagination the sense may be discoverable.

Potiphar may combine *poter* "a breaking out" (closely akin to *peter* "firstborn") with *yipha* "splendour," and *par* "bull." The idea would be, "He is breaking forth as a great bull," or, more simply, "Firstborn Bull."

Poti-phera would contain two of the same elements, substituting *pera* "prince" for the third.

In Gen. 37:36 and 39:1, where the title "Potiphar" appears, the words that follow are *seris pare'oh*. AV translates "an officer of Pharaoh's." Better is the LXX rendering, "the eunuch of Pharaoh." But *seris*, being the construct form of *saris* "eunuch", should modify the word that follows. The full reading would be, "Firstborn Bull of the Eunuch Pharaoh."

This could not be taken literally, of course. Nor would it be official. It would be an esoteric title accorded by the Hebrews to Joseph's master.

The term "Eunuch Pharaoh" could identify only Akhenaton.

That he was physically abnormal is evident in every representation. A colossal nude statue, now in the Cairo Museum, shows him totally devoid of genitalia. The subject has been broached, and hushed repeatedly, for many years. It has been given its most complete and scientific treatment in a recent study by Cyril Aldred who concludes that Akhenaton's "peculiar physical characteristics were the result of a complaint known to physicians and pathologists as Fröhlich's syndrome."[1] This endocrine disorder, frequently caused by lesions of the pituitary gland, produces precisely the symptoms displayed by this unusual king. It is an inheritable weakness which would account also for the abnormal cranial formation of his daughters — if indeed they are his and not in fact offspring of his father Amenhotep III. The records which should determine this, as Aldred points out, are disturbingly vague.

One wonders if it was not Akhenaton's infirmity rather than

his religion for which his people rejected him. It was certainly no secret from his subjects, including the Hebrews of the Delta.

While it is possible that Akhenaton did have daughters, it is certain he had no sons. His immediate successor was his brother Smenkhare who had for a time before Akhenaton's death assumed the name, and the role, of Akhenaton's queen Nefertiti.

After a brief reign, Smenkhare was replaced by the young Tutenkhamen, possibly a third brother, who married one of the "king's daughters." Upon his death, his widow ruled as queen for a time with the Pharaohnic title being assumed by the aged vizier, Aye, identified as the husband of Nefertiti's "nurse," which may mean he was her father and, therefore, grandfather to Tutenkhamen's widow.

In any event, Aye lasted but a short time. The country was in trouble, in danger of dissolution. A military dictatorship was established, and shortly, with the connivance of the priests of Amen, the dictator was legitimized as Pharaoh Horemhab.

Writing after the fact, the Hebrew scribes could have identified only one man as "Potiphar" and "Poti-phera" — Firstborn Bull (of 'The Strong Bull' as the pharaoh was termed) and First-born Prince, meaning, in either case, "pharaoh to be." That man is Horemhab.

They also called him "Pharaoh" in connection with events that occurred before he had the title, as one might say he had gone to school with the "governor", or the "general", if that were the case, though the man in question was only a schoolboy at the time.

This dual identification is confirmed by one passage which is so precise it is utterly confusing in its brevity. That is Gen. 41:5 which says the Pharaoh gave to Joseph in marriage the daughter of Poti-phera priest of On. Even in Egypt a daughter would be given in marriage by her father, not by the king, unless her father happened to be the king. Here, though he was not at the time of the wedding he was by the time of the writing, so the title could properly be used. But it could not be applied to his daughter. She was not of royal blood. She never became the 'daughter of the Pharaoh', but remained the daughter of the priest of On, a title that automatically devolved upon the governor of the Delta, of which On (Heliopolis) was the capital.

The identification of "Potiphar—Poti-phera" with Horemhab enables us to understand how Joseph's career as servant of the captain of the guard, son-in-law to the priest of On, and "Conservation Chief" appointed by the Pharaoh, could weather that stormy period from Akhenaton through Horemhab. During all the turmoil Joseph served one master, from his sale in -1382 at age 14 until his death.

There is left no room to doubt that the "sojourn" begins with the death of Abraham, which makes the rendering of his terminal age especially interesting.   Most of the terminal ages end with "sheba"[10]. It would be quite unexpected to find so many lives terminating in a round number of years, suggesting the ages are not exact.   But Abraham's terminal age is not a round number.   Furthermore, even when reduced by transposition, from "175"[205] ≈ 103, the figure seems excessive.   And there is good reason to believe that Abraham's actual death came much earlier, as E. A. Speiser points out.

Commenting on Gen. 24:1, 2, Speiser calls attention to the statement, "Abraham was old, and well stricken with age."   He then requires his servant to take a vow, saying, "Put, I pray you, your hand under my thigh."   Speiser feels the nature of this ritual indicates that Abraham anticipates death.   Then, in verse 65, when the servant has returned with Rebekah, he identifies Isaac as his "master," affirming that Abraham is no longer living.[1]

Our calculations show that Abraham was then [140] ≈ 77.   If he died at that age, the age of "175" given in Gen. 25:7 is artificial, and must have been introduced for a reason.

Earlier it was suggested that the "sojourn" would most logically begin with the sale of Joseph.   If this event is dated -1382 the duration of the "sojourn" would be 1382 - 1207, when the Exodus occurred, or by our arithmetic 175 years.

The text would state the duration of the "sojourn" in base-7 terms.   To find the base-7 equivalent of a base-10 number we divide first by the highest power of 7 which will go into it.   The remainder is then divided by the next lower power of 7, and so on.   The arithmetic looks like this:

$$
\begin{array}{ll}
\text{Dividing by } 7^2\text{:} & 49 \;)\; 175 \;(\; 3 \\
 & \quad\; \underline{-147} \\
\text{Dividing by } 7^1\text{:} & 7 \;)\;\; 28 \;(\; 4 \\
 & \quad\;\; \underline{-28} \\
\text{Dividing by } 7^0\text{:} & 1 \;)\;\;\; 0 \;(\; 0
\end{array}
$$

The answer appears vertically on the right.   The base-7 equivalent of a base-10 175 is [340].

No mistake is easier to make in copying a number than to reverse the position of adjacent digits.   It is easy to do when writing a number that has just been spoken, or in reading a number aloud. Such reversal happens to a remembered number. Conceivably the duration of the "sojourn" was first recorded as [340] years, beginning with the sale of Joseph. If, through subsequent error in transcription, the figure was changed to [430], there would be no event with which the "sojourn" could begin.

The need to define such an event might lead to the attribution of a terminal age for Abraham of [205] ≈ 103 years.

Perhaps it was not intended that Abraham's terminal age be taken literally. It may be thought of as marking the end of an era rather than the actual death of an individual. In the idiom of the day this terminal age might have been understood in the same sense as if it said, "[205] years after the birth of Abraham," the literal meaning being too improbable.

From the *death* of Abraham to the sale of Joseph was [60] years. From the sale of Joseph to the Exodus was [340] years. If at one time these figures appeared in the text, a redactor thinking in base-10 terms would add 60 + 340 = 400. The "four-hundred year" prediction in Gen. 15 might thus be explained.

These speculations are not vital to the chronology. There is an indication that the "sojourn" was originally associated with the sale of Joseph and lasted for [340] years. Josephus, perhaps reflecting an earlier tradition, begins the "sojourn" with Abraham's entry into Canaan for the express reason that "430" years is much longer than the actual time his ancestors spent in Egypt. Other commentators have made the same point. But the text now shows that the "sojourn" began with the death of Abraham, whether or not his terminal age is to be interpreted literally.

Following through on this basis we can very quickly write:

Jacob was born (Isaac being [60] ≈ 42) in	-1436
Isaac was born (Abraham being [100] ≈ 49) in	-1478
Abraham was born (Terah being "70"[100] ≈ 49) in	-1527
Terah was born (Nahor being "29"[32] ≈ 23) in	-1576
Nahor was born (Serug being [30] ≈ 21) in	-1599
Serug was born (Reu being [32] ≈ 23) in	-1620
Reu was born (Peleg being [30] ≈ 21) in	-1643
Peleg was born (Eber being [34] ≈ 25) in	-1664
Eber was born (Salah being [30] ≈ 21) in	-1689
Salah was born (Arphaxad being [35] ≈ 26) in	-1710
Arphaxad was born (Shem being [100] ≈ 49) in	-1736
Shem was born in	-1785

To write, "Shem was born (Noah being [500] ≈ 245)" would be going too far.

The ages given (Gen. 5) for the first ten generations may have been counted in still another system. But no pattern is to be found, and base-10 arithmetic is in evidence; for instance, Adam was 130 when Seth was born, lived 800 years more, total 930.

Actually, Gen. 5:3 does not say Adam was 130 when Seth was born. It says, "Adam lived one hundred thirty years, and begat a son...Seth." This may be his terminal age, Seth being born

at an unspecified time. The additional years and total given in
the next two verses may well be a fanciful appendage by a later
hand. This thought applied to the whole chapter leaves nothing
but terminal ages, useless for chronology since lifetimes overlap. Perhaps recognition of this fault in the records prompted
inclusion of the flood story, borrowed from the Babylonians,
who borrowed it from the Sumerians, to wash out the earlier
history and establish a new starting point.

It may be that Noah's age of paternity, [500] ≈ 245, is an estimate of the entire span of the generations back to Adam. The
average age of paternity would be 24.5 years. The generations
might alternate [30], [40]; i.e., 21, 28, much like the apparently
artificial sequence 26, 21, 25, 21, 23, 21, 23, for Arphaxad
through Nahor. This sequence seems intended to use up a
known number of years while clinging as close as possible to an
ideal age for paternity of the firstborn, [30] ≈ 21.

We set out to find, as one objective, the beginning of the
Hebrew calendar. It counts back to -3761. We seem to be
stuck at -1785 with the birth of Shem. The word *shem* meant,
or came to mean, "name". He is the eponymous ancestor of
all Shemites (Semites). It is not an illogical place to stop.
How close is it to the goal?

The number 1785 belongs to a continuing base-10 sequence.
From Shem to Ahaz the Hebrews used base-7. The first year
of Ahaz is -741 by our count. In the Hebrew sequence it would
have been [3021]; i.e., 3761 - 740. To find the position of the
birth of Shem we must go back another 1044 years. But we
cannot subtract 1044 from [3021]. We must first transpose
1044 to its base-7 equivalent and subtract by base-7 rules.

The procedure is the same as that used on page 105.

Dividing by 7^3:   343) 1044 (3

                               -1029

Dividing by 7^2:   49)   15 (0

                               - 0

Dividing by 7^1:   7)   15 (2

                               -14

Dividing by 7^0:   1)   1 (1

The answer is [3021] !

Shem was born in the year [0000] of the Hebrew calendar.

The counting proceeds in a base-7 sequence to [3021] and
continues thereafter in the base-10 sequence. If base-10 had
been used from the beginning, the Jewish Mundane Epoch would
be 1785. The Gregorian 1969/70 would have been the Hebrew
3,754 instead of 5,730.

Even so, this is the longest consecutive count of years of

which we have certain knowledge, and the Hebrew calendar remains by far the oldest still in use.

Shem was born in the year "zero." How do you say "zero" in Biblical Hebrew? The word is not found in the Bible. But the concept is expressed. In the beginning the world was *tohu va bohu* "emptiness and emptiness," translated "without form and void" (Gen. 1:2).

The word "nothing" appears in the English many times, but in the Hebrew the negative is usually applied to the verb. So, in Gen. 11:6, where AV reads, "nothing will be restrained from them," a more literal translation would read, "from them will not be restrained a thing." But in some instances "nothing" is a direct translation of *efes*, and in other instances of *ayin*, which is also the name of the 16th letter of the Hebrew alphabet, written in square characters, ע , but in Old characters, O .

A dictionary of modern Hebrew shows both *ayin* and *efes* for "zero." It also shows *shem*.

It would be difficult to explain how *shem* acquired the meaning "zero" unless by ancient tradition. Though it does not appear in the Bible with this meaning, we do find *shemama* meaning "desolation, devestation," and a short form, *shamma*, with the same meaning. Several related words, such as *shamad* "to be annihilated" — in the causative form, *hashemed*, "to destroy,"— convey the same basic connotation, and appear to have *shem* as their root.

If in biblical times, as seems indicated, *shem* meant "zero" as well as "name", to find that Shem was born in the zero year is hardly surprising, especially when we recall that his father, Noah, is literally named "rest."

We can now set up a basic chronological framework. It is divided into two very unequal portions, the Base-7 Period, from the birth of Shem to the first year of Ahaz, [3021] ≈ 1044 years, and the Base-10 Period, lasting only ········ 154 years, to the conquest of Jerusalem. Altogether there are 1198 years of history recorded from Gen. 11:10 to II K. 25:21; II Chron. 36:20.

The Base-7 Period divides into five portions. These are dictated by the data and are not, perhaps, those which might be chosen for historical perspective, but they will be useful here. Into these periods we shall fit the chronological details.

This framework provides every assurance that we are dealing with a rigorously dated history, not a jumble of meaningless numbers.

BASE – 7 PERIOD

		Calendar Year	
		Hebrew	Gregorian
Patriarchal Era[a] [516] ≈ 258 years.			
From the birth of Shem		[0]	−1785
To the birth of Abraham		[516]	−1527
Abramic Era [205] ≈ 103 years.			
From the birth of Abraham		[516]	−1527
To his death at age "175"[205] ≈ 103		[1024]	−1424
Sojourn [430] ≈ 217 years.			
From the death of Abraham		[1024]	−1424
To the Exodus		[1454]	−1207
Exodus + [510] ≈ 252 years.			
From the Exodus		[1454]	−1207
To the beginning of Solomon's Temple, his 4th year, "480"[510] ≈ 252 years later		[2264]	− 955
Judah's Kings[b] [424] ≈ 214 years.			
From Solomon's 4th year		[2264]	− 955
To the first year of Ahaz		[3021]	− 741

BASE – 10 PERIOD

Judah's Kings[c] 154 years.		
From the first year of Ahaz	3021	− 741
To the last year of Zedekiah	3175	− 587
(Adding	586	586
(Year	3761 =	−1

[a] p. 106
[b] p. 88
[c] pp. 25–27, 88

Before going further with the chronological details it may be
wise to clear up a few random points. For instance, the reader may be puzzled by the suggestion that the Hebrew chroniclers
expressed an affection for Joseph's master, Horemhab.

On the other hand, those who are familiar with the character
of Horemhab may find it difficult to imagine him as Potiphar,
who seems to have done Joseph a gross injustice by casting him
into prison on the false accusation of a faithless woman.

Horemhab was one of Egypt's finest administrators. Though
his career began in the military service, and he distinguished
himself as an officer of the highest rank, his reign as Pharaoh
was notably non-bellicose. He instituted laws to curb extortion
by tax collectors, judges, and military men. He rooted out the
corrupt among local officials, asking, "How shall those like you
judge others while there is one among you committing a crime
against justice?"

The two viziers he placed at the head of his administration —
one in Thebes, the other (possibly Joseph) in On, he charac-
terized as "perfect in speech, excellent in good qualities, knowing how to judge the heart, hearing the words of the palace, the
laws of the judgement hall."[1]

Joseph and his people could easily have both respect and
affection for such a man. But how could it have been he who
cast Joseph into prison? The difficulty stems, I believe, from
a misinterpretation of the story.

In Gen. 39 we read that Joseph was overseer of his master's
house and trusted in all things. The master's wife tried to se-
duce Joseph and, failing, reported to her husband that Joseph
tried to "mock," "insult," or "make a laughingstock" of her, as
this euphimism is variously translated.

Whereupon her husband's wrath was kindled:

> And Joseph's master took him and put him into the
> prison, a place where the king's prisoners were
> bound; and he was there in the prison. (v. 20)

> And the keeper of the prison committed to Joseph's
> hand all the prisoners that were in the prison. (v. 22)

It would seem that Joseph was a victim of injustice who tri-
umphed in adversity. But immediately we read that the Pharaoh
was wroth with two of his officers:

> And he put them in ward in the house of the captain
> of the guard, into the prison where Joseph was
> bound. And the captain of the guard charged Joseph
> with them... (Gen. 40:3, 4)

Later, Joseph speaks to the officers, who are with him in

"the ward of his lord's house" (40:7). Still later, one of these officers, the chief butler, speaks familiarly with the Pharaoh, recalling the time he was put "in ward in the captain of the guard's house" (41:10), where he talked, not to a prisoner, but to a "servant of the captain of the guard" (41:12), meaning Joseph.

When we read that Joseph was put into prison, and that he was "bound," we suppose he is a prisoner in ropes or chains. But this is a totally false impression. Joseph is not tied. He is *bound* in the sense of being "required" to work, to serve his master. And Joseph's master is "captain of the guard." The prison is "in the house of the captain of the guard." Either Joseph's master is the "keeper of the prison" himself, or this is one of his subordinates, who trusts Joseph just as he had been trusted before.

The captain's anger must have been directed against his wife. Joseph is not a prisoner. He is still the "servant of the captain of the guard." He is simply "there in the prison." His duties have been changed from overseer of the private quarters, where he must come in contact with the captain's wife, to overseer of the prison the captain maintains.

It is important to realize that the "chief of the butlers" and the "chief of the bakers" are not common men, as we might suppose, but nobles of considerable rank and prestige, capable, if they were so inclined, of carrying out a plot against the king's life. One, the "chief of the bakers," was apparently judged guilty of such an attempt and executed, while the other was returned to favor. These are no ordinary prisoners.

To accept this story in the more usual way is to suppose 1) that a man would take a slave for whom he had paid good money, and who had proved himself extraordinarily competent and trustworthy, and throw that slave in prison, abandoning his investment totally, on the trumped-up charge of a woman who, if she were capable of such behaviour, could hardly have had her husband so completely hoodwinked as such an interpretation would require; and 2) that the slave of a relatively low-ranking officer could be committed by that officer to a prison reserved for the king's prisoners.

Since neither of these is feasible separately, and still less credible in combination, the story cannot be interpreted in that way. As clarified, the story in no way detracts from the identification of Joseph's master with Horemhab.

Terminal Ages and Sheba

It was mentioned that many of the terminal ages end with *sheba*, and would appear to be round numbers. But there is a

further point that might be made in this connection.   Since
sheba meant [10], most of the terminal ages could have been
written more simply.   For instance, Sarah's terminal age,
meah v'esrim v'sheba, [100]+[20]+[10], could have been *meah
ushelshim*, [100]+[30]. Jacob's terminal age, *sheba v'arbaim
umath*, [10]+[40]+[100], could have been expressed *kameshim
umath*, [50]+[100].

But *sheba* is a form of *shabath* "to cease, to rest, to come
to an end," and of *shabbath* "day of rest, holy day, sacred year."
Including *sheba* in the terminal age would convey a sense of
finality and of blessing.

When *sheba* could not be conveniently included the effect
might be achieved by including *shibim*, which would account for
the form used to express Abraham's terminal age. (See p. 94.)

The same reasoning might explain the use of *shibim* for
Terah's age of paternity, the object being to bless the birth of
Abraham. It might also explain the number "29" given for the
age of paternity of Terah's father Nahor.

To bless the birth of Terah, Nahor's age may have been
written *sheba ushtayim v'esrim*, [10]+[2]+[20], the equivalent
of [32]. But a later editor, thinking in base-10 terms, would
read 7 + 2 + 20 and rewrite the number *tesha v'esrim*, as it
now appears. (This is an alternative to the suggestion that in
the base-7 number vocabulary *tesha* was used for [12].)

Joseph's terminal age presents an interesting case. We read:

> Joseph lived an hundred and ten years. And Joseph
> saw Ephraim's children of the third generation; the
> children also of Machir the son of Manasseh were
> brought up on Joseph's knees. (Gen. 50:22,23)

At [110] ≈ 56 Joseph would be barely old enough to be a grandfather. Either he lived much longer or the statement is grossly
exaggerated. We might suppose it was written by one who did
not know the base-7 numbers, but with other terminal ages for
comparison this makes a weak excuse. It would seem more
probable that the number suffered a change.

Joseph's terminal age could have been written to include
both *shibim* and *sheba* in the form *shibim ushelshim ushalosh
usheba*, meaning [100]+[30]+[3]+[10], a total of [143]. This
transposes to 80, which would suit the text much better. A later editor, understanding 70 + 30 + 3 + 7, would get a sum of
110 and rewrite the number as *meah va'eser*, as it now stands.

At 80 Joseph's death would occur in the year -1316, the final
year in the reign of Horemhab. If this is not literally the year
in which Joseph died, it is certainly the end of his era.

The Twelve Sons of Jacob

It seems to be fashionable to suppose that the twelve tribes of Israel are not literally descended from twelve sons of Jacob. The relationship is taken to be symbolic. No reasons are given for rejecting a literal interpretation of the text in this instance; it is simply assumed to be universally unbelievable that Jacob could have so many sons in only seven years.

It would be easy to bypass the question. The text from Gen. 29:32 through 30:24 where the sequence of births is given is rather difficult to follow. I have said that Joseph must have been born in the fifth year of Jacob's marriage. He was evidently the last son born in Syria. This compresses the time span that is usually assumed and might seem to make a literal interpretation impossible. To accept the idea that it is all symbolic would be convenient. But in that case, none of this information is of any chronological value whatsoever. What difference does it make when Levi, for instance, is said to have died if he is not a real person with a real relationship to Jacob or to Joseph? So suppose we examine the text to see whether a literal interpretation is or is not possible.

These, in brief, are the stated conditions:

Leah bore Reuben	(Gen. 29:32)
Leah bore Simeon	(29:33)
Leah bore Levi	(29:34)
Leah bore Judah "and left bearing."	(29:35)
Bilhah bore Dan	(30:6)
Bilhah bore Naphtali	(30:8)
Zilpah bore Gad	(30:11)
Zilpah bore Asher	(30:13)
Leah bore Issachar	(30:18)
Leah bore Zebulun	(30:20)
Leah bore Dinah "afterwards."	(30:21)
Rachel bore Joseph	(30:24)

The only acceptable restrictions are physical. Customs, ritual laws, and the like, which were later established cannot be thought to apply. The normal gestation period is 280 days. After a child has been delivered pregnancy may recur without delay. There is no natural law that requires the passage of a month, or even a few days. Ovulation will normally occur within one month of delivery and may occur in any shorter time. The average would be two weeks.

Allowing two weeks between the delivery of one child and the conception of the next, the children arrive at intervals of 294 days. We are not restricted to this figure; it is used only for convenience.

We are not told the season of the year in which Jacob's wed-

ding took place.   No month names are given in this portion of
the text.   So our dating must be relative rather than absolute.
Again, for convenience, assume alternate months of 30 and 31
days.   The error —only 4 days in 5 years— is of no consequence
in this situation.

For the first child we allow only 280 days.   Thus Reuben
was born to Leah about the 6th day of the 10th month of the 1st
year of the marriage.

Simeon was born to Leah, 294 days later, about the 25th day
of the 7th month of the 2nd year.

Levi was born to Leah about the 14th day of the 5th month of
the 3rd year.

Judah was born to Leah about the 3rd day of the 3rd month
of the 4th year.

Rachel gave Jacob her handmaid Bilhah to wife. Bilhah bore
Dan sometime after Judah was born.   There is no need to allow
a long interval.   It could be a matter of minutes.   Suppose we
put Dan's birth on the 4th day of the 3rd month of the 4th year.

After Judah was born, Leah stopped bearing; that is, she
menstruated, an experience she had not had in 39 months.   This
was the first time she had failed to conceive on the first ovulation following childbirth.   Having received this sign that she
had "left bearing" she gave Jacob her handmaid Zilpah to wife.

Bilhah, having conceived again promptly after the birth of
Dan, bore Naphtali about the 24th day of the 12th month of the
4th year.

Zilpah, having conceived about a month after Judah's birth,
bore Gad about the 8th day of the 1st month of the 5th year.

Leah was not really through.   Conceiving about two months
after Judah's birth, she bore Issachar about the 8th day of the
2nd month of the 5th year.

Zilpah conceived after the birth of Gad and bore Asher about
the 28th day of the 10th month of the 5th year.

This reverses the order in which the text mentions Asher
and Issachar, but note that when Issachar was born:

> Leah said, "God has given me my hire, because I
> have given my maiden to my husband:" and she
> called his name Issachar. (30:18)

This makes sense if the name is chosen when the act of giving is a recent act, for instance, at the time of Issachar's conception, a month after Leah gave Zilpah to Jacob, not after
Zilpah had born him two sons.

The name Asher is explained:

> And Leah said, "Happy am I, for the daughters will
> call me blessed" (30:13).

Since *asher* means "happiness, luck, blessing," it would be especially appropriate for the [10]≈ 7th son born under the auspices of Leah, and if Asher follows Issachar, he is that 7th son. So reversing the order puts no strain on the sense of the text, but clarifies it instead.

Leah bore Zebulun about the 27th day of the 11th month, the 5th year.

Rachel finally bore Joseph, in the 12th month of the 5th year of Jacob's marriage.

Leah bore Dinah "afterwards," not before Joseph's birth. Dinah may have been born about the 16th day of the 9th month of the 6th year, or somewhat later. Dinah would then be about one year younger than Joseph, and about one year old when the family went into Canaan.

Thus it is not only possible for the sons of Jacob to be born in the time allowed and in an order that agrees with the sense of the text, it seems quite probable that a factual account has been given; a fictitious account would be simpler, more easily understood, and more readily accepted.

Perhaps the major reason for supposing that the population of the twelve tribes was not truly descended from these twelve brothers is found in the census figures given for the time of Exodus, in Num. 1:20-46 and repeated in chapter 2. But these figures deserve to be challenged.

The census includes only males "from twenty years old and upward, able to go to war." The sum, derived by base-10 rules of arithmetic, is 603,550. Since males under "twenty", those too old for battle, and all of the women are excluded, this sum would represent no more than one-third and perhaps only one-fourth of the total population which must fall somewhere in the range from 1.8 to 2.4 million.

This figure rivals the population of modern Israel. In light of other elements in the story it is utterly incongruous. Even a well disciplined army of such proportions could not manuever in the manner described in the text. For Pharaoh to pursue with 600 chariots would be altogether senseless and nothing to be frightened about.

For such reasons some scholars have supposed this census might actually have been taken in the time of David. But there are certain incongruities. The twelve five-digit figures all end in '0'; eleven of them in '00'. This could hardly happen in an actual count of people.

Of the 60 digits only four are greater than '6'. If these were base-10 numbers we should expect three to four digits greater than '6' in each of the first four columns.

In Num. 26:7-51 there is a second census said to have been

taken "in the plains of Moab by Jordan" by Moses and Eleazar, after the death of Aaron. These numbers are different from the others. Some of the changes are large, too large for a matter of only "forty" years. But the total is very nearly the same.

In this case there are only three digits larger than '6', all of them '7's. Again every figure ends in '0', all but one in '00'.

Had Joshua led an army of 600,000 men Canaan could have been conquered in a walk. Why stop with Canaan? No ancient conqueror led such a force. Joshua could have put all Asia to tribute.

Such numbers are not encountered again. In Josh. 7:4 3000 men attacked Ai, but fled in defeat. In 8:3 Joshua set an ambush of 30,000 men, but in 8:12 this is repeated as 5000. The total population of Ai is given as 12,000 in 8:25.

The census figures are way out of line and tell us nothing as far as chronology is concerned. Are they fictitious? Are they base-7 numbers corrupted by misunderstanding?

Each number is written in the same form as that given for the tribe of Reuben—six and forty *elef* and five hundreds—with two exceptions. After "hundreds," "fifty" is added in one case, "thirty" in another.

elef means "thousand." It also means "a community, family, part of a tribe." Perhaps it is to be read in the latter sense and not as a number. Then the count for Reuben would be 6 and 40 and 5 hundred; i.e. [546] ≈ 279.

If all the numbers are interpreted in this way the total is 3163 for the first census, 3242 for the second. The total population would be between 10- and 12-thousand. This is a much more probable figure, but we cannot be confident that this treatment of the census figures is correct. It will not work in the case of the Levites, who are counted separately.

Num. 26:62 says "all males from a month old and upward" of the Levites number '3 and 20 *elef*', translated as "23,000." If *elef* is not given numerical value the number becomes [23] ≈ 17 and this can hardly be correct. Unless it means those that are one-month and upward to two-months, or six-months, or one-year, perhaps, and is not at all a census of the tribe.

We are on safer ground with the genealogies. From the time of Joseph's marriage, in the year of his promotion, to the time of this second census, we count 196 years. After the census:

> Then came the daughters of Zelophehad, the son of
> Hepher, the son of Gilead, the son of Machir, the
> son of Manasseh...the son of Joseph (Num. 27:1)

There have been 6 generations in Joseph's line in this period. Presuming Manasseh was born the year after Joseph's marriage, and that Zelophehad's eldest daughter is 20 years old, the average age of paternity for these generations is a very reasonable 35 years.

In Levi's line at the same time there has been one less generation. Aaron has just died at age [123]≈66 (Num. 33:39). His son Eleazar has replaced him as priest. Phinehas, the son of Eleazar, has begun to play an active role (see Num. 25:1-8).

Since Aaron's death precedes the death of Moses by only a month or two it is apparent that Aaron was three years older. His birth must come in -1245. Presuming Kohath was born in the year Jacob died, -1352, when Levi was 50, the average age of paternity for Kohath and Amram would be 52-53. Aaron may have been about 30 when Eleazar was born, Eleazar about 22 when Phinehas was born, and Phinehas would be at this time about 16. This is not fixed. Eleazar might have been 13 at the time of Exodus, born when Aaron was 25. He would then be 41 when Aaron died and Phinehas about 20, born when Eleazar was 21. The exact figures are not so important as the fact that there are reasonable possibilities, as there obviously are.

There are some details of the "sojourn" and an archeological find known as the "400-year" stele which have yet to be considered.

The Sojourn and the "400-year" Stele

Rameses I, already well along in years, succeeded Horemhab. There is no evidence regarding their relationship, but Horemhab must have been more than 80 years old when he died and it is quite possible that Rameses I was his son. After only two years as king Rameses I retired, in -1313, in favor of his son Seti I, who was then about 30 years old. Seti conducted a military campaign in Canaan and restored much of the territory to the empire. When Seti I died his son Rameses II took the throne (-1292) to rule for 67 years. His was the longest reign of any Pharaoh.

By -1292 Joseph had been dead for 48 years if he died at age [110]≈56. Seti I might have remembered him though he would have been only about 3 years old when Joseph died. The proposed extension of Joseph's terminal age, adding 24 years to his life, would assure Seti's vivid recollection. But by -1292 Joseph would have been 24 years dead, and Rameses II was probably not more than 24 years old when he became king. So he would qualify for identification by the line:

> Now there arose up a new king over Egypt which knew not Joseph. (Ex. 1:8)

Rameses II was, undoubtedly, Egypt's most prolific builder,

though his reputation was unnecessarily enhanced by stamping his name on work his predecessors had built or started, such as the rock-cut temple at Abu-Simbel begun by his father. (This temple, by a marvel of modern engineering and international cooperation, was freed from the living rock and raised, to prevent inundation in Lake Nasser behing the High Aswan Dam.)

Much of what Rameses II built has survived, but the city of Rameses on which the Hebrews labored disappeared so completely that Breasted, in 1909, could only report, "it has often been thought to be identified with Tanis."[1] Twenty years later Pierre Montet, excavating at Tanis, modern San el-Hagar, uncovered evidence sufficient to convince him and many others that this identification was correct. Moreover, the discovery of remains of massive fortifications led him to believe that this was also the ancient city of Avaris, the Hyksos capital.

"San el-Hagar in the Delta...is thought to have possessed the successive names of Avaris before 1500 B.C., 'House of Rameses' from about 1300-1100 B.C., and finally Tanis after 1100 B.C."[2] Not all scholars are convinced. Many "believe that Rameses was located, not at Tanis, but at Qantir, a few miles to the South."[3]

At San el-Hagar there was found a stele now known as the "400-year" stele. Montet claimed its inscription commemorated the 400th anniversary of the founding of the city of Avaris by the Hyksos. Davis and Gehman add, "or an important date in its earliest Hyksos history,"[4] which would be more to the point if the stele is to be associated with the Hyksos at all, for they were not the founders of the city. Remains from the XIIth Dynasty (-2000/-1788) have been found there.[5] And Manetho (see p.32) specifically states the city was *rebuilt* by the Hyksos and was known as Avaris before their time.

Wright points out that "some are doubtful as to the interpretation of the '400-year' stele."[6] And John Bright wisely concludes, "Whether there is a connection between this and the traditional four hundred and thirty years (Ex. 12:40) of Israel's stay in Egypt (in Gen. 15:13, four hundred years), and whether this could place their coming there in the Hyksos period, is uncertain and should not be pressed."[7]

Supposing that the Hebrews called this city "Zoan", the same inscription is cited in an effort to determine the date of the founding of Hebron, mentioned quite casually with the report of the spies who went up from Kadesh-barnea.

> They ascended by the south, and came unto Hebron, where Ahiman, Sheshai, and Talmai, the children of Anak, were. (Now Hebron was built seven years before Zoan in Egypt.) (Num. 13:22)

Even if the stele can be correctly dated and the time of the founding of Avaris established it seems hardly likely that the chroniclers of Numbers intended to date the founding of Hebron in terms of the founding of an Egyptian city, especially since that event is not dated elsewhere in the text. Yet "Zoan" is mentioned later. Psalm 78:12,43 refer to "the field of Zoan" in Egypt. Isaiah speaks of the "princes of Zoan" in Egypt (19: 11,13; 30:4). Ezekiel names "Zoan" in a prophetic vein (30:14). And in each case the LXX renders "Tanis" (as we anglicize the Greek).

The basis for the identification becomes clear when we note: first, that "Zoan" is intended to transliterate צֹעַן (tso'an); and second, tso'an is closely related to tsa'an "to migrate", which lexicographers associate with טָעַן (ta'an) "to load" (as in Gen. 45:17, "load your beasts and go.")

Tanis in its day was a vital port where cargo was re-loaded from shallow draft river craft to deeper bottomed sea-going vessels, and vice-versa. Its name reflects that activity, and there is no reason to doubt that tso'an was the Hebrew version. But that does not mean that this word is to be read as the name of the city in every case. Since tsa'an means "to migrate", tso'an may be rendered "migration." This would be appropriate in Psalm 78:12, 43—Goshen may well have been known as "the field of migration." And it should also be rendered thus in Num. 13:22, which then reads, "Hebron was built seven years before the migration to Egypt." That is, "7"[10] ≈ 7 years before Jacob's migration to Egypt, the year in which he visited Kiriath-ha-arba—the city called Arba (Four), which is Hebron (Union).

The occasion of Jacob's visit would be the uniting of four towns into one community, the founding of Hebron. The event is dated in terms of the Era of Isaac, year "180"[210] ≈ 105, that is, -1373.

(Very likely a later redactor, misunderstanding the reason for the date, and assuming its mode indicated that Isaac was still living, transferred the lines regarding Isaac's death to this position in the text. Three anachronistic references to Hebron, prior to the founding of the city —Gen. 13:18; 23:2, and 37:14— obscure the matter further, as do later references to Mamre and Kiriath-arba. These last are understandable. The old name for a place often continues in use long after an official change has been made. These names may in fact refer to specific sections of the new, larger city.)

Once the reason for Jacob's visit to Kiriath-arba is understood, and Isaac's death is put in its proper time, there is no need to wonder that Jacob did not rush home to see his father as soon as he came back from Padan-aram. Then the details regarding Dinah and Shechem, and the birth of Benjamin come into focus. (See pp. 95 ff.)

None of this was realized until an examination of the theories regarding the "400-year" stele drew my attention to Num. 13:22. But without the base-7 concept to bring out the 7-year interval between Jacob's visit to Hebron and his migration into Egypt the truth would still have lain hidden.

The "400-year" stele opened avenues of thought, but whatever bearing it may prove to have on Egyptian history it is now clear, I believe, that it has no bearing at all on Hebrew history though Hebrew laborers may have helped carve and erect it.

This discussion has moved us past the Exodus. We must go back to:

The Birth of Moses

In the city of Rameses in the year -1242 the son of Amram and Jochebed was born. She is said to be the daughter of Levi but this cannot be literally true; Levi died in -1321, 79 years before. But she was of his line, and might be said to be 'of the daughters of Levi.' Like Abraham, Isaac and Jacob, Amram married his cousin. First-cousin marriages are still common among the Arabs.

The placing of the child in the bullrushes where pharaoh's daughter bathes sets the scene within the palace grounds. The child's parents are not among the herdsmen but must be servants in the royal household.

Moses was born in a very special year —the 50th year of the reign of Rameses II, an important jubilee. Only one or two other pharaohs lived to celebrate a 50-year jubilee. No records exist of any special customs pertaining to that event. But the Hebrew practice of forgiving debts and freeing slaves in the Jubilee year may reflect an Egyptian custom. And in this there may be an explanation of the reported attempt to destroy the male offspring of the Hebrew women.

Most, perhaps prefering not to dwell on this bit of horror, read of it superficially, but the details are worth considering. The motive is said to be population control. But why only the males? Destroying both sexes would better serve the stated purpose. If only one sex were to be chosen it would be the females. The number of births in a year depends upon the number of child-bearing women and has little to do with the number of men. The motive must have been other than the writer has suggested.

A determined pharaoh would have used more direct methods of population control, if that were the purpose, and more effective means of destroying the male offspring if that were all he intended. The surreptitious nature of the effort marks it as the work of someone other than the reigning pharaoh.

The one child saved was protected by the pharaoh's daughter. Even she could not have protected him from her father.

The attempt is limited in time as well as place. Had there been a continuing, widespread, systematic destruction of male children until the time of the Exodus there would have been no young men in the population at that time. But assuredly this is not the case.

What we have is an attempt by someone other than the pharaoh to eliminate the male children born in the royal household in the 50th year of the pharaoh's reign.

Might such a child have had some claim to the throne?

Rameses II had many sons. "As the years passed the sons of his youth were taken from him...One by one they passed away until twelve were gone, and the thirteenth was the eldest and heir to the throne."[1] This was Merneptah. By now he was well up in years. He had been waiting a long time for his father to die and would wait another seventeen years. He may well have been motivated by a desire to prevent the birth of a contender.

Unfortunately, though logical arguments can be mustered in support of the hypothesis, the custom suggested cannot be documented. But in any case, once Moses had been adopted by Merneptah's sister he had a claim, a protectress, and a potential sponsor. Merneptah had a thorn in his side, and his sister probably enjoyed his discomfort.

The time for Moses to make good his claim would be the year -1221, the year of his maturity, age [30] ≈ 21. This age is indicated in the line: "when Moses was grown...he went out unto his brethren." (Ex. 2:11). By that time Merneptah was on the throne, having acceded when Rameses II died in -1225.

Moses' slaying of the Egyptian may represent an aborted coup, failing, it would seem, because at that time he had not the support even of his own people, one of whom asks, "Who made you a prince and a judge over us?" (2:14).

It was then that Moses left Egypt. That same year Merneptah led a military expedition into Canaan.[2] The obvious intention was to secure his continued power in that area. Perhaps he thought to find Moses preparing an army for a further attempt to take the throne, or to establish himself as head of an independent nation. But Merneptah found no trace of Moses, and it was written on his victory stele, erected the following year: "Israel (a people) is desolated, her seed is not."

No doubt Merneptah thought the "seed of Israel" dead, but

Moses had not gone north into Canaan. He had gone directly east through Ezion-geber into Arabia where he joined a band of Midianites.

Moses' flight recalls the story of Sinuhe, an ancient and popular tale in Egypt. The parallel is interesting and Breasted's comments are particularly instructive. — When Amenemhet died in -1970, after a reign of thirty years, "swift messengers were dispatched to inform Sesostris of his father's demise. (He quickly) assumed the throne before any pretender among the sons of the harem could forestall him. (And) a certain Sinuhe, one of the nobles...fled into Asia, where he remained for many years. Whether...he had some indirect claim upon the throne which became valid at Amenemhet's death is uncertain."[1]

As the story of Moses' flight reminds us of Sinuhe, the story of his mother's effort to save her child recalls the more ancient tale of Sargon of Akkad. This parallelism is sometimes held to mark such events as fiction. But this is a dangerous assumption. The original is more to be suspected than the copy.

Much of our behaviour is imitative. The patterns are drawn from history, from fiction, from the experiences and example of friends and family, sometimes knowingly, often unconsciously. We follow patterns because, not unreasonably, we hope to succeed where others seem to have found success. The original may be fiction, but the copy is real.

Moses was well aware of his family and his people. After all, Pharaoh's daughter hired Moses' mother to be his nurse. During his exile from Egypt there would be communication with his brother Aaron. When Merneptah died in -1215 Moses would be told that it was safe to return. Aaron would come out to meet him in Sinai and learn, probably for the first time, what Moses now hoped to accomplish. Then leadership of their own people had to be established.

> And Moses and Aaron went and gathered together all the elders of the children of Israel; and Aaron spoke all the words which the Lord had spoken to Moses, and did the signs in the sight of the people, and the people believed. (Ex. 4:29-31)

Aaron spoke for Moses because Moses had said, "I am not eloquent...but I am slow of speech." (Ex. 4:10). Later Moses overcame this handicap. Perhaps he meant only that he did not speak Hebrew fluently at that time. His Egyptian education and several years with the Midianites would account for that.

Allowing two or three years for Moses to fully establish his following is not unreasonable. That brings us to -1212. His efforts to gain permission to lead the people into the wilderness in order to hold a religious festival must have continued for several years. Pharaoh's frequent change of heart may be due, in part, to the bureaucratic process — tentative permission is granted by local administrators but refused by higher authority, and in part by a change in pharaohs. As noted earlier, there was a succession of weak pharaohs with short reigns during this time. For reasons we can only surmise the Hebrews were not the only inhabitants of Egypt ready to rebel. In -1207, co-incident with the total disruption of the central government, and possibly precipitating it, Moses led his people out of Egypt.

The escape into Sinai is generally described as involving a considerable amount of confused motion along the border of Egypt. If Pharaoh had wanted to stop them, he would seem to have had every opportunity. Exodus 12:37-41, however, gives a very straightforward account. The only place mentioned between the city of Rameses and the border of Egypt is Succoth, which has been identified with a city whose ruins have been found along the route of the canal that once connected the Nile to the Bitter Lakes and hence to the Gulf of Suez. Once this canal served the same purpose the Suez canal was built to serve. It was maintained for hundreds of years, one of the engineering marvels of ancient Egypt, but it is not certain that the canal was in use at the time of Exodus. Some years later, we know, it had filled with wind-blown sand.

This identification of city ruins with "Succoth" makes little sense. The word is Hebrew for "booths." It refers to the sort of enclosure made of branches as a temporary corral for cattle still used by the Masai. We find the same term used when Jacob was leading his family back to Canaan.

> And Jacob journeyed to *succoth*...and made booths (*succoth*) for his cattle: therefore the name of the place is called *succoth*. (Gen. 33:17)

Such booths would be built whenever the cattle were rounded up. In order to move quickly across the border it would be necessary to have the cattle close to the crossing point well in advance. They could then be stampeded across, to be herded again more or less at leisure. So *succoth* were on this occassion strategically located in anticipation of the Exodus.

As to the route followed after leaving Egypt proper, there are two lists of encampments. One can be followed through the book of Exodus and the first 32 chapters of Numbers. Then in Num. 33 a review of these travels is given. It includes places not previously mentioned, and omits some named earlier. Most of the places on these lists are unidentifiable. Supposedly authoritative maps of the route, of which there are numerous versions, are in fact highly conjectural.

Whatever route was followed, they must have arrived in a relatively short time in Kadesh-barnea, for spies were sent from there into Canaan early in the first year after they left Egypt.

The spies brought back a discouraging report:— the land "flows with milk and honey" but "the people are strong and the cities are walled, and very great," and "the children of Anak" (giants) are there (Num.13:27,28). Of the twelve spies only Caleb and Joshua expressed confidence and recommended an invasion. The others then redoubled their efforts to discourage the people, stressing the number and size of the giants.

The people cried, and murmured against Moses and Aaron, and said:

> Would God that we had died in Egypt!...Why has the
> Lord brought us into this land, to fall by the sword,
> that our wives and our children should be a prey?
> were it not better for us to return to Egypt?(Num.14:1-3)

Then Moses spoke in the name of the Lord, saying:

> Your carcases shall fall in this wilderness; and all
> that were numbered of you...from twenty years old
> and upward...shall not come into the land which I
> swore to make you dwell in, except Caleb and Joshua.[a]
> But your little ones, which you said would be a prey,
> them will I bring in, and they shall know the land
> which you have despised...
> Your children shall wander in the wilderness forty
> years, and bear your whoredoms, until your carca-
> ses are wasted in the wilderness.
>
> And the men which Moses sent to search the land,
> who returned, and made all the congregation murmur
> against him, by bringing up a slander upon the land
> ...died by the plague before the Lord.
> But Joshua ben-Nun, and Caleb ben-Jephunneh...
> lived still. (Num.14:29-38)

Since the whole period of Moses' leadership was "forty" years, this incident must have taken place very soon after the people came out of Egypt. And in fact, Numbers 20:1 says:

> Then came the children of Israel, the whole congre-
> gation, into the desert of Zin in the first month; and
> the people abode in Kadesh...

---

[a] Caleb and Joshua are thus shown to be more than $[20] \approx 14$ years old.

The first thirteen verses of this chapter repeat with slight variation the story found in Ex. 17:1-7 in which Moses brings water from the rock. But here it is presented as a reason for the Lord to deny Moses himself the right to enter the 'Promised Land'. If in fact this story belongs to the final year of Moses' leadership then it is the second generation who here say:

> Would God that we had died when our brethren died before the Lord! And why have you brought up the congregation of the Lord into this wilderness, that we and our cattle should die there? And wherefore have you made us come up out of Egypt, to bring us in unto this evil place? (Num. 20:3-5)

This differs but slightly from the complaints quoted above from Num. 14:1-3. These cannot be the words of the second generation, for most of them never knew Egypt, and those that did were too young to have had a clear memory of the place [40] ≃ 28 years later. Furthermore, if it is the second generation that Moses addresses, "Hear now, ye rebels..." (Num. 20:9), then he has accomplished nothing in all these years and his people are no more ready to conquer Canaan than they were "forty" years earlier.

We are forced to conclude that these verses are not in their proper chronological position. If this incident does in fact explain why Moses never crossed the Jordan, then we shall have to suppose that he knew for "forty" years that he would not be able to do so.

However the exclusion of Moses from Canaan is to be explained there can be no doubt that Kadesh-barnea was the center of activity for the entire "forty-year" period, of which essentially little is told. This is not to minimize the importance of the events described, such as the giving of the Ten Commandments, but merely to stress the fact that these events actually occupy very little time. Two-thirds of the material in Exodus, Leviticus and Numbers concerns such things as the design of the tabernacle, the numbering of the people, the laws and the rituals. These do not advance the narrative, and have nothing to do with chronology.

Deuteronomy, literally "second telling", is just that. It contains only one item in the chronology which is not found elsewhere, the age of Moses at the time of his death. It is here that we find the line:

> And Moses was an hundred and twenty years old when he died: and his eye was not dim, nor his natural force abated. (Deut. 34:7)

The book of Joshua covers only the period of Joshua's leadership. There are only two items of chronology in that book. The first appears in a conversation between Caleb and Joshua where Caleb says:

> You know the thing that the Lord said to Moses the man of God concerning you and me in Kadesh-barnea. Forty years old was I when Moses...sent me from Kadesh-barnea to spy out the land....My brethren that went with me made the heart of the people melt; but I wholly followed the Lord my God. And Moses swore on that day, saying, "Surely the land whereon your feet have trodden shall be your inheritance. .." And now behold, the Lord has kept me alive... these forty-five years...and I am this day eighty-five years old. (Josh. 14:6-10)

This is 5 years after the death of Moses, therefore -1175. Caleb was given Hebron at this time. In those 5 years considerable headway had been made toward the conquest of Canaan. This passage also confirms an early arrival in Kadesh-barnea. But Caleb's age contains an anomalous digit. Either the Hebrew once read *meah va eser v'kamesh* and was changed, or *kamesh ushemonim* is to be translated $[5] + [110] = [115]$. The latter seems somehow more likely but we cannot be certain. In either case, Caleb was $[40] \eqsim 28$ at the time of the spying; $[45] \eqsim 33$ years later he was "85"$[115] \eqsim 61$.

The second item of chronological data in the book of Joshua simply informs us that Joshua died at age "one hundred ten" (24:29). Since he talked to Caleb $[45] \eqsim 33$ years after the spying episode, he cannot have been more than $[32] \eqsim 23$ when the spying occurred. This finding agrees with Exodus 33:11 which refers to "Joshua ben-Nun, a young man" at the time of the writing of the commandments.

As noted on p. 124 he was more than $[20] \eqsim 14$ at the time of the spying. It seems hardly likely that he was less than $[30] \eqsim 21$ when he was sent on that important mission. If he was just 21 at that time, his death came two years after his talk with Caleb, in the year -1172. He would, in that case, have been $[100] \eqsim 49$ when Moses died. His career as leader would have lasted just $[10] \eqsim 7$ years.

Without the base-7 concept to work with Joshua's age is a problem. The "young man" of Ex. 33:11 would be $110 - 45 = 55$ years old, which is hardly appropriate, unless Joshua lives for many years after his conversation with Caleb. But the longer Joshua lives the more difficult it becomes to resolve the chronology in the book of Judges, which is considered in the next chapter. So far as chronology is concerned, nothing more is to be learned from the book of Joshua.

This chapter was written much later than its position in the book would suggest. You recall, in Chapter 2, the discussion of the difficulty in regard to the data in Judges and the two books of Samuel. We were able to complete the basic chronology only with the help of the figure supplied in I Kings 6:1 that bridges the gap from Exodus to the 4th year of Solomon. That situation kept haunting me, but I could do nothing about it, it seemed.

Time after time I went back over the text looking for some clue to a fresh approach. The rest of the book was nearly finished. I had concluded the previous chapter with the reminder, "Judges and the two books of Samuel contribute no coherent chronology." I had decided against a purely speculative treatment of the material, and had almost resigned myself to leaving the period blank. There seemed no alternative.

Reviewing the problem for what I had resolved would be the last time I read once more:

> And the men of Kirjath-jearim came, and fetched the ark of the Lord, and brought it to the house of Abinadab, in the hill, and sanctified Eleazar his son to keep the ark of the Lord.
> And it came to pass, while the ark abode in Kirjath-jearim, that the time was long; for it was twenty years; and all the house of Israel lamented after the Lord. (I Sam. 7:1, 2)

But I was not lamenting. I was elated. Repeatedly, I had passed this way unimpressed. Suddenly I saw the significance of the passage. This was the key to the chronology of the period of Judges.

Briefly I lamented the number of times I had tossed it aside; wondered how many others had done the same, how many times. No matter. This time I had grasped it firmly and it would not slip away again.

By itself the statement is, today, inconsequential. The importance of the datum can be appreciated only when it is put in context. We must begin at the beginning of the First Book of Samuel, which tells of Eli the priest of Shiloh, Hannah the wife of Elkanah, and her son Samuel who "ministered to the Lord before Eli."(3:1) There are no ages, no time intervals, until we reach Chapter 4. Here we read of Eli's death, after "he had judged Israel for forty years." At the moment that figure is not important. What is important are the unusual circumstances which culminate in Eli's death.

The ark of God had been kept at Shiloh. In hopes that the presence of the ark would help in winning a battle against the Philistines, Eli's two sons brought the ark to the battleground.

In the ensuing fight Eli's sons were both killed, the ark was captured by the Philistines, and when news of this triple trage- dy reached Eli "he fell off the seat, backward...his neck broke, and he died" (4:18).

That left Samuel as the ranking priest of Shiloh. Hereafter he speaks with authority.

The Philistines had nothing but trouble after they captured the ark. They moved it from city to city, but wherever they took it the city was plagued with mice and the people suffered from "emerods" — hemmorhoids. (Some say the term has been corrupted, that it meant "swellings", and the plague which be- set the Philistines was the Bubonic plague, carried by mice. It makes better sense.) When they put the ark in the temple of their god Dagon his image fell over and broke. After "seven" months they decided to return the ark. They loaded it on a wa- gon, added a trespass offering of five golden mice and five golden "emorods," one for each of their major cities, hitched up a team, and let the oxen carry the ark back into Judah.

The ark was not taken to Shiloh, but to the house of Abinadab in Kiriath-jearim where it remained for "twenty" years.

After the ark was captured and returned Samuel anointed Saul king of Israel (I Sam. 10:1).

After David took the city of Jerusalem he removed the ark from the house of Abinadab (II Sam. 6:3).

We can see at once that Saul was king for less than "twenty" years. And it will not be hard to determine how much less, for in II Samuel 1, David learns of the death of Saul—

> And it came to pass after this, that David enquired of the Lord, saying, "Shall I go up into any of the cities of Judah?" And the Lord said to him, "Go up." And David said, "Whither shall I go up?" And he said, "Unto Hebron." (II Sam. 2:1)

> And the time that David was king in Hebron, over the house of Judah, was seven years and six months.
> (II Sam. 2:11)

Neglecting for the moment the extra six months, since David was king for "7"[10] ⇌ 7 years before he took Jerusalem, Saul's reign could last no longer than the difference between [20] ⇌ 14 and [10] ⇌ 7, that is, [10] ⇌ 7 years. In fact, it had to be some- what shorter, for he was not anointed until after the ark was returned. But, now we have it in a bracket, the exact length of Saul's reign is not essential to the chronology so the question may be deferred.

Working back into Judges we find the last two items of data: "The Lord delivered them into the hand of the Philistines forty

years" (Judges 13:1), and Samson "judged Israel, in the days of
the Philistines, twenty years" (15:20).

Samson's time as judge is not necessarily the first "twenty"
years of the Philistine domination. We are not told of his conception until after that period starts, but this may nevertheless
have occurred earlier. In any case, that "twenty-year" period
is not to be added to the chronology, for it is included in the
"forty" years of the Philistine domination. What we must now
determine is the time when that "forty-year" period ended.

The final defeat of the Philistines occurs in two battles in II
Samuel 5, but this is a confusing chapter. Verses 1,2,3, tell
of the anointing of David as king of Israel, which takes place in
Hebron. Verses 4,5, sum up David's full reign, as if he were
already dead. Verses 6,7,8, tell of the taking of Jerusalem.
Verses 9-16, go several years ahead, telling of the building of
David's house, of the concubines and wives he took and the children born to him in Jerusalem. Verses 17-21 tell of one battle
with the Philistines, verses 22-25 of another.

Chapter 6 tells of the removal of the ark from the house of
Abinadab. It was not brought immediately to Jerusalem for
there was an accident. A man named Uzzah put his hand upon
the ark to steady it and "God smote him for his error; and
there he died by the ark of God." The ark was taken into the
house of Obededom and left there for three months. After that
it was moved to Jerusalem. The story is interesting, but the
time involved is not important to the chronology. What is important is the order of events. In these two chapters they are
not in chronological order and must be sorted out.

The two battles with the Philistines would seem to occur
some time after the taking of Jerusalem, but this is not the
case, for it is specifically stated (II Sam. 5:3) that David was
anointed king over Israel while he was still in Hebron, and —

> When the Philistines heard that they had anointed
> David king over Israel all the Philistines came up
> to seek David. (II Sam. 5:17)

So these two battles, following one upon the other (5:17-25),
in which David defeats the Philistines, decisively, take place
as soon as David is anointed king of Israel, while he is still in
Hebron. After these battles David took Jerusalem, and it can
hardly be doubted that this event marks the end of the [40]-year
period of Philistine domination. Thereafter we hear of no incursions by the Philistines; we read instead of David's forays
into Philistia.

As with other aspects of biblical chronology there are, of
course, conflicting views. In his commentary to I Samuel (7:2)

Dr. Goldman,[1] after pointing out that traditional Jewish chronology considers the twenty-year sojourn of the ark in Kiriath-
jearim in the house of Abinadab to end with its removal by David,
expresses the opinion that this twenty years is passed over in
silence between verses 1 and 2 of I Sam. 7. Samuel's victory
over the Philistines at Mizpeh, described in the verses that follow this supposed hiatus, is taken to mark the end of the Philistine domination.[2] Josephus seems to have held a similar view,
regarding the importance of the victory at Mizpeh, as translator
Whiston most certainly did. Whiston declares that Eli died exactly "20 years and 7 months before Samuel put an end to their
(the Philistines') 40 years' tyranny, by the great victory at
Eben-Ezer (the name Samuel gave to the stone he set up as a
memorial)."[3]

The text would seem to support this by saying, after that
victory:

> So the Philistines were subdued, and they came no
> more into the coast of Israel: and the hand of the
> Lord was against the Philistines all the days of
> Samuel. (I Sam. 7:13)

Yet there was still a garrison of Philistines stationed at Geba,
which Jonathan attacked, thus starting the battle of Michmash,
(see I Sam. 13:3ff). Philistine dominance is emphasized by the
statement:

> Now there was no smith found throughout all the land
> of Israel; (for the Philistines said, Lest the Hebrews
> make them swords or spears.) (I Sam. 13:19)

The Philistines attack again at Shochoh, where Goliath's chal-
lenge is accepted by David (I Sam. 17), and again at Keilah
(I Sam. 23:1), before Samuel's death is recorded in 25:1.

The Philistines do not seem to be thoroughly subdued.

However, Geba, Michmash, Shochoh, and Keilah are not in
Israel, as it is distinguished from Judah,[4] and if we understand
"Israel" in I Sam. 7:13 in that sense the statement offers no difficulty. It was not until after Samuel's death that the Philistines
again invaded the northern territory called Israel. On that occasion Saul lost his life on Mt. Gilboa. Indeed, this was the
only time after the victory at Mizpeh that the territory of Israel, as distinct from that of Judah, was violated by the Philistines. The two subsequent Philistine attacks occurred in the
valley of Rephaim (Giants) which Josephus assures us is close
to Jerusalem (*Antiq*. VII, iv, 1).

There is the suggestion of an aggressive sequel to the victory at Mizpeh in a passage which must be carefully examined
and compared with a later verse.

I Samuel 7:14 says:

> The cities which the Philistines had taken from
> Israel were restored to Israel, from Ekron even
> unto Gath: and the coasts (JPSA "borders") thereof
> did Israel deliver out of the hands of the Philistines.

The verse concludes with the non-sequitor:

> And there was peace between Israel and the Amorites.

There seems good reason to believe the first part of this
verse is out of place, having been transferred from its proper
position in II Samuel 8:1. With this sentence removed I Samuel 7:13,14 reads more fluently —"the hand of the Lord was
against the Philistines all the days of Samuel... And there was
peace between Israel and the Amorites."

Now consider II Samuel 8:1. In its present form it is cryptic.

> And after this it came to pass, that David smote
> the Philistines and subdued them; and David took
> Metheg-ammah out of the hand of the Philistines.

Regarding *Metheg-ammah* Dr. Goldman comments, "If the
words represent a name, the place is otherwise unknown. Some
scholars have taken the phrase to mean 'the bridle of the mother city,' i.e. the authority of the metropolis or capital, with
the implication that David assumed supreme power over the
Philistines. The reading in I Chron. xviii,1 is *Gath and its
towns*."

NAB renders the verse with a lacuna:

> After this David attacked the Philistines and con-
> quered them, wresting...from the Philistines.

The editors note, *"wresting...*: the Hebrew text here gives
'the bridle of the cubit'; 1 Chr. 18,1 understood 'Gath and its
dependent villages'; others implausibly read 'dominion of the
capital city'."

The Hebrew in this place is written,   אֶת־־מֶתֶג הָאַמָּה
eth-metheg ha'ammah

This rendering may involve a slight error in transcription
by which מֶתֶג was written for מִגַּת. If so, the original reading
would be *eth-mgath* "near Gath" rather than something about
a "bridle".

The word *ammah* is translated "forearm; cubit; in architec-
ture: foundation; metropolis," With the definite article *ha* one
of the latter might be preferred. We would then have "near the
foundation of Gath." But with this reading the verse is certainly

not complete for, "After this David attacked the Philistines and conquered them, wresting near the foundation of Gath from the Philistines," does not make sense. But the sentence excerpted from I Sam. 7:14 fits in perfectly. II Sam. 8:1 then reads:

> After this it came to pass, that David smote the Phi-
> listines and subdued them; and the cities which the
> Philistines had taken from Israel were restored to
> Israel, from Ekron even unto Gath: and the borders
> thereof David took near the foundation of Gath out of
> the hand of the Philistines. (2) And he smote Moab...

Compare what Josephus writes concerning the same event:

> (David) removed from Jerusalem, and came against
> the Philistines; and when he had overcome them in
> battle, and had cut off a great part of their country,
> and adjoined it to the country of the Hebrews, he
> transferred the war to the Moabites. (*Antiq.* VII, v, 1)

This corresponds very well to the suggested reconstruction. But Josephus could hardly have based this on the present text of II Sam. 8:1, either in the Hebrew or the Septuagint which has the word "tribute" where AV has "Metheg-ammah."

Whether or not this reconstructed reading is correct, the victory of Samuel at Mizpeh, important as it was (and this is not to be minimized), did not terminate the [40]-year period of Philistine domination, as subsequent Philistine attacks prior to their defeat by David make quite clear.

Now we have the event —the taking of Jerusalem— that ends those [40] years, and on p. 129 we put this event at the end of the [10] ⇌ 7th year of David's reign. But there are conflicting statements about this which must be resolved.

II Samuel 5:4, 5 say:

> David was thirty years old when he began to reign,
> and he reigned for forty years.
> In Hebron he reigned over Judah seven years and
> six months; and in Jerusalem he reigned thirty and
> three years over all Israel and Judah.

I Kings 2:11 says:

> The days that David reigned over Israel were forty
> years; seven years reigned he in Hebron, and thirty-
> three reigned he in Jerusalem.

In the first, David is king of Israel for "33" years, in the second, for "40". In the first, David's reign over Judah corres-

ponds to his stay in Hebron; his accession as king of Israel corresponds to his move to Jerusalem. But we have already seen
that he became king of Israel while still in Hebron.

Both statements are oversimplified.   There must be two
equations, one regarding the duration of David's stay in each of
the two cities, the other the length of his reign over each of the
two territories. In each case the sum must be [40] years.

One statement mentions an increment of "six months" but
ignores it in the sum. The other omits this increment entirely.
Following the example of I Kings we shall omit it, supposing
those six months to be part of the year subsequently identified
as the first year in Jerusalem.

The text gives the equation: $33 + 7 = 40$. This is base-10
arithmetic, and that is the reason for the difficulty.

In base-7 terms: $[33] + [4] = [40]$.

Remembering that the word translated "seven" meant [10],
the second equation might be written $[40] - "7" = [30]$.

Since David was king of Israel for a longer time than the
period during which he occupied Jerusalem, the first equation
must be related to length of reign, the second to his stay in the
two cities. Thus, David was king of Judah, only, for [4] years,
king of both Judah and Israel for [33] ≈ 24 years. He made his
capital in Hebron for 7 ≈ [10] years and in Jerusalem for [30] ≈
21 years. His full reign was [40] ≈ 28 years.

The redactor's problem becomes clear if the data is presented in the following way: When David took Hebron he was made
king of Judah; after 4 years as king of Judah he was made king
of Israel; after "seven" years in Hebron he took Jerusalem; he
was king of Israel for thirty-three years and king of Judah for
forty years. Base-10 arithmetic would lead to the conclusion
that David was king of Israel for $40 - 4 = 36$ years instead of
33, that he ruled in Jerusalem for $40 - 7 = 33$ years, or that his
total reign was $33 + 4 = 37$ years rather than 40. Some selection from these data would have to be made. The two versions
in the text are the result.

It seems probable that the text also said, as suspected earlier, that David's 4th year was the year 'Exodus + [440]'. We
can see now why David's 4th year would have been significant
enough to warrant such a statement. In this year "all Israel"
was united under a single monarch.

The Septuagint has the figure "four-hundred forty", but mis-
takenly applied to the 4th year of Solomon. In view of this it
seems most likely that the figure 'Exodus + 480' for the 4th year
of Solomon is a redactor's sum of [440] and [40] by base-10
rules, rather than a mistranslation of *shemonim*, but the result
is the same in either case.

Before arranging this in chart form and setting down the actual dates, suppose we assemble some additional information.

When Saul died his son Ishbosheth became king of Israel. We are told that he reigned for two years (II Sam. 2:10). This would make it seem that Israel was without a king for 2 years, from the time of Ishbosheth's death to the accession of David as king of Israel. Ishbosheth's reign should last for 4 years. Very possibly the statement, "Ishbosheth...reigned two years," is intended to date the battle between Israel and Judah described in the verses that follow. If that battle was fought in the third year, then the assassinations of Abner and Ishbosheth occur in the 4th year of David's reign.

Another point must be clarified. It concerns the anointing of David by Samuel. This came about as a result of Samuel's disappointment in Saul. Two reasons are given: Saul usurped the priestly function and made a burnt offering himself (I Sam. 13:9); Saul disobeyed in the matter of annihilating the Amalekites and saved king Agag and the best of the sheep and cattle alive (I Sam. 15).

Those events follow the line —

> Saul reigned one year; and when he had reigned two years over Israel, (13:1)

This phraseology is peculiar to AV. JPSA renders:

> Saul was — years old when he began to reign; and two years he reigned over Israel.

The literal translation, as Dr. Goldman notes, is 'Saul was a year old...' which is "palpably impossible," as is the idea that Saul's full reign lasted only two years.[1] Most likely this statement is only intended to set the time for the events immediately following, which would show that Samuel's dissatisfaction with Saul stemmed from events in the third year of Saul's reign.

Samuel told Saul that his kingdom could not continue. He made the statement twice, but nearly everything happens twice in this portion of the text. Finally:

> The Lord said to Samuel, "How long will you mourn for Saul, seeing I have rejected him from reigning over Israel? Fill your horn with oil, and go; I will send you to Jesse the Bethlehemite, for I have provided me a king among his sons." (16:1)

Then Samuel anointed David (16:13), and it must have been the fourth year of Saul's reign, but David did not become king at that time. In fact, if Samuel's death is mentioned in chronological sequence, David did not become king until after Samuel died.   This is confirmed in Saul's consultation with the witch of Endor (chap. 28) which shows that Samuel predeceased Saul.

We are now in a position to set the chronology of this period in coherent form.   But the reader who reviews the text will experience some difficulty in fitting all the events described into the chronological framework.   And well he might, for nearly everything is told twice, often in contradictory versions.

For instance: Having chosen Saul in chapter 9, Samuel selects the king by drawing lots in chapter 10.   In 10:24 Saul is made king.   In 11:15 Saul is made king again.

David is introduced to Saul twice —as a musician (16:19-23), and as a warrior (chap. 17).   When David the warrior fights Goliath Saul doesn't know him, has never seen him.   But in the chapter before, he knew David the nusician very well.

Saul tries to kill David in 18:11.   This is repeated in 19:9.

Jonathan warns David of Saul's intention to kill him in 19:2.   In 20:2 David says Saul intends to kill him and Jonathan cannot believe it.   No one seems able to remember what happened a day or so earlier.

David refrained from killing Saul in chapter 24, and Saul was deeply moved.   But in chapter 26 Saul is pursuing David again; David has the opportunity to kill Saul again, but refrains from doing so, and Saul is deeply moved.

These are not different versions of the same incident.   They differ too much for that.   The purpose is to contrast David's character with Saul's.   But the double-telling tends to defeat that purpose.   David's forbearance on one occasion expresses confidence in himself and love for Saul.   On the second occassion it begins to look foolhardy and mocking.   Saul's contrition the first time marks him as a reasonable man, able to acknowledge a mistake, willing to change.   When the whole thing is repeated, as if he had forgotten the previous experience entirely, we must judge him either totally hypocritical and insincere, or quite insane.

The double-telling also distorts the time element, virtually doubling the apparent span.   We cannot gain perspective unless this is kept in mind.

In the chart opposite the years are numbered in terms of Exodus.   It is notable that the year Samuel anointed David was the year 'Exodus + [430]'.   Is there more than a coincidental connection between this and the [430]-year duration of the "sojourn" in Egypt?   Perhaps the suspected alteration of [340] was not accidental.

Far from having a vague sense of time these people seem to have a propensity for making history happen in accord with the

Reference	Event	Year: Exodus +	
Judges 13:1	First year of Philistine domination First year of Samson's term David born	[404] ≈ 200	
I Sam. 15:20 4:11 4:18 6:1	Samson died; judged Israel [20] years Ark of God captured by Philistines Eli died; judged Israel [40] years Ark returned after "seven" months	[423]	213
7:2 10:1, 11:15	First year of Ark in house of Abinadab Saul's first year as king	[424]	214
16:13	David anointed by Samuel, Saul's 4th year	[430]	217
31:4	Saul died in his [10]th year of reign	[433]	220
II Sam. 2:1- 4 2:10	David's first year in Hebron, his first year as king of Judah Ishbosheth's first year as king of Israel	[434]	221
5:3	David anointed king of Israel his 4th year as king of Judah	[440]	224
	David's [40]th year as king of Judah [33]rd year as king of Israel [30]th year in Jerusalem age [100] ≈ 49	[503]	248
I Kings 2:12	Solomon's first year as king	[504]	249
6:1	Solomon's 4th year; Temple begun	[510]	252

More graphically:

```
                         EXODUS +
[404]        [420]        [433]       [446]        [462]        [505]
 200     5    10    15    20    25    30    35    40    45    50
...I....I....I....I....I....I....I....I....I....I....I...
Ark: -Shiloh      P   -Abinadab    ·        -Jerusalem
  :                                                        ·
  :    Philistine domination      :        Jerusalem      : S  t
  :::::::::::::::::::::::::::::::::::::::::::::::::::::::::::: o  e
      Eli          :: Saul  : Hebron    D A V I D          : 1  m
  :::::::::::::::::::::::::::::::::::::::::::::::::::::::::::: o  p
      Samuel            : / : Ish :        Israel          : m  l
  :::::::::::::::::::::::::::::::::::::::::::::::::::::::::::: o  e
                       :  J  ·          Judah              : n
  ::::::::::::::::::::::::::::::::::::::::::::::::::::::::::::
```

P marks the period in which the Philistines held the ark.
The double row of dots indicates the minimum time between
Eli's death and Saul's accession.
Samuel's death occurs in the period marked "/".
"Ish" is for Ishbosheth.
"J" is the period David ruled Judah only.
This plan maximizes Saul's reign. See pp. 138ff.

numbers. In this particular period the emphasis is on number 4, an interesting number in the base-7 system, because it is exactly half of [11].

Counting by fours in the base-7 system produces what seems a curious sequence: [4], [11], [15], [22], [26], [33], [40], [44], [51], [55], [62], [66], [103], [110]...bound to fascinate a numerologist with the repetitious [4], [2], [6], sum of the digits. Then [4] + [2] + [6] = [15] and the sum of the digits [1] and [5] is [6] —the sides of the cube, the points of the hexagram, the days of creation.

[40] had a long standing fascination, probably because of the [40] days in the base-7 calendar month.

[40] years is a month of years.

During the years beginning with 'Exodus + [400]' four is a logical number to be fascinated by, and David is surely the man of the era: — born in 'Exodus + [404]', anointed by Samuel in Saul's 4th year, he occupied Hebron in 'Exodus + [434]', became king of Israel in his 4th year as king of Judah, 'Exodus + [440]', captured Jerusalem and moved the Ark of God in 'Exodus + [444]'. He was king for [40] years. His reign ended with the beginning of 'Exodus + [504]'.

Did David die at that time? At the age of only 49? Or did he simply retire in favor of his son? The text says he died. But it also says he was very old when he died. The phrase, "the king died and his son reigned in his stead," may be a formula not to be taken literally. The year [100] would be jubilee year. The idea of jubilee is rebirth. Perhaps the "king" died while the man was reborn. In Egypt such a ritual rebirth was dramatized as part of the jubilee celebration held in the 30th year of the king's reign. Had he been crowned in his 21st year (age 20) his 30th year as king would be his 50th year of life. Not all kings were crowned at age 20 but the custom of the 30th jubilee may have been based on an ideal, possibly held over from a time when kings were crowned only at that age.

Having established the year of Eli's death as 'Exodus + [423] ≈ 213' we can set the beginning of his term of service [40] ≈ 28 years earlier in 'Exodus + [353] ≈ 185' which would be [21] ≈ 15 years before the beginning of the Philistine domination. Abdon is said to have judged Israel for "8"[11] ≈ 8 years (Jud. 12:13f) preceding that period and before Abdon Elon was judge for [10] ≈ 7 years (Jud. 12:11). The first year of Elon and the first year of Eli must be the same and Eli's career concurrent with those of Elon, Abdon and Samson.

Lest it be thought that only one judge should serve at a time, note that Samuel "made his sons judges...they were judges in Beer-sheba" (I Sam. 8:2), while Samuel himself continued as judge, for "Samuel judged Israel all the days of his life" (I Sam. 7:15).

Tradition dates Hannah's visit to Shiloh in the first year of Eli. Samuel's birth could not occur much before the end of that year. When Eli died,[a] Samuel could not be more than 27 years old. But we need not delay the anointing of Saul to allow time for Samuel to develop a reputation as judge, for it is safe to assume he was already well known. Josephus says, "When Samuel was twelve years old he began to prophesy" (*Antiq*. V, x, 4), and there is no reason to reject this, even though it is not necessarily precise, for the Bible says, even before Eli's death, "all Israel from Dan to Beersheba came to know that Samuel was an accredited prophet of the Lord" (I Sam. 3:19, 20 NAB), and "The word of Samuel came to all Israel" (I Sam. 4:1).

When we read that Samuel "went from year to year in circuit from Bethel, and Gilgal, and Mizpeh, and judged Israel in all those places" (I Sam. 7:16), it is reasonable to project this back in time. That is, we may safely assume that he had been making this circuit for many years and did not just begin to do so from the time the statement is made.

Samuel's death is recorded in I Sam. 25:1. After that, David went down to the wilderness. Some months later he went to Philistia and stayed with king Achish for a year and four months (I Sam. 27:7). When he left it was to set up his capital in Hebron as king of Judah. Thus Samuel seems to have died about two years before David became king. That would place his death in 'Exodus + [432] ≎ 219' and though he may have been active as prophet and judge for 20 years or more, as Josephus avers, he could not have been more than 33 years old when he died, only 5 years after the year in which Eli died.

Yet in I Sam. 8:1, and again in v. 5, we are told that Samuel was "old," while in 12:2 he describes himself as "old and gray-headed." This conflict has long been recognized. Dr. Goldman notes[1] that traditional Jewish chronology holds Samuel's terminal age to be 52, and since he is called "old" it is assumed he aged prematurely.

This explanation may seem a bit too easy, but before we examine the point it is worth noting the source of the figure "52". It derives by base-10 calculation from the same basic assumptions already made regarding the birth of Samuel, the sojourn of the ark, and the taking of Jerusalem. — Samuel was born 1 year after Eli became priest and was therefore 40 - 1 = 39 when

---

[a]Eli is said to be "ninety-eight" when he died. This may mean he was 2 years less than [100], i.e. [65] ≎ 47, but there is no way to check this.

the ark was captured and Eli died. The ark was moved to Jerusalem 20 years later, after David had been king for 7 years. Samuel died before David became king, thus 20 - 7 = 13 years after Eli's death, making him 39 + 13 = 52. This makes no allowance for Davids stay in Philistia, but tradition may agree with Josephus (*Antiq*. VI, xiii, 10) who gives this period as only 4 months and 20 days, or LXX which gives just 4 months.

So far as the order of events is concerned there is complete agreement. But to explain that Samuel only seemed old appears to overlook the fact that he made his sons judges (I Sam. 8:1). Do we not have to allow time for his sons to grow old enough to be appointed as judges? The traditional view may have been satisfied that no allowance had to be made since Samuel was taken to be 39 when Eli died and no minimum age is given for a judge. But application of the base-7 concept makes him only 27. It is hard to imagine that he had one son old enough to be a judge, yet the text says he had two.

Significantly, we are told nothing of Samuel's wife. Nor is there any mention of Eli's wife. Both had "sons," but were they natural sons? Samuel's mother was Hannah and his father Elkanah, yet Eli calls him "my son" (I Sam. 3:6, 16). Merely an affectionate form of address, perhaps, but the relationship between Eli and his "sons" Hophni and Phinehas need be no different than that between Eli and Samuel. These other "sons" may also be Nazarites.

Hophni and Phinehas, who died when the ark was captured, were not the only "sons of Eli," nor was Samuel the only other. For Eli is told by a "man of God" that Hophni and Phinehas will die in one day, that the Lord will raise up a faithful priest, and "Everyone that is left in your house shall bow down to him... (and beg for) one of the priest's offices" (2:34-36 JPSA). Eli was to be punished because he honoured his sons above the Lord, and grew fat on the offerings of the people (2:29). His sons' misconduct is detailed in 2:12-17, 22, and although Eli registers disapproval in vv. 23-25, the Lord told Samuel, "I will judge (Eli's) house for ever, for the iniquity, in that he knew his sons did bring a curse upon themselves, and he rebuked them not" (3:13 JPSA).

If Eli is to blame for the misconduct of his "sons," what are we to think when Samuel made his "sons" judges and they "turned aside after lucre, and took bribes, and perverted justice" (8:3)? Is Samuel at fault? Perhaps the blame still falls upon Eli. For it would seem that Eli, priest of Shiloh, "father" to a group of Nazarites, conducted a school for prophets and judges. The training could not have been good, and the discipline was dreadful. When he and his two eldest "sons" died Samuel, senior surviving member of the group, thereupon became high priest. The remaining "sons of Eli," as predicted, now had to beg for a priest's office from the "faithful priest" who had just been "raised up."

Furthermore, Samuel became "father," and the Nazarites formerly known as the "sons of Eli" became the "sons of Samuel." If their conduct did not immediately improve it is not surprising.

In I Sam. 8:1 Samuel is said to be "old," in Hebrew *zaken*. The same word is used in v. 4 in reference to the "elders" of Israel, yet in v. 5 where it applies again to Samuel it is translated "old." This is not necessary, and probably incorrect.

Samuel is "elder" of Shiloh. If *zaken* is translated "elder" each time, the meaning is clear and there is no problem in respect to Samuel's age.

After anointing Saul Samuel says he is "old and gray-headed" (I Sam. 12:2), except in the Septuagint where he says "I am old and shall rest." The Hebrew is *sabethy*, translated as from *sab* "gray," but by the LXX as from *sabath* "to desist, to cease, to rest, to come to an end." The most appropriate modern rendering might be, "I am old and finished." And in this instance "old" is *zakenethy*, a different form from that previously used. It may express the way Samuel feels rather than his age.

The "sons" Samuel sent to Beer-sheba, called "his firstborn" Joel, and "his second" Abijah, would be the next eldest of the former "sons of Eli," perhaps scarcely younger than Samuel himself. With these ring-leaders out of the way Samuel must have hoped to retrain the younger Nazarites. But the reports from Beer-sheba were so bad that the elders of Israel would not give Samuel time to restore integrity to the system. He was obliged to establish the monarchy, though clearly, despite his speech of resignation, he did not intend to relinquish control entirely. He expected Saul to follow his instructions.

Saul did not comply and Samuel withdrew his support, which did the king no immediate harm for the people followed him. Perhaps hoping to restore the former system, Samuel set up a new school of prophecy, which Saul investigated personally (I Sam. 19:18-24). But he also anointed David to replace Saul as king. Saul had no inclination to step down and David was not immediately able to assume the throne.

Samuel died; Saul and his son Jonathan were killed by the Philistines. David was accepted as king of Judah, but he still had to contend with Saul's son Ishbosheth and his general Abner. Both were assassinated. Israel accepted David as king. The monarchy survived.

The prophets retained a share of influence but lacked power.

If this analysis of the period from the first year of Eli (and of Elon), 'Exodus + [353] ≈ 185', to the 4th year of Solomon, 'Exodus + "480" [510] ≈ 252', results in a much shorter term than is generally assumed, it is not due entirely to the application of the base-7 concept. It is shorter because it does not speculate on how much time should be allowed for each event that is twice described, on how old is "old" and how many years are passed over in silence between chapters 7 and 8, or similar conjectures.

The data in I and II Samuel is now coherent and we have a firm tie between Judges and Kings, thanks to Abinadab's "20-year" tending of the ark. Suppose we look now at the other end of the period of Judges. There are two firm figures —the death of Moses in 'Exodus + [40]' and the conversation between Caleb and Joshua in 'Exodus + [45]'. If Joshua lived two years longer, until 'Exodus + [50]', a reasonably firm figure, there remain only 149 years to be accounted for, from the death of Joshua to the first year of Elon.

From Judges 3:8 to 12:9 there is a series of terms covering the period in question. When these are transposed and added the sum is 248. There are 99 years too many.

Of the fifteen items that make up this sum one is particularly perplexing. In the AV we read, "And that year they vexed and oppressed the children of Israel eighteen years." Other translations render this somewhat differently but with no more success. But we had better put it in fuller context. It is found in Judges 10. We read there of Tola who "judged Israel twenty and three years"(v. 2), and of Jair who succeeded him and "judged Israel twenty and two years"(v. 3). Then Jair died, and we read that the people served other gods and forsook the Lord.

> And the anger of the Lord was hot against Israel, and he sold them into the hands of the Philistines, and into the hands of the children of Ammon.
> And that year they vexed and oppressed the children of Israel eighteen years, all the children of Israel that were on the other side Jordan, in the land of the Amorites, which is in Gilead.
> Moreover, the children of Ammon passed over Jordan to fight also against Judah, and against Benjamin, and against the house of Ephraim; so that Israel was sore distressed. (Jud. 10:7, 8, 9)

Then Jephthah was made "head and captain over them"(11:11) and when he could not negotiate peace with the Ammonites —

> Jephthah passed over unto the children of Ammon, to

fight against them... and he smote them from Aroer
...to Minnith, even twenty cities, and unto the plain
of the vineyards, with a very great slaughter. Thus
the children of Ammon were subdued before the children of Israel. (Jud. 11:32, 33)

Rashi understood *that year* meant the year Jair died,[1] which
hardly seems possible until we read Josephus' paraphrase of
this portion of the text. He tells the story in much the same
way, but without mentioning the time element until Jephthah —

passed over to the land of the Ammonites, and over-
threw many of their cities, and took their prey, and
freed his own people from that slavery they had un-
dergone for eighteen years. (*Antiq.* V, vii, 10)

This is quite plain, and it is seen that the AV translation of
Judges 10:8 will make equally good sense if the tense of the
verb is modified to read, "That year they *had* vexed and oppressed the children of Israel eighteen years."

Not all had been oppressed by the Ammonites, only those
living in Gilead. But "that year" the Ammonites attacked Judah.
And "that year" *is* the year that Jair died. The "eighteen"
years are not part of the main stream of chronology but are
concurrent with the last "18"[21] ≎ 15 of Jair's [22] ≎ 16 years,
or with 14 of them, "that year" being the 15th, and the first
year of Jephthah who "judged Israel six years" (Jud. 12:7).

Since those "eighteen" years are not to be counted the excess
is reduced from 99 to 84 years, which is three times [40].

Two other items stand out as being different from the rest in
that they are not clearly associated with the name of a judge or
a conqueror. The first says:

And Moab was subdued that day under the hand of
Israel. And the land had rest eighty years. (Jud. 3:30)

This figure is vaguely tied to Ehud who killed Eglon king of
Moab and started a battle that ended the era of Moabite supre-
macy. But Ehud is named neither judge nor king and "eighty"
years is abnormally long for one man to serve in any capacity.

The following verse reads:

And after him was Shamgar ben-Anath, who slew of
the Philistines six hundred men with an ox goad; and
he also delivered Israel. (3:31)

No further time period is given for Shamgar, so we might suppose the "eighty" years was shared with Ehud. But the next
two verses spoil that thought quickly.

> The children of Israel again did evil in the sight of
> the Lord, when Ehud was dead. And the Lord sold
> them into the hand of Jabin king of Canaan... (4:1, 2)

Shamgar disappears as rapidly as he came. His name is found
in the Song of Deborah (Jud. 5:6) but associated with events that
occur some [20] years after the "eighty-year" period is over.
That "eighty-year" figure does not seem to belong.

Josephus includes it in *Antiq.* V, iv, 3 saying, "Ehud... held
the government eighty years." Shamgar, he says, "was elec-
ted for their governor, but died in the first year of his government." Then in the next paragraph (V, v, 1) he writes:

> And now it was that the Israelites, taking no warning
> by the former misfortunes to amend their manners,
> and neither worshipping God nor submitting to the
> laws, were brought under slavery by Jabin, the king
> of the Canaanites, *and that before they had a
> short breathing time* after the slavery under the
> Moabites. (emphasis added)

On the one hand Josephus is saying there was an eighty-year
period of peace, but on the other he tells us that there was no
interval at all between the domination by the Moabites and by
the Canaanites. Translator Whiston tries to compromise by
reducing "eighty" to "eight." Though this change is large it is
not sufficient. The terminology Josephus uses does not fit eight
years any better than it fits eighty.

Josephus cannot have written these two paragraphs one after
the other. But an editor, even Josephus himself, might have
inserted the "eighty" years at some later time without thinking
to change the expression about "a short breathing time" in the
opening paragraph of the succeeding chapter.

In the Septuagint Ehud is credited with "eighty" years. But
this does not mean the figure was in the Hebrew text as early
as -285 for only the Torah was translated at that time. Judges
was put into Greek at a much later date.

It would appear that Josephus worked, originally, from a text
that did not contain that "eighty-year" figure.

The second figure in question appears at the end of the Song
of Deborah, in most English translations the last line of Judges
5:31, but in both Hebrew and Greek a separate verse numbered
5:32. It says, simply:

> And the land had rest forty years.

Josephus says Barak governed for this period after personally
killing Jabin king of Canaan. He is the only one who seems to

know these details. In the Bible no name is attached to this interval of time. The line does not read as if it were part of the Song, though AV prints it as if it were.

These two figures, which we have interpreted as "80"[110] ⇌ 56, and [40]⇌28, make up the excess 84 years. If we omit them, we shall have a coherent chronology for the period of Judges, as shown on the following chart.

Exodus to Philistine Domination

Reference	Event	Year: Exodus +	
Deut. 34:7	Moses died, "11th" month	[40]⇌28	
:8	After "30" days mourning and some preparation they crossed		
Josh. 5:10	the Jordan prior to the "14th"		
6:15	of the first month and "seven"		
ff	days later Jericho fell	[41]	29
14:7-10	Caleb given Hebron	[45]	33
24:29	Joshua died, age [110]⇌56, leader for [10]⇌7 years	[40/50]	28/35
Jud. 3:8	Chushanrishathaim dominant "8"[11]⇌8 years	[51/61]	36/43
:10	Othniel judge [40]⇌28 years	[62/131]	44/71
:14	Eglon of Moab dominant "18"[21]⇌15 years	[132/152]	72/86
4:2	Jabin of Canaan dominant		
:3	[20]⇌14 years	[153/202]	87/100
6:1	Midianites dominant "7"[10]⇌7 years	[203/212]	101/107
8:28	Gideon judge [40]⇌28 years	[213/252]	108/135
9:22	Abimelech "king" [3]⇌3 years	[253/255]	136/138
10:2	Tola judge [23]⇌17 years	[256/311]	139/155
:3	Jair judge [22]⇌16 years	[312/333]	156/171
:8	(Ammonites dominate Gilead "18"[21]⇌15 years	[313/333]	157/171)
12:7	Jephthah judge [6]⇌6 years	[334/342]	172/177
:8f	Ibzan judge "7"[10]⇌7 years	[343/352]	178/184
:11	Elon judge [10]⇌7 years	[353/362]	185/191
	(Eli became judge same year)		
:13f	Abdon judge "8"[11]⇌8 years	[363/403]	192/199
	Philistines dominant from	[404]	200

This ties in with chart on page 137.

We cannot simply delete "80" years in one place, "40" in another, without giving some thought to why and under what circumstances those figures were introduced into the text. The chronological confusion in Josephus' work may point to part of the answer. He gives the length of the period from Exodus to the 4th year of Solomon as 592 years (*Antiq.* VIII, iii, 1), and as 612 years (XX, x, 1). Some copies of his work state that Saul was king "for 18 years while Samuel was alive, and after his death two," while other copies add to this, "and twenty," (VII, xiv, 9).

Adding to this confusion we find that Paul in Acts 13:18-21 says Moses led the people for "about 40 years," the judges through Samuel ruled "about 450 years," and Saul was king for "40 years." Adding David's reign and the first 4 of Solomon's years makes the total 574. Thus it is apparent that there was little agreement regarding the chronology of this period in the first century though Judges had long since been admitted to the canon.[1]

The Council of Jamnia is said to have "confirmed the third canon and ratified once and for all the other two"[2] in year 90 of the Common Era. Perhaps corrections were approved in the chronology of Judges at that time and these included the addition of the two items to which attention has here been called. Josephus' work by that time must have passed this point in its composition. Insertion of the new data without careful editing would then account for some of the numerical confusion in the work. Careless transcription, as Whiston believed, may account for such items as the omission of Tola and the 23 years he served as judge, and the absence of any term of years for Abdon. Pure invention may account for other items such as the 25 years of leadership credited to Joshua (*Antiq.* V, i, 29), and the length of Saul's reign.

But why would these two items of "80" and "40" years be added? In what way did this seem to correct the chronological data? It is now surprisingly easy to see what assumptions made these numbers necessary.

First, it was supposed that the 4th year of Solomon's reign was 'Exodus + 480' and the data must add by base-10 rules to this sum. Second, it is assumed that David's accession terminates the period of Philistine domination. Then the following arrangement is feasible, beginning with 'Exodus + 379'.

base-ten				version				
3 3 3	3		4	4 4			4 4	
7 8 8	9		2	3 4			7 8	
9 3 9	7		2	7 3			7 0	
Ark in –Shiloh			P –Abin'd'b	–Jerusalem				
Elon|Abdon	Philistines			David			Solomon	
	Eli		Saul	Ish	Jerusalem		|Temple	
	Samuel			Hbrn				

In this base-10 plan Saul's reign may last as long as 13 years. Ishbosheth has a reign of 7 years. The space allotted to Samuel includes his full, traditional life-span of 52 years.

This leaves 378 years to account for. The text would provide the following information:

	Exodus +	b
Moses died after 40 years, in	40	a
Caleb got Hebron 5 years later, in	45	s
Chushanrishathaim dominated for 8 years to	53	e
Othniel judged for 40 years to	93	t
Eglon of Moab dominated for 18 years to	111	e
Jabin of Canaan dominated for 20 years to	131	n
Midianites dominated for 7 years to	138	
Gideon judged for 40 years to	178	v
Abimelech was king for 3 years to	181	e
Tola judged for 23 years to	204	r
Jair judged for 22 years to	226	s
Ammonites dominated for 18 years to	244	i
Jephthah judged for 6 years to	250	o
Ibzan judged for 7 years to	257	n

The period of Ammonite domination has been presumed to apply to the whole country, not just Gilead, and we are still 121 years short. The one year may be a year that Joshua lived after his conversation with Caleb. It might be "that year" in which Jephthah conquered the Ammonites. But what of the 120?

It is notable that three periods of domination follow each other without interruption. When Ehud killed Eglon of Moab, Jabin of Canaan took over. When Jael killed Sisera the armies of Jabin were defeated, but the Midianites promptly took over.

In fact this is not surprising. The Hebrews were capable of heroic action but lacked a strong, organized system of government capable of sustaining the results. An individual like Ehud could assassinate Eglon and others would rally behind him to capture the fords of Jordan and slaughter a great number of Moabites. But as soon as the Hebrews went home and began to live their peaceful, independent lives again, Jabin assumed power. No doubt his army had kept the Midianites out. When he was overthrown in the rebellion organized by Barak and Deborah, the same thing happened; the people relaxed and Midianites overran the country.

But the chronologer need not think along these lines. Seeing a need for more years in the chronology and supposing that a period of peace might follow each of these victories he might suggest 40 years for Ehud, 40 more for Shamgar, making 80 years of peace between Eglon and Jabin; then 40 more between Jabin and the Midianites. Very likely it had been assumed that the Ammonite domination applied only to Gilead, for the text is really quite clear in that respect, but the years are needed to complete the count. It is safe to assume the chronologer added them in. Some may have preferred instead to assume an 18-year period of anarchy after Joshua's death, as Josephus does, (*Antiq.* VI, V, 4), but this didn't get official sanction.

Very probably the 80- and 40-year periods of peace were entered first as marginal notes and later, accidentally, merged with the text. Had they been written in more deliberately it would not be so easy to identify and remove them. But they must have been approved by some body such as the Council of Jamnia or they would not be found in the canonized text.

Anyone who might wish to insist on the base-10 character of the data can now understand Judges and the two books of Samuel in terms of a chronology that is internally consistent. But this does not defeat the base-7 concept by any means. That base-10 chronology is still not consistent with the history of neighboring countries, and produces no meaningful correlation with the Hebrew calendar.

What has been shown here, I feel, is that those who wrote the numbers knew what they were doing, and those who preserved the Bible over the centuries were not indifferent to the chronological difficulties, though they did not understand the cause. But they were not disinterested or careless in their handling of the data. Their effort to solve the chronological problems in this portion of the text has not been appreciated because the assumption that David's reign began with the end of the Philistine domination is not a common one. Yet it must have seemed sufficiently obvious to those who made it that they felt no need to point it out. We may be thankful for this. Had a note been added to stress the point it would have made the application of the base-7 concept exceedingly difficult.

The major chronological divisions of David's reign have been considered but we have barely mentioned his son Solomon. He married the daughter of a Pharaoh. The wedding may well have been combined with his coronation. It seems, at any rate, to have been in the same year. Since we can date the accession we should be able to tell who the Pharaoh was. The year was 'Exodus + [504] $\approx$ 249', the Gregorian year -958.

Breasted lists, in the 21st Dynasty:

Siamon, -976/958, succeeded by his son,
Pesibkhenno II, -958/945.

A new Pharaoh took the throne of Egypt in the very year that Solomon became king of Israel-Judah. He was probably about the same age as Solomon. It is doubtful he had a daughter old enough to become Solomon's wife. More likely, Solomon married Pesibkhenno's sister, daughter of Pharaoh Siamon. In which case it was Siamon who attacked the city of Gezer and took it from the Philistines as a wedding present for his daughter (I K. 9:16). Perhaps an expensive present; Siamon may have paid with his life. That would account for his son's succession in the same year. Unfortunately we do not have a record of this military event. However, we do know that Egypt was divided in this era into two kingdoms. The priests of Amen ruled a theocratic south from Thebes. The pharaohs of the north had their capital in Tanis. Both were devoid of power and influence in Syria. If Siamon did in fact take Gezer it was possible only because David had thoroughly weakened the Philistines.

The birth of Solomon is reported in II Sam. 12:24. He was the son of David and Bathsheba. David did not take Bathsheba to wife until after he captured Jerusalem. Nor was it immediately after that, but a year or even two years later. And Solomon was not the first child of that union. So it would appear that Solomon was not born until the fourth year of David's occupation of Jerusalem. That would be -976, the year in which Siamon became pharaoh.

That coincidence, the similarity of the names Siamon and Solomon, plus the meaning of that name—*Shelomoh* "the peaceful", suggest that Solomon's marriage to Siamon's daughter was pre-arranged, as part of a treaty between David and Siamon in -976. Such a treaty would have made Israel–Judah a buffer state shielding Egypt, while David would have secured his southern border and the Mediterranean coast against attack, leaving him free to direct his attention north, east, and southeast, establishing a substantial empire.

Whether it included marriage arrangements or not, some treaty with Egypt must have existed. Without it David would have been much more defensive, for although she was weak Egypt still posed a threat, if largely a psychological one. And Egypt was a supplier of horse and chariots. No doubt David owed a part of his military success to this, as Solomon later owed it a large share of his financial success.

> Solomon had horses brought out of Egypt and linen yarn: the king's merchants received the linen yarn at a price. And a chariot came up and went out of Egypt for six hundred shekels of silver, and an horse for an hundred and fifty: and so for all the kings of the Hittites, and for the kings of Syria, did they bring them out by their means. (I K. 10:28, 29)

The suggested treaty, guaranteeing that Solomon would succeed David, would account for the conflict between David and

his son Absolom, and the less strenuous conflict with his son
Adonijah over the succession. (See I K. 1.)   Both Absolom and
Adonijah were senior to Solomon and had by tradition a right to
the throne ahead of him.

Treaty or no treaty, calculation shows that Solomon was not
much more than 18 years old when he became king. The Temple
was begun in the 4th year of his reign. He must have been [30]
≎ 21, an appropriate age to embark on such a project, in a pro-
pitious year — the [40]th year of the united kingdom of Israel-
Judah, established in the year 'Exodus + [440]'.

I K. 6:1 says the Temple was begun "in the month Zif, which
is the second month." II Chron. 3:2 says "the second day of the
second month." I K. 6:38 says the Temple was finished "in the
eleventh year, in the month Bul, which is the eighth month...
So he was seven years in building it." This is the only instance
of the number "eleven" in the chronological data prior to the
change in the counting system. It may very well be a later insertion. The arithmetic is base-10 and not strictly accurate.
The elapsed time would include an additional 6 months.   Furthermore, there is a conflict here with both I K. 8:2 and II Chron.
7:10 where it is stated that the Temple was dedicated in the
"seventh" month.

During the dedication of the Temple Solomon prays.   Then
we read, "Thus Solomon finished the house of the Lord and the
king's house..." (II Chron. 7:11), and "during the night" the
Lord speaks to Solomon in answer to his prayer. The indication is very strong that both Temple and palace were finished
at the same time. Yet II Chron. 8:1 says,

> And it came to pass at the end of twenty years,
> wherein Solomon had built the house of the Lord,
> and his own house...

And I K. 7:1 says, "Solomon was building his house thirteen
years." This is followed by a description of the house. Then
in chapter 8 we read of the dedication of the Temple. Surely
the dedication of the Temple was not delayed for thirteen years
while the palace was being built.

The palace may have been started in the first year of Solomon's reign, the Temple in his 4th year. If the house took
[13] ≎ 10 years to build and the Temple approximately "7" [10]
≎ 7, including year 4, then both may have been completed before the end of year [13] ≎ 10. The dedication of the Temple
would then follow its completion without delay, yet after completion of the house.

The "twenty" in Chron. 8:1 is probably a redactor's sum of
the two construction periods, presumed to have been consecu-

tive rather than concurrent. The month numbers are surely a redactor's addition to the text. The original chronicler would not name the months and also explain the names in numerical terms. His contemporaries were fully familiar with the names. But Babylonian month names were later adopted and for later generations the old names needed clarification.

Age has been mentioned in connection with David and Solomon but for the most part it does not seem worthwhile to draw attention to the ages specified for the kings. There is no way of testing them. In some cases the coronation ages of both father and son are given, and from these the age of paternity can be found when the length of the father's reign is also known. In one instance this works out to 11 years, not altogether credible. In another instance there is a contradiction —the coronation age of Ahaziah is given as "22" (II K. 8:26), and again as "42" (II Chron. 22:2). Rehoboam is said to be "41" when he became king, but Solomon his father was king for only "40" years, which would mean that Rehoboam was conceived almost two years before Solomon became king.

Considering that Solomon, with hundreds of wives, seems to have had no children other than Rehoboam, it may be significant that Rehoboam was born before David died. But we cannot very well accept this age as accurate while rejecting the others.

LXX, III K. 12:24 says, "Roboam his son reigned in his stead in Jerusalem, being sixteen years old when he began to reign, and he reigned twelve years in Jerusalem." But in III K. 14:21, "Roboam was forty and one years old when he began to reign, and he reigned seventeen years." This only adds to the confusion so far as the age is concerned. Perhaps neither one is correct. But the "12-year" figure suggests the possibility that in this case "17" is the sum of 5 and 12, the 5 being the years Rehoboam reigned before the attack by Shishak, the 12 being the years he reigned after that attack. The sum should be [5] + [12] = [20]. The "17" given in the text would then be a redactor's error rather than a matter of translation.

When Solomon died the kingdom was divided. Rehoboam reigned in Jerusalem over the kingdom of Judah. Jeroboam reigned in Tirzah over the kingdom of Israel. We must now work out the chronology for the kings who followed Jeroboam on the throne of the northern kingdom.

We have already pointed to the problem of correlating the kings of Israel with the kings of Judah (pp. 25-29) and set up a chart (pp. 30, 31) based on the synchronisms supplied by the text. It showed that the synchronisms do not produce a correlation that agrees with the length-of-reign figures nor a chronology that agrees with contemporary non-biblical records. This was all done in accord with the rules of base-10 arithmetic.

It would be very nice if the application of base-7 arithmetic eliminated the problems. Unfortunately, but not surprisingly, this is not the case. The problem is changed by application of base-7 rules but not solved.

There is one synchronism, given no special emphasis in the text, that is dictated by events which culminate in the accession of Jehu as king of Israel and Athaliah as queen of Judah.

Jehu, inspired by Elisha, assassinated Jehoram ben-Ahab, then king of Israel, and took the throne himself. The same day his followers killed Ahaziah king of Judah whose mother Athaliah promptly usurped the throne (II K. 9:24, 27; 11:1f). Thus the first year of Jehu corresponds to the first year of Athaliah.

The chronologist who adds by base-10 rules does not find his sums agree with this correlation. He gets 95 years for Judah, 98 for Israel. When the numbers are transposed before adding the sums agree; both lines, Rehoboam-Athaliah and Jeroboam-Jehu, cover a span of [134] ≈ 74 years.

Restoring [10] ≈ 7 years to Abijah's reign upsets that agreement. Evidently an opposite 'correction' was made sometime in the distant past. An ancient editor, noting that the two lines did not agree at this point as they should, and failing to understand II Chron. 14:1 where Abijah loses [10] years of his reign, apparently reduced Nadab's reign by an equal amount. This was easily done by omitting the word *esreh*, reducing Nadab's reign from [12] years to [2]. That 'correction' did not affect the synchronism of '[1] Elah' with '[26] Asa', which is followed only two years later by the synchronism of '[1] Omri' with '31 Asa'. This sequence, which is incomprehensible in base-10, is perfectly correct in base-7.

We must now reverse that 'correction', bringing the total of each line to [144] ≈ 81 years. In doing so we leave those base-7 synchronisms intact.

With the exception of the addition of [10] ≈ 7 years to both Abijah's and Nadab's reigns the chart opposite is based solely on the biblical data for length-of-reign treated as base-7 numbers. Every item of data is included. Those that are wrong are crossed out. Those that have been mistranslated are diagonally slashed. Noted are several variants that appear in the Septuagint (LXX) and Lucian (Luc.) texts.

Kings – According to Length-of-reign Base-7

The table is laid out with JUDAH on the left, the central column of "Regnal years / BCE", and ISRAEL on the right. The content is given below by reign. Quoted numbers are synchronism / length-of-reign ("1-r") values as printed; struck-through labels are reproduced with ~~strikethrough~~.

Ref. I K.	JUDAH King	"synchronism" / "1-r"	BCE	ISRAEL King / "1-r"	"synchronism"	Ref. I K.
14:21	Rehoboam	"17"	930	Jeroboam "22"		14:20
15:1,2	Abijah	"18 Jeroboam" / "3"	917, 916, 915			
15:9,10	Asa	"20-Jeroboam" (II Chron. 14:1, + "10" 13)	914, 907, 906, 905	Nadab "2"	~~"2-Asa"~~	15:25
			888	Baasha "24"	"3-Asa"	15:28, 33
			887	Elah "2"	"26 Asa"	16:8
			886	Zimri	"27 Asa, 7 days"	16:10, 15
			885, 880	Omri "12" ("6 in Tirzah", occupies Samaria)	"31 Asa"	16:23
			879, 878			
22:41f	Jehoshaphat	~~"4-Ahab"~~[a] / "41" / "25"	877, 876	Ahab "22"	~~"38-Asa"~~[b]	16:29
			861			
II K.			860	Ahaziah "2" (ben-Ahab)	~~"17 Jehoshaphat"~~[c]	22:51
8:16f	Jehoram (ben-Jehoshaphat)	~~"5-Joram"~~ / ~~"18-Jehoshaphat"~~ / "2-Jehoram" / "25"	859, 858, 854	Jehoram (ben-Ahab) "2"		**II K.** 3:1
			851			1:17
8:25f	Ahaziah	"12 Jehoram" / "8" "11" / "1"	850			

Regnal-years (BCE) column, top to bottom: 930, 917, 916, 915, 914, 907, 906, 905, 888, 887, 886, 885, 880, 879, 878, 877, 876, 861, 860, 859, 858, 854, 851, 850.

[a] LXX & Luc. "11 Omri"   [b] LXX & Luc. "2 Jehoshaphat"   [c] Luc. "24 Jehoshaphat"

The "17" years given Rehoboam may result from improper translation of *sheba-esreh*, but an earlier text may have said, "He was king for five years when Shishak attacked and king for twelve years after," and "17" would be the sum of those figures by base-10 rules. The synchronism of '1 Abijah' with '18 Jeroboam' may be a mistranslation, or simply the base-10 number next after 17.

The assassination of Elah in '27 Asa' can be explained in the same two ways. It should say [30]. But some may raise an objection here, having heard that the time between '27 Asa' and '31 Asa' is the duration of the contest between Omri and Tibni who opposed him. But we can close the gap and do without the explanation. There is no indication that this conflict lasted for any such period. It is mentioned briefly, almost casually, as if it amounted to very little, though while it lasted "half of the people followed Tibni" (I K. 16:21). The half that followed Omri prevailed, perhaps because his half included the entire army, which had been under his command at the time of Elah's assassination.

The explanation doesn't really work in any case. Omri's reign began the moment word of Elah's death reached the army, then attacking Gibbethon, for "all Israel made Omri, the captain of the host, king over Israel that day in the camp" (I K. 16: 16), and that was before the conflict with Tibni began.

It is notable that aside from '1 Ahaziah'='12 Jehoram' which would be hard to get wrong since both men died the same day, only two synchronisms are correct in all respects — '1 Elah' = '26 Asa' and 2 years later '1 Omri'='31 Asa'; i.e. [26]+[2]=[31].

We still have the period from the first year of Jehu (-849) to the 9th year of Hoshea (-722) to clarify. The chronologist adding by base-10 rules finds the given data adds to 163 for Judah but only 143 years 7 months for Israel. Our problem is only quantitatively different. After transposing, and with a 1-year correction added to Amaziah's reign, we have a sum for Judah that agrees with the dating, i.e., 128 years. But for Israel the same procedure produces a total of only 110 years 7 months, a shortage of 17 years 5 months.

In this sequence we find several anomalous digits. To begin with, Jehu's reign is given as "28" years (II K. 10:36). Understanding *shemona* as [11] the translation would be [20]+[11]= [31]. But "28" could also be a base-10 calculation. Jehu was succeeded by his son Jehoahaz in '23 Joash ben-Ahaziah' (II K. 13:1). Joash began to reign after the six years of queen Athaliah. A redactor would add 6+22=28. So we cannot be certain how the number attained its present form.

Jehoahaz ben-Jehu was king for "17" years (II K. 13:1). This would seem to pose no special problem. We would think that "17"[20] ≈ 14. But a closer look shows this to be incorrect. The pertinent information is contained in four verses:

> In the seventh year of Jehu, Joash began to reign, and reigned forty years in Jerusalem. (II K. 12:1)

> In the twenty-third year of Joash...Jehoahaz ben-Jehu began to reign over Israel...seventeen years.
> (II K. 13:1)
> In the thirty-seventh year of Joash king of Judah began Jehoash ben-Jehoahaz to reign over Israel...
> (II K. 13:10)
> In the second year of Jehoash ben-Jehoahaz king of Israel, reigned Amaziah ben-Joash king of Judah.
> (II K. 14:1)

It is apparent that the first year of Jehoash is the last year of Joash, for otherwise Amaziah could not be king in the second year of Jehoash. We have here an instance in which the Hebrew quite plainly expresses "forty" as *arbaim* and also as *shelshim va·sheba*. To explain the "37" otherwise would require a circuitous and improbable series of calculations and accidental events. The "17" years given Jehoahaz is easily explained, however, as the base-10 difference between 23 and 40. But in base-7, [40]-[23]=[14], which transposes to 11, and this must be the length of Jehoahaz' reign.

A chart should make this easier to follow.

Athaliah		1 is	1	Jehu
		6	6	
Joash "7 Jehu"		1	7 [10]	
	[22]	16	22 [31] "28"	
	[23]	17	1	Jehoahaz "23 Joash"
	[36]	27	11 [14] "47"	
	[40]	28	1	Jehoash "37 Joash"
Amaziah "2 Jehoash"		1	2	

This 3-year reduction in the reign of Jehoahaz increases the deficiency we have been trying to eliminate. We are now short 20 years 5 months. We're making progress in the wrong direction. But many elements are matching up and working out in perfect accord with the work done earlier in connection with the length of Amaziah's reign (pp. 81, 82). —Continuing from above:

Amaziah	[15]	12	13 [16]	Jehoash
	[16]	13	1	Jeroboam "15 Amaziah"
	"20" [33]	24	12 [15]	
Azariah		1	13 [16]	

Jeroboam II (ben-Jehoash) was king for "41" years (II K. 14:

23).   He was succeeded by his son Zachariah.

In the thirty-eighth year of Azariah king of Judah
did Zachariah ben-Jeroboam reign over Israel in
Samaria six months. (II K. 15:8)

But extending the chart we find:

Azariah   [23] 17 is 29 [41] Jeroboam
                 [24] 18   ?

Something has to happen in Israel in the year '24 Azariah'. ?
If Zachariah's reign of six months falls in the year "38" [41] ≏
29 of Azariah's reign, we have a gap of at least [14] ≏ 11 years
duration between the end of Jeroboam's reign and the brief reign
of his son and successor.
That is the key word, "successor."

Jeroboam slept with his fathers, the kings of Israel;
and Zachariah his son reigned in his stead. (14:29)

Something has been left out. The words "fourteen years" have
been omitted, and perhaps more. The full line should read:"In
the twenty-fourth year of Azariah began Zachariah to reign and
he ruled over Israel fourteen years...and in the year '38' [41]
Azariah did Zachariah reign six months." His total reign then,
would be 11 years 6 months, since [14] ≏ 11.
Fading of inks, damage to the scroll, or human error would
easily account for the omission. Restoring these years reduces the shortage from 20 years 5 months to 9 years 5 months.
Recognizing this omission in the reign of Zachariah started
a chain reaction. Two more omissions promptly showed up.
First, by extending the reign of Zachariah into prior years
it became possible to answer the question: Which six months of
the year called "thirty-eight" did Zachariah reign? The answer
has to be — the first six. If he had not served in the previous
year, any six-month period within the year could be indicated.
It had seemed that he must have been king during the last of
the year, because:

Shallum ben-Jabesh conspired against him and smote
him before the people, and slew him, and reigned
in his stead. (II K. 15:10)

And: Shallum ben-Jabesh began to reign in the thirty-
ninth year of Uzziah (Azariah) king of Judah; and he
reigned a full month in Samaria. (15:13)

Knowing that Zachariah reigned the first six months of the
year in which he was killed, it follows that his assassin ruled
the remaining months of that year. Shallum's total reign must

be 7 months, not just 1. And this does not contradict the text, for *malak*, here translated "began to reign," is elsewhere taken to mean "did...reign," as in II K. 15:8 quoted above.

Even as translated, the meaning is ambiguous. "He began to reign" is not necessarily the same as "his reign began." It may mean only that he started the year but did not complete it.

But why does the text not mention the remaining months of the year "38 Azariah"? Perhaps they are omitted because the text once said, "Zachariah was king for 6 months of that year and Shallum was king for the other 10 months."

This would be perfectly correct in terms of the base-7 calendar divided into [16] ≈ 13 months. But a redactor who knew nothing of that calendar would see it as a ridiculous mistake.

The text would go on to say: "Shallum began to reign in the following year, but he reigned one month and Menahem ben-Gadi smote him and slew him and reigned in his stead for the 15 months remaining in that year."

What it now says is:

Menahem ben-Gadi went up from Tirzah and came to Samaria, and smote Shallum ben-Jabesh in Samaria and slew him, and reigned in his stead. (15:14)

In the thirty-ninth year of Azariah king of Judah began Menahem ben-Gadi to reign over Israel, ten years in Samaria. (15:17)

In the fiftieth year of Azariah king of Judah, Pekahiah ben—Menahem began to reign over Israel in Samaria, two years. (15:23)

No mention is made of the remaining months in the year called "39". If Menahem's reign begins in the second month of "39" and continues until his son becomes king in the year "50", then his reign covers a period of very nearly 11 years, not just 10, except that this is a base-10 calculation. The ancient text would not have given Menahem "10" years at all. The year "39" is really year [42]. Menahem's reign extends from the second month of '[42] Azariah' through '[46] Azariah' a matter of less than five years. The original text must have given him [4] years and [15] months.

That would be enough to convince a redactor that he had discovered a series of errors in the text. He would be impelled to make corrections. Base-10 calculations with the numbers, as he understood them, would give Menahem 10 years, and the problem with the months would be most easily solved by dropping all mention of them from the text. If the result was a bit vague, at least there was no flagrant error.

Had we been thinking in terms of the [16]-month calendar from the beginning of our analysis of this period we would have counted [6] months for Zachariah and [1] month for Shallum for a total of [10] months. The deficiency would have been given as [23] years [6] months. This would hàve increased to [26] years [6] months when we took [3] years from Jehoahaz. The [14] years restored to Zachariah would have reduced it to [12] years [6] months. The addition of [10] months to Shallum's reign would bring it down to [11] years [15] months.

We had allowed [10] years for Menahem. Now we find he was king for only [4] years [15] months, which is [2] years [1] month less. This adds to the deficiency, bringing it up to [14] years, exactly.

Thinking in terms of a twelve-month calendar is perfectly satisfactory. We had reduced the deficiency to 9 years 5 months. Shallum has been restored an omitted 6 months. This leaves a shortage of 8 years 11 months. Menahem's loss of 2 years 1 month increases the deficiency to 11 years.

Either way it is the same thing: [14] ≈ 11.

Again we have made some progress backwards. Before going further, let's bring the chart up to date.

Azariah	[23] 17	is 29 [41] Jeroboam II
	[24] 18	1 Zachariah
	[40] 28	11 [14]
1st-half	[41] 29	11½ [14]½ "3̸8̸ Azariah, 6 m."
2nd-half	[41] 29	6 months. Shallum
1st month	[42] 30	1 month: Total, 7 months
remainder of	[42] 30	11 months. Menahem
	[46] 34	4 years: Total, 4 yrs. 11 m.
	[50] 35	1 Pekahiah

Pekahiah began his reign in the "fiftieth year of Azariah." He was king for two years, (15:23). Then:

> Pekah ben-Remaliah, a captain of his, conspired against him, and smote him in Samaria...and killed him, and reigned in his room. (II K. 15:25)

> In the fifty-second year of Azariah king of Judah Pekah ben-Remaliah began to reign over Israel in Samaria, and reigned twenty years. (15:27)

> In the second year of Pekah ben-Remaliah king of Israel began Jotham ben-Azariah king of Judah to reign...and he reigned sixteen years in Jerusalem.
> (15:32, 33)

Adding this to the chart:

Azariah	[51] 36	2	Pekahiah "2"
"52"	[52] 37	1	Pekah ben-Remaliah
Jotham "2 Pekah"	1	2	\"52 Azariah"
"16"	[16] 13	14 [20] "20"	

The reigns of Jotham and Pekah ben-Remaliah end in the same year. And it is noteworthy that every item of data regarding length of reign, and the correlations between the two lines of kings as well, is perfectly correct in these several verses, providing strong confirmation for the several adjustments we have made prior to this point.

> Hoshea ben-Elah made a conspiracy against Pekah ben-Remaliah, and smote him, and slew him, and reigned in his stead, in the twentieth year of Jotham ben-Azariah. (15:30)

That is what it says, right after telling us that Jotham was king for only sixteen years. We noted this earlier (p. 29). The explanation given then was rather lame because we were thinking in base-10 terms. In base-7 terms this is no problem, for [20] follows next after [16]. Whether or not Jotham was king for part of that year the meaning is perfectly clear.

> In the seventeenth year of Pekah ben-Remaliah Ahaz ben-Jotham king of Judah began to reign... and reigned sixteen years in Jerusalem. (16:1, 2)

The number "seventeen" is a mistranslation for [20]. Ahaz became king in the latter part of '[20] Pekah'.

The first year of Ahaz and the first year of Hoshea correspond. But the chroniclers do not correlate them this way for a very good reason. To say, "Ahaz became king in the first year of Hoshea, and Hoshea became king in the first year of Ahaz, " would provide no historical continuity. And indeed, though the system might be called a nonaccession-year system it appears that the king did not have a "first" year. There is the year in which "he began to reign," one word, *malak*, in Hebrew, which for equal brevity might be translated "acceded." Then there is the "second" year. The term "first year" may have been avoided because it was in most cases less than a full year.

Events are not in strict chronological order in the text. We read that Hoshea killed Pekah in 15:30, and in 15:32 we are told of Jotham's accession in the second year of Pekah. Then in 16:1 Ahaz becomes king in the "17th" year of Pekah, and Pekah with Rezin of Syria as his ally attacks Ahaz (16:5).

When we read in 17:1 that Hoshea "began to reign" in the twelfth year of Ahaz it is easy to suppose that 15:30 is in error, and Hoshea did not become king in a year called '20 Jotham', a year that did not exist in the first place.

When the verses are read in chronological order the events become clear.

Ahaz became king in "17"[20]-Pekah, which is Pekah's last year, not three years before the last. Soon after Ahaz became king Pekah and Rezin laid siege to Jerusalem. Ahaz called on Tiglath-pileser the king of Assyria for help, (16:1-7).

Tiglath-pileser attacked Damascus. Rezin rushed to the defense of his city, breaking off the siege of Jerusalem, and Ahaz was saved, for Pekah could not sustain the siege by himself.

Ahaz was therefore indebted to Tiglath-pileser and went to Damascus to pay him tribute, but that was somewhat later.

Besides attacking Damascus —

> In the days of Pekah king of Israel, came Tiglath-pileser king of Assyria, and took Ijon, and Abel-beth-maacah, and Janoah, and Kadesh, and Hazor, and Gilead, and Galilee, all the land of Naphtali; and carried them captive to Assyria.
> And Hoshea ben—Elah made a conspiracy against Pekah ben-Remaliah, and smote him, and slew him, and reigned in his stead, in the twentieth year of Jotham ben-Azariah. (15:29, 30)

The year designated "the twentieth year of Jotham" is in fact the year in which Ahaz became king, and since this happened before Pekah besieged Jerusalem, it obviously happened before Hoshea killed Pekah. Jotham was already dead, and his reign was not in the final analysis even credited with this year. That year was included in the reign of Ahaz. But then it was known as "twentieth Jotham", and so it is called in the book.

But what of the twelfth year of Ahaz when Hoshea "began to reign over Israel nine years"? This is another example of the ambiguity of the word "began." Hoshea had been king since the year '20 Jotham'. In the twelfth year of Ahaz Hoshea began to count what turned out to be his last nine years. The text neglects to state the total length of Hoshea's reign.

Since Ahaz and Hoshea began to reign in the same year, the twelfth year of Ahaz would also be the twelfth year of Hoshea, if they were both using the same counting system. Ahaz, you recall, changed the counting system in Judah. He was counting his years with base-10 numbers. Apparently Hoshea's chroniclers were still using the base-7 numbers up until the 12th year of Ahaz. So the record would have shown that the year '11 Ahaz' was the year '14 Hoshea'.

In the twelfth year of Ahaz the chroniclers of Israel began to count with the new system. That was the year -730, only two years after Tiglath–pileser III conquered Damascus. It was probably -731 that Ahaz went to Damascus to meet Tiglath-pileser and learned to count in the new way. Hoshea learned of this innovation about as quickly as could be expected and adopted the new system at once. But Ahaz made the system retroactive to the beginning of his reign, so far as the historical record was concerned. Hoshea's chroniclers began to count a new sequence of years beginning again with the year 'one'.

Hoshea's reign lasted [14]+9 years. Taking both figures as base-10 numbers the total is 23. Ahaz and Hoshea both became king in the same year. Ahaz ruled for 16 years. Hoshea, it would seem, continued as king for 7 years after Ahaz died. Those years were numbered 3 through 9. It followed that:

> In the third year of Hoshea ben-Elah king of Israel,
> Hezekiah ben-Ahaz king of Judah began to reign. (18:1)

This is not correct. The [14] must be transposed before the 9 can be added. Since [14] ⇌ 11, the correct total is 20.

Hoshea was king for only 4 years after Ahaz died, and those years were numbered 6 through 9. It was in the 6th year of Hoshea (actually the 17th from the beginning of his reign) that Hezekiah became king of Judah, as the synchronism regarding the twelfth year of Ahaz clearly informs us.

Ahaz (base-10)	1 is	1	Hoshea
	11	11 [14]	
	12	1	beginning base-10 in Israel
	16	5	
Hezekiah	1	6	
	4	9	(Total reign: 20 years.)

We had a deficiency of 11 years; it has now been eliminated. The correlation of the kings of Israel with the kings of Judah is complete.

The work on these last several pages is summarized on the following page in a chart that continues the one on p. 153.

Kings – According to Length-of-reign Base-7 (cont. from p.153)

JUDAH				ISRAEL			
Ref. II K.	King	"synchronism" "1-r"	Regnal years "1-r" — BCE	Regnal years "1-r"	King "1-r"	"synchronism"	Ref. II K.
11:1-3	Athaliah		[1 ... 6] — 1 / 849, 6 / 844	[1 1], [6 6]	Jehu		10:36
11:4	Joash	"7 Athaliah"	[1] — 1 / 843	[7 10]			
12:1		"7 Jehu" /	[22] 22 / 828, [23] 23 / 827, [36] 36 / 817, [40] "40" 40 / 816	[22 31] "2̶8̶", [23 16→17], [27], [28]			
				[1 1] "1̶7̶", [11 14]	Jehoahaz "23 Joash"		13:1
				[1 1], [2 2]	Jehoash "3̶7̶ Joash"		13:10
14:1, 2	Amaziah	"2 Jehoash"	[1] 1 / 815, [15] 15 / 804	[13 16] "16", [12 15]			
14:17		"lived 15 years after Jehoash"	[16] "2̶9̶" 16 / 803, [33] 33 / 792	[13 16]	Jeroboam "15 Amaziah"		14:23
15:1, 2	Azariah	"27 Jeroboam"	[1] 1 / 791, [23] 23 / 775, [24] 24 / 774, [40] 40 / 764, [41] 41 / 763	[29 41] "41", [1 1], [11 14]	Zachariah	(Total: 11 yrs, 6 mons.) "6 months, 3̶8̶ Azariah"	15:8
			[42] 42 / 762	11½ [14½], ½	Shallum	(Total: 7 months) "½"	15:13
			[46] 46 / 758	½ "1 month.", 11 mos.	Menahem "3̶9̶ Azariah"	"1 month, 39 Azariah"	15:17
			[50] 50 / 757, [51] 51 / 756, [52] "52" 52 / 755	+4 yrs. (Total: 4 yrs.11 mos.), [1 1], [2 2] "2"	Pekahiah "50 Azariah"		15:23
15:32, 33	Jotham	"2 Pekah"	[1] 1 / 754, [16] "16" 16 / 742	[1 1], [2 2], [14 20] "20"	Pekah "52 Azariah"		15:27
16:1, 2	Ahaz	"17 Pekah"	[1] 1 / 741	[1 1]	Hoshea "20 Jotham"		15:30
		(changed to base-10, retroactive to 1st year)	[11] 11 / 731, [12] 12 / 730	[11 14] (end of base-7 in Israel), [12 1]	"12 Ahaz began 9 years"		17:1
18:1	Hezekiah	"16" [16] 16 / 726 "2̶ Hoshea" → "3 Hoshea"	[1] 1 / 725, [4] 4 / 722	[16 5], [17 6], [20 9]	Israel taken captive.		17:6

With the chronology established many things can be understood that were formerly unclear. The restoration of Abijah's reign to its full length, for instance, has interesting consequences.

The battle described in II Chron. 13:3-29 between Abijah and Jeroboam is seen to be of greater significance than previously seemed to be the case. Jeroboam was defeated. Sometime later, perhaps in the following year, "The Lord struck him and he died." This may imply something other than a natural death. When a king loses a battle he often loses his throne, and his life, in consequence. Whether this was the case with Jeroboam or not we cannot be certain. But one other fact is strongly indicated—that the battle occurred in Abijah's first year as king.

It is a commonplace of history that a king attacks or is attacked in his first year. There are reasons why this tends to be true: A new king sets out to establish his authority, or someone else decides to test it; an incipient revolt is brought to a climax because it seems most likely to succeed when power is in the process of transfer... So the battle between Abijah and Jeroboam would be expected in Abijah's first year.

With the defeat of Jeroboam, Israel became subordinate to Judah. When Nadab succeeded to the throne it would be normal for an effort to be made to restore the independence of his kingdom. Very probably there was a battle between Nadab and Abijah though it is not mentioned. There were [10] ⇌ 7 years of peace in Abijah's reign. If there had been no war with Nadab there must have been [11] ⇌ 8 years of peace.

When Abijah died and Asa became king Nadab should have improved the opportunity to re-establish the prestige of Israel. Either he did not try, or he tried and failed. Presumably the former, since no battle is recorded between Nadab and Asa. In that case, it was Nadab's submissive complacency that motivated Baasha to assassinate him, for Baasha promptly made war upon Judah.

That war continued, indecisively, for years. Then Baasha began to build Ramah, a lofty fortification, to halt all traffic between Israel and Judah (II Chron.16:1; I K.15:17). Asa bought assistance from Ben-hadad I of Syria who attacked Israel in the north. Baasha withdrew from Ramah. Asa tore down what had been built and re-used the material to build a watch-tower of his own.

II Chron. 16:1 dates this event in the "thirty-sixth year of Asa." But I K. 16:18 says Baasha was replaced by his son Elah in the "twenty-sixth year of Asa," and our chronology concurs. Since Baasha's defeat very probably ended his reign, Ben-hadad's attack must have occurred in the year '[25] Asa', or very early in '[26] Asa'. A few verses later (II Chron. 16:12), "Asa,

in the thirty-ninth year of his reign, was diseased of his feet."
His full reign was "forty-one" years, so we deduce he was af-
flicted during the last two years. This then is where the number "thirty-six" belongs, because [36]+[2]=[41].

When Ahab was king of Israel, Ben-hadad of Syria besieged
Samaria. Ahab defeated him (I K. 20:1). The next year, Ben-
hadad tried again. Ahab not only defeated him the second time
but took him captive. Ben-hadad said, "The cities my father
took from your father I will restore, and you shall make streets
for yourself in Damascus, as my father made in Samaria" (I K.
20:34).

This cannot be Ben-hadad I speaking. His father, Tabrim-
mon, died before Samaria was built, and even before Ahab's
father, Omri, became king. The words must be those of Ben-
hadad II.

There followed three years without war between Syria and
Israel (22:1). Then Ahab, in alliance with Jehoshaphat of Judah,
fought Ben-hadad at Ramoth-gilead where Ahab was mortally
wounded. Since Ahab died in -861 the three years of peace with
Syria must be -864, 3, and 2. The capture of Ben-hadad II must
have been in -865.

Though we can be certain that the attack in -865 was led by
Ben-hadad II it does not follow that it was he who led the attack
of the year before. That may well have been Ben-hadad I, and
his defeat by Ahab may have ended his career. The complete
revamping of the Syrian military structure (20:24) supports this
thought, strongly suggesting a change in top leadership.

Ben-hadad I began to reign about -900. To have named any
streets in Samaria he must have been king in -879 when that
city was completed. He was probably king in -866 and could
not have been king in -865. Ben-hadad II might have ruled in
-866, but it is unlikely that he was king before that or we would
have heard of him sooner. The uncertainty is of the order of +
or - 1 year. Ben-hadad I had a reign, beginning in -900, of 34
or 35 years. Ben-hadad II must have ruled for 25 or 24 years.
He was succeeded by Hazael in -842.

From the Syrian records historians have not been able to
determine even an approximate date for the accession of Ben-
hadad II. Contemporary records have helped us confirm the
fact that the Bible dates itself. In return the Bible now supplies
a missing date in Syrian history. — Nor is this its only contri-
bution.

In Chapter I we discussed, briefly, two Assyrian inscriptions that refer to biblical kings but in connection with events
that are not mentioned in the Bible. As a result, these inscriptions took no part in the development of the biblical chronology.

Now we must re-examine the text for possible allusions to the events in question.

The earlier of the two, the Monolith Inscription of Shalmaneser III, refering to his battle with a coalition led by "Hadadezer of Aram," names "Ahabbu the Sirilean" as leader of a force of "2,000 chariots and 10,000 soldiers." There is no difficulty in identifying "Hadadezer of Aram" with Ben-hadad II of Syria. Recognizing "Ahabbu the Sirilean" as Ahab of Israel has seemed equally easy. Explaining the omission of this battle from the Bible is more difficult.

Some scholars, despite obvious conflicts, have thought to identify the battle against Shalmaneser III with the battle at Ramoth-gilead in which Ahab of Israel was killed. The battle of the inscription was fought at Karkar, but this location is not certainly known, so it is suggested that Karkar is another name for Ramoth-gilead. But Ahab went to Ramoth-gilead to fight *against* Ben-hadad. To twist this into an *alliance with* Ben-hadad against Shalmaneser is totally unwarranted.

Thiele suggests, more logically, that the battle at Karkar preceded that at Ramoth-gilead; that Ahab, after his success at Karkar, thought to even an old score against his erstwhile ally, Ben-hadad.[1]

This does not tell us why there is no reference in the biblical text in the time of Ahab to Karkar, Assyria, or Shalmaneser III. But the chronology makes the reason clear:

Ahab died in -861.
Shalmaneser became king of Assyria in -858.
The battle at Karkar was fought in -854.

Then: Who is "Ahabbu the Sirilean"?

The chart on page 153 shows that the king of Israel in -854 was Jehoram ben-Ahab. The king of Judah was Jehoram ben-Jehoshaphat. These two kings must be the allies of Ben-hadad II who fought Shalmaneser III at Karkar.

Rather than his father, it must be Jehoram ben-Ahab who is identified by the inscription.

Did the Assyrian scribe confuse these two men? Possibly. Was the dynasty rather than the man being named? Then it should have said "Omri". There is a simpler answer. With two kings named Jehoram one could not be distinguished from the other by using that name alone; the full name, "Jehoram ben-Ahab of Israel," would take too much work and too much space on the stone, so the scribe omitted "Jehoram ben-".

This change in identification does no violence to the Bible, only to the history books. There is no mention of Karkar in the Bible in any case.

That omission can hardly be deliberate, for Shalmaneser, though his records seek to disguise the fact, met defeat on that occassion. The chroniclers of Israel could not have been un-impressed. Those of Judah may have ignored the battle. The inscription mentions "500 soldiers of the Gueans"[1]—Judeans?—a token force. But the omission from the records of Israel suggests a damaged scroll. Suppose we examine this thought.

Of Ahab we are told a great deal and the story seems per-fectly coherent. Of his son Jehoram we are told very little, yet he ruled Israel for nine years. In this part of the text there is a garbled verse which may well be the scar of an excission:

> And in the fifth year of Jehoram ben-Ahab king of
> Israel, Jehoshaphat being then king of Judah, Jeho-
> ram ben-Jehoshaphat king of Judah began to reign.
> (II K. 8:16)

The fifth year of Jehoram ben-Ahab was -854, the year of the battle at Karkar. Jehoshaphat was not king of Judah, nor was that the year in which Jehoram ben-Jehoshaphat began to reign. It appears that two incomplete and dissociated verses have been joined, with the clause regarding Jehoshaphat inser-ted. After the words, "And in the fifth year of Jehoram ben-Ahab king of Israel —" a description of the battle at Karkar would be in order.

To further support the idea that the record at this point suf-fered some damage, first: there is the confusion in the corre-lating data which gives two dates for the beginning of the reign of Jehoram ben-Jehoshaphat; second: while Jehoram ben-Ahab lost credit for the battle at Karkar he has been given credit for another battle in which he could have taken no part. This is the battle described in II K. 3:4 ff, beginning, "Mesha of Moab was a sheepmaster... "

In the story that follows the principal characters are Jeho-shaphat king of Judah, the prophet Elisha, the king of Moab whose name appears on the somewhat dubious Moabite Stone, an ephemeral king of Edom who was no king — for in the days of Jehoshaphat "There was no king in Edom; a deputy was king." (I K. 22:47), and the king of Israel — whose title is repeated many times but whose name is given only once, and that some-what cryptically:

> And king Jehoram went out of Samaria the same
> time, and numbered all Israel. (II K. 3:6)

The chronology shows that Jehoram ben-Ahab king of Israel could not have been allied at any time with Jehoshaphat king of Judah. Either the king of Israel or the king of Judah must be incorrectly identified here.[2] The question is: Which?

We might hastily conclude that Jehoshaphat is out of place in this story for we have already read of his death in I K. 22:50. In that case we should have to substitute the name "Jehoram ben-Jehoshaphat" wherever the name "Jehoshaphat" now appears in this portion of the text. But Elisha says to the king of Israel:

> As the Lord of hosts lives, before whom I stand, surely, were it not that I regard the presence of Jehoshaphat the king of Judah I would not look toward you, nor see you. (II K. 3:14)

Elisha might have spoken so to either Ahaziah ben-Ahab or his brother Jehoram ben-Ahab, for he despised them both. But the name "Jehoram ben-Jehoshaphat" would not be an appropriate substitute for "Jehoshaphat" in the mouth of Elisha; he held that Jehoram in the same low regard as the sons of Ahab, for Jehoram ben-Jehoshaphat was their brother-in-law. He was married to the daughter of Ahab and the Baal-worshipping Jezebel, arch enemy of Elisha's mentor, the prophet Elijah.

So the king of Judah in this tale is indeed Jehoshaphat, and the king of Israel must therefore be Ahaziah.

This makes eminently good sense, for Ahaziah is king in the beginning of II Kings which opens with the line:

> Then Moab rebelled against Israel after the death of Ahab. (1:1)

> Mesha of Moab was a sheepmaster... (3:4)

should follow immediately. The name "Jehoram" in v. 6 should be changed to "Ahaziah" or the verse omitted. Then vv. 6-27 complete the story.

The episode reported in I K. 22:48, 49, where Jehoshaphat refused to let Ahaziah participate in his intended expedition to Ophir must follow.

Jehoshaphat's death is recorded (v. 50), and thereafter we read (II K. 1:2-18) of the injury and death of Ahaziah, a story in which Elijah the prophet is a principle figure.

In this latter point we may discern at least a partial cause for the chronological confusion. The stories involving Elijah and those involving Elisha are separated into two groups. The general impression is that Elisha succeeded Elijah, and this is perfectly true. II K. 2 tells how Elijah "went up by a whirlwind into heaven" and his mantle passed to Elisha. But their careers overlap in part, and it is significant that during the expedition to Moab Elisha is identified only as the man "who poured water on the hands of Elijah," not as one who had inherited Elijah's mantle, indicating Elijah had not yet gone up (II K. 3:11).

In chapters 4-7 of II K. the miracles of Elisha are related.
There would seem to be no datable history here, though beginning in 6:24 Samaria is besieged by Ben-hadad of Syria. But
the king of Israel involved in the siege has no name.

The famine in the city was so great:

> An ass's head was sold for twenty pieces of silver,
> and the fourth part of a cab of dove's dung for five
> pieces of silver. And as the king of Israel was
> passing by upon the wall, there cried a woman unto
> him, saying, "Help, my lord, O king." And he said,
> "If the Lord do not help you, whence shall I help you?
> out of the barnfloor or out of the winepress?"

Seeing she was not amused —

> The king said, "What ails you?" And she answered,
> "This woman said to me, 'Give your son, that we
> may eat him today, and we will eat my son tomor-
> row.' So we boiled my son, and did eat him; and I
> said to her on the next day, 'Give your son, that we
> may eat him;' and she has hid her son." (6:25-29)

Then the king tore his clothes in anguish and walked on.

Elisha predicts that prices will drop dramatically, that food
will be plentiful and cheap. Four lepers, reasoning that they
will surely die if they stay where they are and the Syrians can
do no worse than kill them, go to the Syrian camp to beg for
food. They find the camp deserted.

> For the Lord had made the host of the Syrians to
> hear a noise of chariots, and a noise of horses, the
> noise of a great host; and they said one to another,
> "Lo, the king of Israel has hired against us the kings
> of the Hittites, and the kings of the Egyptians to
> come upon us." Wherefore they arose and fled in
> the twilight, and left their tents, and their horses,
> and their asses, even the camp as it was, and fled
> for their lives. (7:6, 7)

This explanation would seem to be formed in the imagination
of the four lepers. But how can they imagine that the Syrians
could be frightened by Hittite kings who had not existed for 400
years, or Egyptians who had not been seen in that part of the
world for an equally long time? However, the lepers notified
the king of Israel. He suspected a ruse, so:

> They took therefore two chariot horses; and the king
> sent after the host of Syrians, saying, "Go and see."

> And they went after them unto Jordan; and, lo, all
> the way was full of garments and vessels, which the
> Syrians had cast away in their haste... (7:14, 15)

Confident, now, that the Syrians were really gone, the king
ordered the gates to be opened. The people plundered the Syrian camp, and Elisha's prediction was fulfilled.

It reads like a myth. It might be a legendary account of a
real siege. But when? If only the king of Israel had a name.

After this battle, in II K. 8, the king is speaking to Gehazi,
the servant of Elisha. He asks to hear all the wonderful things
Elisha has done. Gehazi is telling him of the child that Elisha
restored to life, when a woman appears, seeking the king.

Gehazi says, "This is the woman, and this is her son, whom
Elisha restored to life."

The woman, a Shunammite, has just returned from the land
of the Philistines where she sojourned for seven years. She
now wants her house and land returned to her. She had gone to
Philistia because Elisha warned her there would be a famine of
seven years duration and advised her to "sojourn wheresoever
thou canst sojourn."

Looking back in chapter 4 we find the story of Elisha and the
Shunammite woman, and her son. As Elisha was working to
restore life to the child, "the child sneezed seven times, and
the child opened his eyes"(4:35). This may have been interpreted by Elisha as an omen of seven year's famine, but if so, the
passage has not survived in its proper place, or in detail.

Elisha could not have warned the woman at any other time,
however, for he dismisses her in 4:37 and we do not hear of her
again until the seven years are up.

In the very next verse (4:38) we find mention of a famine, or
dearth, in the land, but it would be a mistake to make much of
this. The stories concerning Elisha are not in chronological
order, and perhaps never were. They had a purpose other than
history.

We now have a seven-year period defined, but we don't know
where to put it. Reading on in chapter 8:

> Elisha came to Damascus; and Ben-hadad the king
> of Syria was sick; and it was told him, saying, "The
> man of God is come hither." And the king said to
> Hazael, "Take a present in your hand, and go, meet
> the man of God, and enquire of the Lord by him,
> 'Shall I recover of this disease?'" (8:7, 8)

Hazael did as he was told, and Elisha answered him, somewhat cryptically —'Tell the king he will recover; but he will die,
and you will be king of Syria.'

Hazael understood. He told Ben-hadad that Elisha had said the king would recover. Then "he took a thick cloth and dipped it in water, and laid it on the king's face, so that he died. And Hazael reigned in his stead." (8:15)

From Syrian records we know that Hazael became king in -842. The siege described in II K.7 must have been in -843. Then Elisha's warning to the Shunammite woman was given in -850. It was at that time that Elisha had Jehu anointed king of Israel. His warning to the Shunammite woman anticipated the upheaval that would result when Jehu assassinated both Jehoram ben-Ahab and Ahaziah, wiped out the house of Ahab, destroyed the Baal worshippers and tore down their temple, all of which is reported in chapters 9 and 10.

Elisha may or may not have foreseen the attack by Ben-hadad, but there can be no doubt the king of Israel during that siege was Jehu. This removes part of the mystery, but what put an end to the siege? Why did the Syrians withdraw, leaving their camp intact? Or should we discount this part of the tale?

We recall reading how Rab-shakeh stood outside the walls of Jerusalem and cried in a loud voice in the Jews' language, pouring forth a torrent of propaganda, hoping to effect the surrender of the city in the days of Hezekiah. And Isaiah, speaking in the name of the Lord, said, "Be not afraid of the words which you have heard... Behold, I will send a blast upon him, and he shall hear a rumor, and shall return to his own land" (19:7).

No doubt a 'blast' was sent on Ben-hadad, and the Syrians heard a rumor — not about Hittites and Egyptians; these names must have been filled in by a later redactor whose sense of history was not precise, perhaps to complete a damaged and partially unreadable verse. The "noise" heard by the Syrians may have been that of a crier, or it may have been the persistent murmur of voices throughout the camp, repeating the report of a prophet (?).

In either case, the "noise" was, 'Jehu has hired Shalmaneser king of Assyria who is even now on his way with his chariots and his horses and his host to destroy Damascus. He will burn your homes. He will slaughter your wives, your mothers, and your fathers. Your children will be taken captive into Assyria. Your daughters will be whores and your sons eunuchs in the service of Shalmaneser.'

The Syrians believed, and fled, rushing to the defense of Damascus. Had they taken their tents and supplies, Jehu would have seen at once what was happening. His army would have pursued, and harried their retreat. A pack train would only slow them down. If they did not defend it, Jehu would plunder it anyway. They had to reach the Jordan before their flight was

detected or the bowmen of Israel would cut them down by the
hundreds as they crossed the river. So they fled under cover
of darkness, leaving almost everything behind, and lightening
their burdens further as they rushed toward the river.

The story is neither myth nor legend. It could be told only
by a witness.

Imagine the scene when they reached Damascus — an army
in tatters, exhausted, broken, no plunder, no string of captives, without even their tents and their beasts of burden. But
they had reached the city ahead of Shalmaneser. The people
were warned of impending attack; the city was prepared for a
siege. Guards were posted; men slept in their clothes with a
weapon at hand. Nervously they waited —— and waited. But
Shalmaneser did not come. There was no need. The noise of
his coming had saved Samaria.

No wonder Ben-hadad was sick. — Hazael put him out of his
misery. The city was opened. The people came in and went
out as usual. Defense was forgotten.

Then Shalmaneser came and put Hazael to tribute, in -841.

When Tiglath-pileser broke the siege of Jerusalem by Rezin
of Syria, attacking Damascus to save king Ahaz of Judah, Ahaz
paid him a handsome tribute. Jehu might be expected to have
done as much for Shalmaneser a hundred years earlier. The
Bible says nothing of any tribute paid by Jehu, but the Black
Obelisk of Shalmaneser does. It is dated in the 18th year of
Shalmaneser who became king of Assyria in -858. The tribute was paid in -841.

The mysterious battle of II K. 6:24-7:15 is not only authentic
in every detail, when the verses are read in the intended order
the battle occurs in the 7th year of Jehu, and again the Bible
dates itself.

Doubts concerning the inscription naming "Jaua bit-Humri"
are resolved by concluding that the Assyrian scribe meant 'Jehu
of the city of Omri', a conclusion I find I am not the first to
reach. Albright notes, "It cannot be emphasized too strongly
that the expression 'Jehu son of Omri' in Assyrian means simply 'Jehu of Beth-Omri', and has nothing to do with the man
Omri as such."[1]

As the text has stood since before the Septuagint translation
was made Elijah was taken up and his mantle passed to Elisha
after Ahaziah ben-Ahab died. Elisha's career began with the
reign of Jehoram ben-Ahab. Then we are asked to accept the
following sequence of occurrences:

Elisha publicly insults the king of Israel (3:14), then warns

him of a Syrian ambush and saves his life more than once (6:10).
The king of Israel, calling the prophet "my father," asks permission to kill a band of Syrians but Elisha refuses and the king
submits to advice (6:21ff). Elisha allows himself to be trapped
in Samaria when Ben-hadad has the city under siege, though he
might have escaped, for Ben-hadad respects him. He refers
to the king of Israel as "son of a murderer," yet promises the
siege will end in 24 hours. After the siege is broken the king
asks Elisha's servant Gehazi, "Tell me, I pray thee, all the
wonderful things that Elisha has done." And takes great interest in the woman whose son Elisha restored to life. But soon
thereafter Elisha has Jehu anointed with instructions to assassinate the king and annihilate all his relatives.

It is hard to imagine that this sequence represents the relationship between Elisha and one king of Israel. But, given the
chronological misunderstandings that produced the synchronism
of '1 Jehoram ben-Ahab' with '18 Jehoshaphat' (II K. 3:1), there
was not much else to do.

The corrected chronology shows our suspicions are justified;
the "king of Israel" referred to in these several instances is
not always the same man, and never Jehoram ben-Ahab.

Here, in abbreviated form with emendations ( ), events are
put in chronological order, beginning with the death of Ahab:—

I K. 22:40, Ahab died and Ahaziah became king of Israel.

:41-47, Jehoshaphat was king of Judah from (the [12]th year
of Omri) for [25] years.

:51-53; II K. 1:1, Ahaziah was king from (the [24]th year) of
Jehoshaphat for 2 years. Moab rebelled when Ahab died.

3:4-27   Mesha of Moab paid tribute to the king of Israel in
the form of wool sheared from many sheep. After Ahab died
Mesha refused to pay. The king of Israel (Ahaziah) asked Jehoshaphat of Judah to go with him to war against Moab, and
Jehoshaphat agreed. After seven days' journey through the wilderness of Edom a water shortage led Jehoshaphat to ask for
a prophet of the Lord. A man of Israel said, "Here is Elisha
who poured water on the hands of Elijah." Elisha scorned the
king of Israel, but agreed to prophesy for Jehoshaphat.

Elisha solved the water shortage, and predicted success for
the mission, which ended with Mesha's sacrifice of his son as
a burnt offering upon the city wall. (Such sacrifice was a common sign of submission, by which cities were saved from destruction, but the text does not interpret it in this way.)

I K. 22:48-50   Jehoshaphat built ships to sail to Ophir for
gold. He refused to let Ahaziah join in the venture which never
came off anyway because the ships were all wrecked.

Jehoshaphat died and Jehoram his son became king (-858).

2:1-3:3 tells of the end of Elijah's career and the passing of his mantle to Elisha who then "healed" the water at Jericho. At Bethel the children who mocked Elisha, saying, "Go up, you bald head." were torn by bears.

Jehoram ben-Ahab began to reign in (the [25]th year) of Jehoshaphat and reigned [12] years.

4:1-7 tells how Elisha helped a widow, supplying her with an ever-flowing pot of oil.

4:38-44 tells of poisoned stew rendered harmless;

6:1-7 tells of Elisha's causing an iron axe head to float.

8:16-29   In the fifth year of Jehoram ben-Ahab (the fifth year) of Jehoram ben-Jehoshaphat who reigned "8"=[11] years (-854, Shalmaneser III was defeated at Karkar by these two and several other kings allied under Ben-hadad king of Syria).

Edom and Libnah revolted against domination by Judah.

Jehoram ben-Jehoshaphat died.   In the [12]th year of Jehoram ben-Ahab of Israel Ahaziah was king of Judah for one year. He went with Jehoram ben-Ahab to fight Hazael (captain of the host of the) king of Syria for possession of Ramoth-gilead. Jehoram was wounded.   They went together to Jezreel (-850).

4:8-35   Some years before in Shunem a woman had provided food and shelter for Elisha.   She was childless and her husband was old.   Elisha blessed her with a son.   When the child was grown, one day his head hurt.   Sitting on his mother's lap, he died.   She went to Elisha who returned with her and revived the child.   The boy sneezed seven times before opening his eyes.

4:36,37 blended with 8:1,2 —
He called Gehazi and said, 'Call this Shunammite woman.' So he called her. Elisha said, 'There will be a famine for seven years. Take your son and sojourn wherever you can.' She took her son and sojourned in Philistia seven years.

9:1-10:30   Elisha had Jehu anointed king of Israel with instructions to destroy the house of Ahab. Jehu and his followers went to Jezreel.   They assassinated Jehoram ben-Ahab and his nephew Ahaziah.   Jezebel was thrown down from a window at Jehu's command, and the dogs ate her flesh.

The seventy sons of Ahab were beheaded and their heads sent to Jehu; and Jehu slew all that remained of the house of Ahab, all his great men, his kinsfolks, and his priests, and he slew the brethren of Ahaziah.

Jehu proclaimed a solemn assembly for Baal, and when all the worshippers of Baal were in the house of Baal Jehu ordered them slaughtered, and the doors were guarded so none could escape.   Then the images and the house of Baal were destroyed completely.

For his good work, the Lord said, Jehu's sons for four generations would sit on the the throne of Israel.

6:8-7:20 The king of Syria (Ben-hadad) warred against Israel (Jehu), and the man of God (Elisha) warned the king where
the Syrians would attack. The Syrians tried to capture Elisha,
but they were smitten with blindness and he led them into Samaria where their eyes were opened. Jehu wanted to kill them
but Elisha ordered them fed and returned to Syria. Then the
bands of Syrians came no more into Israel.

But Ben-hadad brought his army in and laid siege to Samaria. The famine was so bad some resorted to cannibalism.
Elisha promised the king the siege would end in 24 hours. His
prediction proved true when four lepers discovered the Syrian
camp deserted.[a]

8:3-15 The Shunammite woman returns with her son whose
life was restored by Elisha, after 7 years' sojourn in Philistia.
Jehu has asked Gehazi to tell him of all the wonderful things
Elisha had done, and the woman appears at the appropriate moment in Gehazi's tale. The king attends to her needs.

Elisha goes to Damascus and instigates Hazael's assassination of Ben-hadad. Hazael becomes king of Syria (-842).

5:1-27 Elisha heals Naaman captain of the host of the king
of Syria of leprosy. Gehazi accepts payment from Naaman and
is punished by receiving Naaman's leprosy.[b]

10:31-36 Hazael takes all the land east of Jordan away from
Israel. Jehu dies (-828) after ruling "28"[31] years.

---

[a] The king called Elisha "ben-shaphat" which may be a play on
shaphat "to judge" and shapha "to be bald" and somehow linked
to the inexplicable story of the children torn by the she—bears.
Elisha calls the king "son of a murderer," understood to mean
"murderer" with no reflection on his father.[1] Directed at Jehu,
whose murders Elisha approved, this may be taken as ironic
humor, similar to the king's retort when the woman cries for
help and he asks, "out of the barnfloor or out of the winepress?"
Either would involve a step not over two feet high. The king is
expressing his impotence in this situation.

There is an expression of this same kind of bitter humor in
the fact that the man who scoffs at Elisha's prediction is tram-
pled to death in the rush when the people go out to plunder the
Syrian camp.

[b] This episode has been postponed because it cannot be thought
that the king converses with a censured and leprous Gehazi in
chapter 8.[2] Furthermore, since Hazael was apparently captain
of the host of Ben-hadad,[3] Naaman must serve in this capacity
under Hazael.

From here on the text is in good order. In chapter 11 we go back to -850, the first year of Jehu, to tell the story of Athaliah who began to rule Judah in that year. This saw-tooth effect is, of course, inevitable when the history of two nations is being told. Simultaneous but separate events can only be related consecutively. It is not this sort of chronological problem that we have been concerned with in the first ten chapters of II Kings. There it appears the ancient editors were faced with the problem of reconstructing the events from a book about Elijah and Elisha in which the kings of Israel and Syria were usually, if not always, nameless, and the stories were not necessarily in chronological order.   This was necessary, presumably, because the historical chronicles were damaged and little more could be read than each king's name, and length of reign.

When we read the expression – 'the rest of the things that he did, and his sayings, and his acts, are they not written in the book of...?' – with the name of a document no longer extant, we may suppose it means only that the editor found nothing else of particular interest in that document. It may also mean, "The rest is unreadable, for the scroll has crumbled and the ink has faded, but who can deny it was written?"

Athaliah was assassinated after 6 years and Joash, the only surviving prince of the line, was made king.   This was the 7th year of Jehu, -843 (II K. 12:1). There is mention of the 23rd year of Joash (12:6) in connection with repairing the temple. Sometime after that, though we are not told exactly how long, Hazael conquered Gath, a Philistine city about 30 miles southwest of Jerusalem. Joash paid tribute to Hazael to avoid war. We then read of his assassination and the accession of his son Amaziah.   That would be -816/-815. Whether this happened because of the tribute is uncertain.

In 13:1 we saw-tooth back to the 23rd year of Joash (-827) when Jehu died and his son Jehoahaz became king of Israel. Here we read that Hazael has oppressed Israel, leaving her in a very much weakened condition. Then Jehoahaz died and his son Jehoash became king. This is -817/-816, the last year of the reign of Joash of Judah.

In 13:5 we are told, "The Lord gave Israel a saviour, so they went out from under the hand of the Syrians." But this is premature, as is the announcement of the death of Jehoash in 13: 12, 13. The defeat of the Syrians does not occur until after the death of Hazael and the accession of his son Ben-hadad III (13: 24, 25) which took place in -810, according to Syrian records. And the death of Jehoash is cited again, in its proper time, in 14:15, 16, after he has defeated Judah in battle and plundered Jerusalem.

In 14:13 it says, "Jehoash king of Israel took Amaziah king of Judah." This is taken to mean that Amaziah was captured, and it is presumed he was taken prisoner to Samaria. But the text does not actually say this. It says that Amaziah lived for 15 years after Jehoash died, and that he fled Jerusalem in the face of a conspiracy, but they pursued him to Lachish and slew him there. Obviously, if Jehoash captured him he subsequently released him, possibly in exchange for the loot he took from Jerusalem without taking him to Samaria at all. It does say he took hostages, presumably to protect his retreat. But these need not have included the king.

The point is that Amaziah's supposed captivity cannot be made an element in the chronology for it has no ascertainable duration. We can only say that he was defeated, possibly taken prisoner and held a short time, in his [15]th year, -804, the year Jehoash of Israel died.

Suppose we see how this portion of the text fits with the history of Assyria. In -841 Shalmaneser III had defeated Hazael, and received tribute from Jehu of Israel. What next?

Civil war weakened Assyria in the last years of the reign of Shalmaneser III and throughout the reign of his son and successor Shamshi-Adad V (-823/-811). This accounts for the fact that Hazael was able to take the land east of Jordan while Jehu was still alive (probably in Jehu's last year, -828), then to devestate Israel, conquer Gath, and collect tribute from Judah in the following year, '[23] Joash' (-827).

When Shamshi-Adad died his son Adad-nirari III (-810/-753) was still very young. Though nominally king, his mother Sammuramat — the legendary Semiramis — in fact controlled the government. Despite her fabulous reputation little is known of her deeds. It may be no coincidence that Hazael was replaced by his son Ben-hadad III in -810, and that Jehoash of Israel was then able to throw off the Syrian yoke, but there is no certain connection here.

We do know that in his first year of effective reign, -805, Adad-nirari III invaded Syria, conquered Damascus, and took tribute from the neighboring nations, including Israel.[1] The stele discovered in 1967 which names Jehoash of Samaria as one who paid has already been mentioned (pp. 7 ff). Though the biblical text offers no confirmation of the Assyrian inscription submission to Assyria in -805 could account for the fact that -804 was the last year of Jehoash who was succeeded by his son Jeroboam (II) in the [15]th year of Amaziah of Judah (14:23).

Whether there is a cause-effect here or not, the chronology which application of the base-7 concept to the biblical data has given us matches contemporary Syrian and Assyrian records.

Jeroboam II may have continued tribute to Assyria, but it seems unlikely; Adad-nirari turned his attention to the kings of Kaldu (Chaldea) and, from his death in -783 until -745 when his youngest son Tiglath-pileser III took the throne, Assyrian power was at a low ebb.[1]

Tiglath-pileser III used the title *Pul* on becoming king of Babylon in -729.[2] He is referred to by this title in the Bible.

> Pul the king of Assyria came against the land: and Menahem gave Pul a thousand talents of silver, that his hand might be with him to confirm the kingdom in his hand. And Menahem exacted the money of Israel, of all the mighty men of wealth, of each man fifty shekels of silver, to give to the king of Assyria. So the king of Assyria turned back, and stayed not there in the land. (II K. 15:19)

If later known values applied at this time, the silver shekel weighed 224.5 grains. Thirty-five shekels would have weighed about one pound (avoir.), and the talent was 3,000 shekels. At [50] ≈ 35 shekels each it would take 29,000 contributors to raise [1000] ≈ 343 talents, weighing about 16 tons. Even as reduced by transposition these figures are implausibly large, but this is not our special concern.

Essentially, the statement agrees with one in the annals of Tiglath-pileser: "As for Menahem, terror overwhelmed him... he fled and submitted to me... silver, colored woolen garments, linen garments...I received as his tribute..."[3]

But Tiglath-pileser III was king of Assyria -745/-728, and Menahem was king of Israel -762/-758, for 4 years 11 months. How could Menahem pay tribute to Pul?

Even if we could justify giving Menahem the full "ten" years he is said to have ruled Israel (II K. 15:17), and included the 11 months the Bible disregards, his reign would end in -752, seven years before the accession of Tiglath-pileser III.

Taking the data just as they are given in the text — Hoshea 9 years, Pekah 20, Pekahiah 2—adding these to -722, the last year of Hoshea, yields -753 for the end of Menahem's reign, eight years too early. So the difficulty does not result from use of the base-7 key; it is in the text of the Bible.

The Assyrian and Hebrew records agree that Menahem paid tribute to Tiglath-pileser III. But the earliest year in which it could conceivably have been paid is -741, the first year of Ahaz king of Judah, more than 16 years after the end of Mena-hem's reign. We must suppose that Menahem stepped down in favor of Pekahiah in -758, but did not die at that time.

What is being suggested is something in the nature of a coregency, which I hesitate to do. Some chronologists assume coregencies, but only once does the Bible suggest anything of the kind — II Chron. 26:21, where Jotham is said to judge the people during the reign of his father Uzziah (Azariah). The duration of the coregency is not given. The length of Jotham's reign does not include that period. The figure for Azariah's reign does. So the coregency has no effect on the chronology.

To call for a coregency in order to correlate the Hebrew history with the Assyrian record is not desirable if there is no biblical justification. But in fact the text may not be silent on this subject. The names "Pekahiah" and "Pekah" suggest that coregency is exactly what we are expected to understand.

Either the transliteration of these names from the Hebrew is not quite accurate, or we do not pronounce them as the transliterator intended. The third consonant in each case is not the letter *he*, which sounds like 'h', but the letter *cheth*, which sounds like 'ch' in Scottish "loch".

This slight change in pronunciation is itself unimportant, but we are now able to see that the name "Pekah", as originally written, without the Masoretic vowel points, is indistinguishable from the word for "open eyed, seeing, intelligent," — qualities that would be required in an "overseer, prefect, or commander," *pakid*, from the verb *pakad* "to appoint, to entrust." We also find in Biblical Hebrew the phonetically similar *pechah*, representing the Babylonian or Persian title "governor, prefect, pasha."

The suggestion is that "Pekahiah" (pekachyah), and "Pekah" (pekach), are not the given names of the men so identified, but two forms of a title which might well be translated "coregent."

Neither the Bible nor the Assyrian record dates the year of Menahem's tribute. As Luckenbill points out, the records of Tiglath-pileser III were found in a fragmentary state and chronological order is not firmly established. The history of his reign appears in several versions, differing markedly in the details, so the content is also open to question. It would appear that "Rasunna (Rezin) of Aram" and "Menihimmu (Menahem) of Samerina (Samaria, Heb. ⌈Shomeron)" both paid tribute sometime between the third and the ninth year of Tiglath-pileser, thus between -743 and -737.[1] This is well before the year in which Damascus was actually taken (-732), and the year -741 indicated by our chronology is certainly possible though not definitely confirmed.

Luckenbill has inadvertently introduced an additional item of confusion. In translating a clay tablet from Nimrud which bears a portion of the record of Tiglath-pileser's reign he puts down, "Iauhazi (Jehoahaz) of Judah."[2] But there was no king of

Judah named Jehoahaz until -607.[a] No doubt the name "Iauhazi" identifies Ahaz of Judah whose name is not otherwise represented in the Assyrian record.

Another name found in the records of Tiglath–pileser III raises some interesting questions. That name is "Azriau of Iaudi," rendered by Luckenbill, without comment, "Azariah of Judah."[1] Some would make this the biblical Azariah, but A. T. Olmstead writes, on the basis of Syrian inscriptions:

> Hebrew Judah in the south was closely paralleled in language, in thought, in the name of a ruler, most startling of all, in his commemoration of Yahweh in his name, by a country in north Syria called by the scribe Iaudi.[2]

Thiele, who dates the biblical Azariah -792/-739, feels:

> It is extremely unlikely that at the very time that Judah had such an outstanding king, possessing such marked abilities as a warrior and statesman (II Chr. 26:6-15), another state of a similar name should possess a king with a name that is almost identical and with the same outstanding characteristics.[3]

But that argument does not determine which of these two was contemporary to Tiglath-pileser III, and weighs as heavily against Thiele's conclusions as it does in their favor. We have found Azariah's reign runs from -791/-755. On this basis he could not be the king referred to by Tiglath-pileser III. Rather than an extraordinary coincidence we may have in the case of "Azriau" only another example of many in which a king has taken the name of an illustrious predecessor from his own or, as in this case, another country.

There is nothing in the account of Azariah's reign that would connect him to the battle of which Tiglath-pileser III reports:

> 19 districts of Hamath, together with the cities of their environs, which (lie) on the shore of the sea of the setting sun, which had gone over to *Azriau* in revolt (lit., sin) and contempt of Assyria, I brought within the border of Assyria. My officials I set over them as governors. 30,300 people (I carried off from) their cities...[4]

Had the kings of Hamath had the support of Azariah's army of "307,500 men" with its "2,600 leaders" (II Chron. 26:12,13) the outcome might have been quite different. At a later date a

[a] Ahaziah is called Jehoahaz in II Chron. 21:17, but his year as king (-850) is too early for Tiglath-pileser III.

force of about 50,000 men repulsed Shalmaneser III at Karkar.

It is not within the scope of this book to discuss at greater length the intriguing kingdom of "Iaudi", but its existence is not at all in doubt. Nor does there seem any reason to doubt that in the time of Tiglath-pileser III it had a king "Azriau" who led an unsuccessful revolt against Assyrian domination. Syrian and Assyrian records agree on this point and there is no conflict with the Hebrew record.

Tiglath-pileser III also notes, regarding Israel:

> Pakaha, their king they deposed and I placed Ausi' (Hoshea) over them as king.[1]

The Bible agrees, at least in part.

> Hoshea ben-Elah made a conspiracy against Pekah ben-Remaliah, and smote him, and slew him, and reigned in his stead... (II K. 15:30)

Conceivably, Tiglath-pileser was party to the conspiracy. And so, very possibly, was Menahem, then eager to appease the Assyrian king who had come to the aid of Ahaz of Judah, if not with force then at least diplomatically with the threat of force.

Then in fact, Hoshea may have been, at this point, a third coregent under Menahem, a third "Pekah," and the record may have shown that Pekah replaced Pekah in '20 Jotham'. Then if Menahem died in -731, Hoshea would have ceased to reign as Pekah and begun to reign under his own name in '12 Ahaz'. Here it might have said that Hoshea replaced Pekah. Understandably, this statement would be moved forward to 'correct' the seeming confusion in '20 Jotham', leaving Hoshea to begin to reign in '12 Ahaz' (II K. 17:1) without replacing anyone.

These details cannot be insisted upon, but they may explain the confusion in regard to synchronisms and the total reign of Hoshea.

The biblical account now indicates that Menahem died when Pekahiah took the throne. If in fact he lived longer, a slight rearrangement of verses alters the time element in the text to match the fact. From II K. 15 take verses 19-22, 30, and 31. Discard verse 22. Let the other five verses follow 16:9. Presumably, this would be the original arrangement, changed at one time with the thought that it would clarify the text to collect the verses relating to Menahem in a continuous sequence, thus eliminating any interruption to the sequence relating to Ahaz. The resulting distortion in the time element relative to these events may have escaped notice.

As the text now stands, 16:9 and 16:10 seem closely related in time. In fact there is a decade between them. Tiglath-pileser's first attack or threatened attack on Damascus must have come in -741 if it was to help Ahaz. At that time he collected tribute but did not occupy the city. He returned in -732. This time he took the city, and that would be the earliest year in which Ahaz could have gone to Damascus to meet him.

Hoshea evidently paid tribute to Tiglath-pileser throughout the remainder of that Assyrian monarch's reign. He must also have paid the succeeding king of Assyria, Shalmaneser V, in -727, as indicated in II K. 17:3. But in -726 Hoshea failed to pay and in -725 Shalmaneser V laid siege to Samaria.

It seems doubtful that Hoshea was actually bound in prison, as 17:4 is translated. More likely, the passage is intended to convey something comparable to what Sennacharib wrote concerning Hezekiah —"Himself like a caged bird, I shut up in Jerusalem, his royal city."[1] For if Hoshea had been imprisoned as a captive in the hands of Shalmaneser, Israel would have been without a king, and a three-year siege would not have been required to effect its surrender.

Of course, we must understand that the siege was not continuous for three years, but rather that it was repeated annually for that period. No city could hold out under an effective siege for three full years. The only alternative interpretation would be: the siege was continuous but not effective, so the city was not cut off completely from supplies.

The Assyrian records become very thin at this point. Luckenbill shows only one brief, unimportant passage from the reign of Shalmaneser V. But the biblical account is confirmed by the Assyrian Eponym List[2] which indicates Samaria was besieged in -725, 4 and 3. Thus it was -722 that the inhabitants of Samaria were deported and Isreal ceased to exist as a nation.

That year (-722) was the last year of the reign of Shalmaneser V. His successor Sargon II takes credit in his records for the defeat of Samaria, boasting, "I besieged and captured Samaria, carrying off 27,290 of the people who dwelt therein."[3] This is not confirmed by the biblical account. Shalmaneser is said to besiege Samaria (II K. 18:9), and the "king of Assyria" is said to take Israel captive (18:11). Sargon's name does not appear. It has been said that Sargon, whose reign did not begin until -721, usurped credit for this military exploit. But it may be, as H. W. F. Saggs suggests, that Sargon was the general directing the operation on behalf of Shalmaneser V.[4] In any event, the date -722 is not in question.

The next Assyrian name in II Kings is that of Sennacherib. We read of an attack on Judah "in the fourteenth year of king Hezekiah" (II K. 18:13). Our chronology shows this would be -712. But Sennacharib did not come to the throne until -704.

The year -712 falls in the reign of Sargon. Concerning that year Georges Roux writes:

> The Egyptians fomented another revolt in Palestine. This time the leader was Iamani, King of Ashdod, followed by Judah, Edom and Moab, and supported by *Pir'u of Musru*, i.e. Pharaoh of Egypt (probably Bocchoris).[1]

Isaiah introduces his 20th chapter with a reference to this event, and here we find the name of Sargon.

> In the year that Tartan came unto Ashdod, when Sargon the king of Assyria sent him... (Is. 20:1)

Tartan is the Assyrian title "Second in Command." Conceivably, Sargon's son, Sennacherib, was serving his father in this capacity at the time. This could account for the confusion. At any rate, it would seem that the tribute paid by Hezekiah, as detailed in II K. 18:14-16, was paid in -712. Part of the propaganda barrage of Rabshakeh, or one very similar to that found in II K. 18:17-35, belongs to that year.

We should probably read II K. 20:1-20 at this point. Here Isaiah tells Hezekiah that the Lord "will add unto thy days fifteen years" (20:6) which, added to 14, completes the 29 years which Hezekiah reigned. There is also in this chapter a communication from Berodach-baladan (Merodach-baladan in Isaiah 39:1), identified with Marduk-apal-iddina king of Babylon from -721/-711 when he was reduced by Sargon II to vice-regent. In -705 Sargon died and his son Sennacherib became king. It must be at this time that Hezekiah received the Babylonian ambassador. In -703 Merodach-baladan rebelled. He lost, but escaped with his life, and continued to foment rebellion among the Assyrian provinces until his death in -699. He is no doubt in part responsible for the revolt of Hezekiah in -701.

By that time Hezekiah would have completed "a pool, and a conduit, and brought water into the city" (II K. 20:20), a construction also mentioned in II Chronicles 32:3,4, and:

> This same Hezekiah also stopped the upper water-course of Gihon, and brought it straight down to the west side of the city of David. (II Chron. 32:30)

The "conduit" was a large tunnel, discovered in 1880. An inscription on the wall describes the "boring through." Tunnelling from both ends, through nearly 600 yards of solid rock, "the stone-cutters struck pick against pick, one against the... other;... and a hundred cubits was the height of the rock above the heads of the stone-cutters."[2]

By that excellent feat of engineering the city was prepared for a siege. II K. 18:17 - 19:36 would follow. Here we find a description of the siege of Jerusalem in -701, which would be the 24th year of Hezekiah, and the associated attack by Sennacherib upon Egypt, defended by "Tirhakah king of Ethiopia" (19:9), in fact, Taharkah, then leading the Egyptian army for his uncle, the pharaoh Shabaka. Some 12 years later Taharkah became the third and last of the pharaohs of the "Ethiopian" (actually Nubian) dynasty that ruled Egypt from -712/-663.

Hezekiah withstood the siege; Jerusalem was not taken. But many other cities of Judah were thoroughly plundered. Sennacherib in his annals says:

> As for Hezekiah the Jew, who did not submit to my yoke, 46 of his strong walled cities, as well as the smaller cities in their neighborhood...I besieged and took...[1]

The tribute and presents Sennacherib claims to have received at this time are very possibly the spoils he took from the cities he overcame, and may include the tribute paid by Hezekiah some years earlier.

During the siege Hezekiah appeals to Isaiah for advice. Isaiah assures him the Lord will deliver them. Hezekiah prays. The result is impressive:

> It came to pass that night, that the angel of the Lord went out, and smote in the camp of the Assyrians a hundred fourscore and five thousand; and when they arose early in the morning, behold, they were all dead corpses. (II K. 19:35)

Though it spoils an amusing line, we should probably give the writer credit for intending "they (the Jews) arose early in the morning" and found that "they (the Assyrians) were all dead corpses." The number should probably be understood as 180 + 5000 = 5,180 and not as 185,000.

Herodotus relates an Egyptian version of Sennacherib's defeat. In that story the Egyptian army refused to fight. The Pharaoh recruited a rabble of tradesmen, artisans and the like and camped with this force opposite the Assyrians at Pelusium (Mud-town), which commanded the entrance to Egypt. His actions were prompted by a dream in which his god had promised help. He waited throughout the night. A multitude of field-mice came in the night and devoured the quivers, bowstrings, and leather shield-straps of the Assyrians. Thus disarmed the Assyrians fled the Egyptian attack, and many were killed.

The Egyptian and Hebrew accounts are readily reconciled by

supposing the mice to be agents of the *malach*, "messenger,"
(in Greek, *angelos*, hence "angel") of the Lord.

Historians have surmised that mice indicate an epidemic of
plague. Others, due to the swamps around Pelusium, guess
that malaria was a factor in Sennacherib's retreat. But these
diseases would be readily recognized by the Egyptians. Divine
intervention could still be supposed without inventing a story
about mice.

Hezekiah had been informed of the word of the Lord by the
mouth of Isaiah, saying, "Behold, I will send a blast upon him,
and he shall hear a rumor, and shall return to his own land..."
(19:7). The rumor may have pertained to mutiny, attempted
assassination, and a real or fancied threat of usurpation in
Ninevah. In response, Sennacherib may have withdrawn to secure his throne, hastily in the night, as voluntary termination
of a siege requires. A genuine mutiny sparked by the rumor
might account for 5,180 dead mutineers, left unburied because
of their treason.

The Egyptians, finding the field overrun with mice interested in many things, including discarded weapons with broken
bowstrings and leather straps, may have credited the mice for
lack of a better explanation. A few sick or wounded stragglers
may have fallen to the Egyptian weapons, enhancing their sense
of victory.

Had Isaiah some hand in events, as Elisha had in the assassination of Ben-hadad by Hazael, and of Jehoram by Jehu? In
II K. 6:9-12 we learn that military intelligence was a function of
the prophet Elisha. Elsewhere are indications that Elisha was
not the only prophet to perform this service. Did Isaiah delay
transmission to Hezekiah of news regarding Sennacherib's withdrawal until he had made a 'prediction'?

In any event:

> Sennacherib king of Assyria departed, and went and
> returned, and dwelt in Ninevah. And it came to pass
> as he was worshipping in the house of Nisroch his
> god, that Adrammelech and Sharezer his sons smote
> him with the sword; and they escaped into the land
> of Armenia. And Esarhaddon his son reigned in
> his stead. (II K. 19:36, 37)

There is no dispute regarding the historic accuracy of this
report. Obviously the writer was informed about current events
in other countries. But it has been said that he dated the event
incorrectly. Sennacherib did not die until -681, twenty years
after his abortive attack on Jerusalem.

In fact, the biblical chronicler did not date this event at all.

He merely inserted it in the text at the end of the story of Sennacherib. He may have been pleased to think, and not averse to creating the impression, that Sennacherib's ultimate demise was in answer to the prayers of Hezekiah, and as predicted by Isaiah. But that does not mean he supposed it took place immediately upon Sennacherib's return to Ninevah. Certainly the first chronicler to enter the item into the record knew better.

Of Esarhaddon we are told nothing beyond the fact that he succeeded Sennacherib. Nothing is said of the Assyrian invasion of Egypt. The name of Ashurbanipal does not even appear. During the reigns of Manasseh, Amon, and Josiah, the Hebrew chroniclers seem almost oblivious to contemporary events.

We are told that:

> ...the Lord brought upon them the captains of the
> host of the king of Assyria, which took Manasseh
> among the thorns, and bound him with fetters, and
> carried him to Babylon. (II Chron. 33:11)

Then Manasseh "besought the Lord his God, and humbled himself, (and was returned) to Jerusalem into his kingdom"(33:12, 13). But the Bible does not date this event. It would seem to correspond to Esarhaddon's record, which states:

> I summoned the kings of Syria and those across the
> sea—Baalu king of Tyre, Manasseh king of Judah...
> Musurri king of Moab...twenty kings in all. I gave
> them their orders...[1]

Except that this summons brought the kings to Ninevah rather than Babylon, evidently about -679, the second year of Esarhaddon.

Since it is hardly conceivable that Sennacherib, having failed to conquer Hezekiah, was able to force Manasseh to visit him, and it is unlikely that Esarhaddon issued a further summons later in his reign when he was engaged in efforts to conquer Egypt, it is improbable that Manasseh was taken once to Ninevah and, on a separate occassion, to Babylon. But the kings summoned by Esarhaddon may have been shown, as an object lesson, the ruins of Babylon, destroyed by Sennacherib in -689. Esarhaddon rebuilt the city, but had not done so at that time.

Regarding Manasseh we are also told that he "shed innocent blood very much, till he had filled Jerusalem from one end to another" (II K. 21:16), which may indicate that Hebrew youths were conscripted for service in the Assyrian army, as is known to be the case for other tributary nations under Ashurbanipal.

It bears only indirectly on the biblical account but a further point regarding the Assyrian records deserves to be examined.

Both Sargon II and Sennacherib attacked Egypt and withdrew, seemingly defeated. Their records express satisfaction and scholars have sneered, perhaps incorrectly.

In -712 Sargon put down a rebellion in Canaan led by Iamani of Ashdod supported by Pharaoh Bocchoris. When he left, the Nubian, Shabaka, held the throne and Iamani, given asylum by Bocchoris, had been extradited.

In -701 Sennacherib faced a similar situation. An Egyptian army led by Taharka was supporting rebellion in Canaan. It is not at all certain that Shabaka had any hand in this. For all we know he was dead. Taharka was driven back into Egypt. When Sennacherib withdrew Shabaka's son, Shabataka, was king.

In each case, the western provinces were secure and Egypt was in the hands of a friendly Pharaoh. Egypt had not been conquered, but there is no reason to believe that this was even contemplated. Sennacherib's withdrawal may have been hastened by other factors already mentioned, but except for his failure to fully subjugate Hezekiah his campaign had succeeded.

In -674 Esarhaddon led his troops into Egypt at the express invitation of the several governors of the Delta, then without a central government, who were threatened by the same ambitious Taharka. He had made himself Pharaoh in the south in -688 and was now moving north. Control see-sawed back and forth. In -668 Ashurbanipal took on the task when Esarhaddon died. In -665 Taharka died. His son-in-law Tanutamon fought on for another year before he retired to Napata. Ashurbanipal was then able to set a friendly Pharaoh, Psamtik, on the throne of Egypt, but 12 years later Psamtik rebelled, drove the Assyrians out and made Egypt independent again.

When Ashurbanipal died the Assyrian Empire rapidly disintegrated. The Chaldean, Nabopolassar, c.-626, made Babylon independent. Cyaxares the Mede destroyed Ashur c.-614. He was joined by Nabopolassar in the destruction of Ninevah and the empire was divided between them. Ashur-uballit II held out at Harran until -609. When we read in II K.23:29 that Pharaoh Necho went against the king of Assyria it must be Ashur-uballit who was to be prevented from holding Syria or Canaan. In this Necho succeeded, but 4 years later he lost the the territory to Nebuchadnezzar, heir to Nabopolassar.

Further details of Assyrian history fall outside our province. More than enough has been given to show the biblical dating is sound. But certain other questions remain unresolved.

On page 78 a base-7 vocabulary was proposed. But every anomalous digit has been explained without resort to that vocabulary, except *sheba* =[10]=*eser*. The use of other alternative forms is neither affirmed nor denied.   We cannot reconstruct with assurance the early Hebrew number vocabulary.   This is regrettable but not serious.   No obstacle to our basic thesis is presented by any of the number-word forms in the extant text.

It would be interesting to know whether the year numbers were included in the earliest text.   The current year could not be known if the count had not been kept.   But the count could have been kept and not used in the text.

One number in particular seems to indicate that the year numbers were included.   That is the length of the "sojourn". In the present text there is not sufficient data in that period to determine or verify the given figure.   But essential items may have been lost after the total was derived.

If the year numbers were part of the original text, there is no reason to be surprised at their absence now.   We need only consider the reaction of a later redactor reading, for instance, that the Exodus occurred in "1454" and the Temple was begun "480" years later in "2264".   His arithmetic would make the interval 810 years.   Or, consider the "7-year" period of Midianite domination.   It began in "1660" and lasted until "2000". Base-10 arithmetic makes that a period of 340 years.

Failing to deduce the true nature of the problem the editors must have concluded that the year numbers were in some way strangely defective prior to 3021.   If those numbers were left in, the whole text might be rejected as incredible.   But why not retain the year numbers after 3021?   Perhaps because it would invite the question: Why are there no year numbers in the earlier part of the text?

Furthermore, given a starting point, someone would surely try to calculate year numbers for the earlier events.   But unless these were identical to the original numbers they could not be acknowledged as correct, despite the fact that the original numbers were, to say the least, imponderable.

Chapter X - WHERE IS HARAN ?

One item of data remains:

Terah's Terminal Age

Discussion of this item was deferred because it is not a factor in the chronology, and it leads into the question that heads this chapter. Since the location of Haran is a matter of geography it is not strictly within the scope of this book, but there are several items in the chronology that are associated with it so intimately it would be a mistake to leave it out.

Terah's terminal age is the same as Abraham's terminal age though expressed differently. It is written *kamesh umathayim* "five and two-hundred," while Abraham's is written, as pointed out earlier, *math v'shibim v'kamesh*, translated "175" but interpreted here as [100] & [100] & [5] = [205].

Whether Abraham's terminal age is real or artificial, it is probable that Terah's was chosen to match, and is not his true terminal age, for it does not fit the text. And this has bothered many generations of scholars.

In the story, Terah took his son Abram, his daughter-in-law Sarai, and his grandson Lot, and left "Ur of the Chaldees" to go into Canaan. They travelled as far as a place called Haran (sometimes rendered Harran) and here they stayed until Terah died. Then Abram took his wife and his nephew and continued the journey, for —

> The Lord had said to Abram, "Get thee out of thy country, and from thy kindred, and from thy father's house, unto a land that I will show thee; And I will make of thee a great nation, and I will bless thee, and make thy name great..."(Gen. 12:1, 2).

But Abram was devoted to his father. He could not desert the aged Terah, despite the Lord's promise. He waited until his father died before setting out on his own.

This interpretation suits the order in which the events are narrated, but simple arithmetic shows the events took place in another order.

> Terah lived seventy years, and begat Abram, Nahor, and Haran. (Gen. 11:26)

> The days of Terah were two-hundred and five years; and Terah died in Haran. (11:32)

> Abram was seventy-five years old when he departed out of Haran. (12:4)

Base-10 arithmetic would make Terah 145 years old when Abram was 75, and this is the terminal age which the Samaritan Pentateuch gives Terah, an obvious correction, yet not far from the base-7 figure for Terah's age when Abram went into Canaan. We found that Abram was [42] $\approx$ 30 at that time. And Terah must have been "70"[100] + [42] = [142] $\approx$ 79. Whether or not he died at that age we cannot say. If he lived to be [205] $\approx$ 103, he had yet 24 years to go.

Base-10 calculations based on the AV translation would show that Terah lived for 60 years after Abram left, far from the land of his nativity, among strangers. One wonders how he survived, and who reported his death so that his terminal age could be entered in the family record. Surely there is a flaw here, and a review of the text shows this very clearly.

Terah died in Haran. Years later, Abraham learned that his brother Nahor and his wife Milcah had children, including a son Bethuel. And Bethuel had a daughter Rebekah. Abraham told his servant to "go into my country, and to my kindred, and take a wife unto my son Isaac" (Gen. 24:4). The servant went "unto the city of Nahor" (24:10), which could be a city named Nahor, or an un-named city in which Nahor lived. There he found Rebekah and her brother Laban, her mother, and her father Bethuel. He told them of his errand, saying his master Abraham had charged him to "go unto my father's house" (24:38) and "take a wife for my son of my kindred, and of my father's house" (24:40).

Years later again, Isaac told his son Jacob to —

> Go to Padan-aram, to the house of Bethuel, your mother's father; and take a wife from thence of the daughters of Laban, your mother's brother. (28:2)
> And Jacob went...toward Haran (28:10)...and came into the land of the people of the east. (29:1)

He came to a well where people watered their sheep.

> And Jacob said unto them, "My brethren, whence be ye?" And they said, "Of Haran are we." (29:4)

Then Rachel came to the well. Jacob told her who he was and she ran and told her father. (29:12)

Clearly, the place Abraham calls "my country," the "city of Nahor," the place the servant quotes Abraham as calling "my father's house," the place Isaac identifies as "Padan-aram," "the house of Bethuel," and "Haran," are one and the same.

Most scholars agree that the term "Chaldees" or "Chaldeans" in Gen. 11:31 where Abraham, Sarah, Lot and Terah are said to leave "Ur of the Chaldees" (LXX "land of the Chaldees") is anachronistic. The Chaldeans do not appear on the stage of history until about -1000. In the time of Abraham they were surely not in control of the ancient Sumerian city of Ur.[1]

Furthermore, Terah's group cannot have travelled to Haran leaving Nahor and Milcah behind, whatever their point of departure, for Haran is where Nahor and Milcah and their descendants for at least four generations lived. Haran is where Jacob worked for Laban, where 11 of his 12 sons were born.

Some ancient scholars recognized this. The Samaritan Pentateuch and some of the Greek texts (not LXX) include Nahor and Milcah in Terah's migration. But that does not offer a full solution of the problem for, as Speiser points out, "according to 12:1 and 5, Haran was Abraham's birthplace."[2]

If Terah's terminal age is factual, he lived for 24 years after Abram went into Canaan. But not among strangers. He was with his son Nahor, and Milcah his grand-daughter who was Nahor's wife. We can safely assume he was well cared for.

In connection with Laban's pursuit of Jacob to the mountains of Gilead, we found the distance could not be more than 250 miles, from Haran to the fords of Jordan. This ruled out the city called Haran on the Balikh branch of the Euphrates, but it left an important question unanswered:

Where is Haran?

According to AV and LXX, Abraham's servant, when he was sent to get a wife for Isaac, went to "Mesopotamia"(Gen.24:10). JPSA and NAB, transliterating the Hebrew אֲרַם נַהֲרַיִם, say he went to "Aram-naharaim." *Naharaim* is "river" with a dual ending. In Greek *Mesopotamia* is "between rivers." The meaning would seem to be the same, except that Aram means high land.

Where the present translations speak of "Padan-aram" the Septuagint invariably says "Mesopotamia," sometimes adding, "of Syria." The Masoretic version is sometimes פַּדַּן אֲרָם , *padan-aram*, but more often פַּדֶּנָה אֲרָם ,*padenah-aram.* The LXX seem to have read in each case, פְּדַ נַה אֲרָם ,*pada naharim* "redeemed (from) rivers."

The LXX never heard of a place called "Padan-aram."

The Greeks quite logically called the Tigris-Euphrates valley *Mesopotamia.* It has been supposed that the LXX and the chroniclers of Genesis had the same area in mind. But the text says Aram, or Syria. The Tigris was never a river of Syria.

When Jacob left Laban "he rose up, and passed over the river, and set his face toward the mount Gilead" (31:21). But all three verbs are future tense in the Hebrew, denoting incompleted action, and *abar*, translated "passed over," may also be translated "to travel." The verse may be understood, "he started travelling toward the river, setting his course toward mount Gilead."

About fifteen days later Jacob entered Shechem "which is in Canaan, when he departed out of Mesopotamia of Syria" (LXX, Gen. 33:18).

Abraham's servant went directly from Canaan into Mesopotamia. Jacob went from Mesopotamia directly into Canaan.

There is no land between. Mesopotamia of Syria is bounded on the west by the river Jordan. The eastern boundary of this *high* land between rivers must be the Euphrates. We must look for Haran here, about 250 miles from the fords of Jordan.

If we strike an arc on the map we find it includes an ill—defined area anciently called Hauran. We also find, at 33.03° N., 36°E., a peak of 1093 meters called Jabal al-Harrah, by a town called Al-Harrah.[1] But we are too far west, only 20 miles from the Jordan at a point about 10 miles north of Yam Kinneret, the Sea of Galilee.

From a point due east of Damascus a great mountain of lava stretches southeast into the northwest corner of Saudi Arabia, terminating about 250 miles east of the Dead Sea. It forms the natural divide between the Euphrates and the Jordan watershed. This mountain is also Al-Harrah.[2] (*hrh*, or *harah*, is the verb "to conceive" and the adjective "pregnant"; its masculine form *hrn*, *haran*, or *heron*, is the noun "conception.")

A chain of such lava mountains runs south from Al-Harrah, parallel to the Red Sea coast. These bear such names as Harrat Hutaym, Harrat Khaybar, and Harrat Al-'Uwayrid, for in Arabic "lava flow" is *harrat*.

Since it too is a lava flow, Al-Harrah may properly be called Harrah Harrat, and we hear the name of the mountain made famous by Noah, the mountain of the Deluge — Ararat.

You will find, even on small globes, and maps of Turkey, at about 39°N 44°E, a mountain labelled Ararat. Its real name is Büyük Ağri Daği. A long way back this was the mountain of Ziusudra (Utnapishtim), the hero of Sumerian (Babylonian) legend.[3] It would hardly be chosen by storytellers of the western plains for the landing place of their hero Noah. To call it Ararat is a mistake, though one dignified by time.[4]

Noah's mountain is farther south and west, rising from the plains of northern Arabia. It still bears the name Harrah harrat, and on its summit or in its shadow was Haran. This is the land of Shem and Arphaxad, of Terah and Abram, of Nahor, of Bethuel and Laban. It is desert today, but it was not always so. It was once well watered, as was all Arabia (and for that matter all north Africa where the Sahara desert now lies).[5]

Arabia is the land of Khabiri, the land of *ha 'ibri*, Hebrews, "the burners" who grazed their flocks and herds and fired the grass, and dug the fork-rooted Mandrakes that greened again quickly, an omen of fertility rising from the ashes.

This is the land of the Midianites, *medanim*, "people from Eden," an alternate name for Khabiri. Here was the garden of creation. But the Lord hung over Eden a "flaming sword which turned every way" — from east to west daily, from north to south and back annually. And Cain, the "edge, or point," of the plow perhaps, but mostly of the sharp hooves of cattle, killed Abel, "the pasture." And Adam, "man," gave birth to another son, Seth, the lord of the desert.

At first the desert was little more than a barren patch in the center of the peninsula. Then it stretched southward and north- ward, until it cut the land in two. It widened, as torrential rains cut wadis, wind sifted out the humus and spread the bar- ren sand to smother the surrounding plains.

The desert reached its present limits about the time of the Amarna letters. The time-table in Arabia was about the same as in Africa where man left a record in paintings, in the Tas- sili N'Ajer of Algeria, and in Libya. They tell of a land of trees and lakes where elephant, rhino, hippo, and all manner of small animals roamed. Then there are herds of cattle, numberless herds. Ever increasing. For man drank the blood, and the milk, and did not slaughter.

Sheep and goats replaced the cattle. For a time there were horses, but then only burros. Now camels and a few scrawny sheep and goats remain, a vestige of the thousands that once the land had supported.

Here and there where natural springs continued to flow, or dug wells still gave water, small communities of farmers ma- naged to survive, learning to cope by irrigating the land from their wells, moving to adjacent ground when salination des- troyed the soil. Here their descendants subsist. (The farming communities of the Sahara, and their number is by no means small, could never have been created by outsiders entering an existing desert; they have to be remnants.)

From the growing desert of Arabia families and groups of moderate size migrated steadily into the river valleys to the north. In the northwest they reached the sea and applied their knowledge of navigation to that element. Others, like Abraham, crossed the Jordan into Canaan. Some moved into Egypt.

Sometimes the Khabiri swept in as raiding parties, intent on plunder. After a particularly devestating sand storm they mo- ved as a relentless horde. Armies could kill them, but could not turn them back. There was nothing behind them but death.

At last the migration of the Khabiri ceased. The supply was exhausted. The land they once inhabited, once called Eden, is now the Empty Quarter.

The charts of "Detailed Chronology", the next 8 pages,   include every dated biblical event, and some (marked *) that the text omits which can be interpolated from the data.

Some items of contemporary history in other countries have been included for clarity in the "Detailed Chronology." A more comprehensive chart of "Historical Correlation" follows.

Hopefully, the reader has found here a new sense of reality, regarding the people and events in an altogether remarkable book.

DETAILED CHRONOLOGY

	PATRIARCHS	ABRAHAM	SOJOURN

Reference	Event	Hebrew	Gregorian
Gen. 5:32	Shem was born to Noah	[0000]	-1785
11:10	Shem was [100] ⇒ 49, Arphaxad was born when	[100]	1736
:12	Arphaxad was [35] ⇒ 26, Salah was born when	[135]	1710
:14	Salah was [30] ⇒ 21, Eber born when	[165]	1689
:16	Eber was [34] ⇒ 25, Peleg born when	[232]	1664
:18	Peleg was [30] ⇒ 21, Reu born when	[262]	1643
:20	Reu was [32] ⇒ 23, Serug born when	[324]	1620
:22	Serug was [30] ⇒ 21, Nahor born when	[354]	1599
:24	Nahor was "29" [32] ⇒ 23, Terah born when	[416]	1576
:26	Terah was "70" [100] ⇒ 49, Abraham was born when	[516]	1527
	Sarah was born when Abraham was *[10] ⇒ 7 (see 17:17)	[526]	1520
12:4	Abraham was "75" [42] ⇒ 30, Sarah *[32] ⇒ 23, when they went into Canaan	[561]	1497
16:3	Abraham wed Hagar after [10] ⇒ 7 years in Canaan	[601]	1490
:16	Ishmael born to Hagar, Abraham "86" [53] ⇒ 38	[602]	1489
17:24f	Circumcision: Abraham "99" [66] ⇒ 48, Ishmael [13] ⇒ 10	[615]	1479
21:5	Isaac born to Sarah age "90" [60] ⇒ 42, Abraham [100] ⇒ 49	[616]	1478
23:1	Sarah died age "127" [130] ⇒ 70; Abraham *[140] ⇒ 77	[656]	1450
25:20	Isaac wed Rebekah at age [40] ⇒ 28 ......)	[1006]	1436
:26	Jacob and Esau born to Rebekah, Isaac age [60] ⇒ 42	[1024]	1424
:7	Abraham died, age "175" [205] ⇒ 103 ...)	[1042]	1412
	"Sojourn" of [430] ⇒ 217 years begins ...)		
:17	Ishmael died, age "137" [140] ⇒ 77	[1046]	1408
26:34	Esau married two Canaanite girls at age [40] ⇒ 28 ....)	[1056]	1401
28:5	Jacob went to Padan-aram, age *[40] ⇒ 28; Isaac *[130] ⇒ 70 (died?)...)	[1060]	1400
29:18-28	Jacob, age *[50] ⇒ 35, wed Leah & Rachel after "7" [10] ⇒ 7 years with Laban	[1061]	1399
:32	Reuben born to Leah (c. 6th day, 10th month)	[1062]	1398
:33	Simeon born to Leah (c. 25th day, 7th month)		
:34	Levi born to Leah (c. 14th day, 5th month)		

(sojourn)

Reference	Event	Year: Hebrew	Gregorian
Gen.29:35	Judah born to Leah (c. 3rd day, 3rd month).........	[1063]	-1397
30:5f	Dan born to Bilhah (c. 4th day, 3rd month)........		
:7f	Naphtali born to Bilhah (c. 24th day, 12th month)....		
:10f	Gad born to Zilpah (c. 8th day, 1st month).......		
:17f	Issachar born to Leah (c. 8th day, 2nd month).....	[1064]	1396
:12f	Asher born to Zilpah (c. 28th day, 10th month)....		
:19f	Zebulun born to Leah (c. 27th day, 11th month)....		
:22f	Joseph born to Rachel (in the 12th month).........	[1065]	1395
:21	Dinah born to Leah (c. 6th day, 9th month)	[1066]	1394
31:38,41	Return to Canaan after [20] ⇌ 14 years in Padan-aram, Jacob *[60] ⇌ 42	[1113]	1383
34:2,25	Dinah defiled by Shechem, avenged by Simeon and Levi ...		
35:18f	Benjamin born to Rachel, who died. Jacob *[104] ⇌ 53.....	[1114]	1382
37:2	Joseph sold into Egypt, age "17"[20] ⇌ 14,... *[340] ⇌ 175 years of "sojourn" remain.....	[1124]	1375
41:46	Joseph made "Conservation Chief" at age [30] ⇌ 21	[1126]	1373
35:27,28	Founding of Hebron, year "180"[210] ⇌ 105 Era of Isaac (cf. Num. 13:22)	[1134]	1368
41:47	"7"[10] ⇌ 7-year period of plenty following Joseph's appointment ends	[1136]	1366
45:6	Jacob goes to Egypt after 2 years of famine, age [130] ⇌ 70 (47:9)		
	*Kohath born, Levi *[64] ⇌ 46..........................	[1156]	1352
47:28	Jacob died after "17"[20] ⇌ 14 years in Egypt, age "147"[150] ⇌ 84....	[1204]	1340
50:26	Joseph age [110] ⇌ 56, died (?)	[1232]	1321
Ex. 6:16	Levi died age "137"[140] ⇌ 77	[1240]	1316
	*Amram born, Kohath *[105] ⇌ 54	[1264]	1298
1:8	Accession of king "who knew not Joseph", Rameses II	[1303]	1292
6:18	*Kohath died age [133] ⇌ 73	[1322]	1279
	*Miriam born, Amram *[100] ⇌ 49	[1364]	1249
	*Aaron born, Amram *[104] ⇌ 53 (see Num. 33:38f)	[1401]	1245

Detailed Chronology

	MOSES	JOSHUA	JUDGES
	(sojourn)	Exodus +	

Reference	Event	Year: Hebrew	Gregorian
	Moses born, Amram *[110]⇌56 (see Deut. 1:3; 31:2; 34:7)	[1404]	-1242
	*Caleb born (see Josh.14:7-10)	[1414]	1235
	*Joshua born (see Josh. 24:29)	[1424]	1228
Ex. 6:20	*Amram died, age "137"[140]⇌77 ..)	[1434]	1221
2:15	Moses left Egypt, *age [30]⇌21.....)	[1435]	1220
	*Merneptah's stele –"Israel is desolated, her seed is not."– erected	[1446]	1212
4:27f	Moses and Aaron meet in "wilderness," return to Egypt	c.[1446]	1207
12:40	EXODUS, [430] years after the death of Abraham.. Ex. 7:7, Moses "80"[50]⇌35 Aaron "83"[53]⇌38	[1454]	
Num.13:1-14:34	Spies sent into Canaan from Kadesh-barnea..		
33:38f	Aaron died, age [123]⇌66 .....)– Exodus + [40]⇌28	[1524]	1179
Deut.1:3; 31:2;34:7	Moses died, age [120]⇌63....)		
34:8f	Joshua became leader, age *[100]⇌49, in 11th month..	[1525]	1178
Josh.1:1,10f	Battle of Jericho, c. [33]⇌24 days after Moses' death	[1532]	1174
14:7f	Caleb gets Hebron, age "85"[115]⇌61; Exodus + [45]⇌33	[1534]	1172
24:29	Joshua died age [110]⇌56; Exodus + *[50]⇌35	[1535]	1171
Jud. 3:8	Chushan-rishathaim of "Mesopotamia"(Aram-naharaim) dominant "8"[11]⇌8yrs, f.	[1546]	1163
:10f	Othniel judge for [40]⇌28 years, from	[1616]	1135
:14	Eglon of Moab dominant for "18"[21]⇌15 years, from		
:30	("80" years omitted)		
4:2f	Jabin king of Canaan dominant for [20]⇌14 years, from	[1640]	1120
5:31	("40" years omitted)		
6:1	Midianites dominant for "7"[10]⇌7 years, from	[1660]	1106
8:28	Gideon judge for [40]⇌28 years, from	[2000]	1099
9:22	Abimelech ben-Gideon king for 3 years, from	[2040]	1071
10:1f	Tola judge for [23]⇌17 years, from	[2043]	1068
:3	Jair judge for [22]⇌16 years, from	[2066]	1051
:8	Jephthah ends "18"[21]⇌15-year Ammonite domination of Gilead ...	[2121]	1035
12:7	Jephthah judge for [6]⇌6 years, from......		

196

Detailed Chronology

Period markers (left to right across the chart): ELI · SAMUEL · SAUL · DAVID

Reference	Event	Hebrew Year	Gregorian Year
Jud. 12:8f	Ibzan judge for "7"[10] ⇌ 7 years, from	[2130]	-1029
:11	Elon judge for [10] ⇌ 7 years, from	[2140]	1022
	Eli judge for [40] ⇌ 28 years (I Sam. 4:18), from ...Samuel born in...	[2150]	1015
:13f	Abdon judge for "8"[11] ⇌ 8 years, from		
13:1	Philistines dominant for [40] ⇌ 28 years, from ...	[2161]	1007
	*David born (II Sam. 2:1, 4; 5:4),...............		
15:20	Samson judge for [20] ⇌ 14 years, from ...		
16:30	Samson destroyed the Philistine temple and died...		
I Sam. 4:11	Ark of God captured, Hophni and Phinehas died....	[2210]	994
4:18	Eli died, making Samuel "elder" and judge........		
6:1	Ark of God returned after "7"[10] ⇌ 7 months...		
7:1f	Ark kept for [20] ⇌ 14 years in house of Abinadab, from...	[2211]	993
10:1; 11:15	Saul made king by Samuel.................		
13:1; 15:1f	Saul's 3rd year he lost the support of Samuel	[2213]	991
16:13	David anointed by Samuel; *Exodus + [430].	[2214]	990
25:1	Samuel died, *age [45] ⇌ 33.	[2216]	988
27:7	David with Philistines 1 year 4 months, from end of 8th month of...	[2220]	987
31:6	Saul died after reign of c. [10] ⇌ 7 years, end of	[2221]	986
II Sam. 2:1, 4	David occupied Hebron, made king of Judah (5:4, age [30] ⇌ 21)...		
2:10	Ishbosheth (Ishbaal) king of Israel.		
5:3	David made king of Israel when Ishbosheth died, the end of his	[2224]	983
	*4th year as king of Judah; *Exodus + [440] ⇌ 224.		
[40]th year of Philistine domination................			
[10]th year of David's residence in Hebron.........			
[20]th year for the Ark in the house of Abinadab...		[2230]	980
5:17f	Two battles in the valley of Rephaim end Philistine domination...		
5:7	Jerusalem occupied, David's *4th year as king of Israel....	[2231]	979
6:17	Ark of God moved to Jerusalem; *Exodus + [444]............		

Detailed Chronology

Gregorian	Hebrew	EMPIRE / SOLOMON / DIVIDED MONARCHY — Reference	Event
-959	[2260]	I K. 2:12	[40]th year of David's reign as king of Judah...
			[33]rd year of David's reign as king of Israel...
			[30]th year in Jerusalem; *age [100] ≏ 49 ......
958	[2261]	3:1	Solomon made king of Israel-Judah......
			Solomon married Pharaoh's daughter; *began to build his house •
955	[2264]	9:16	Pharaoh (Siamon) took Gezer to give her as a wedding present...
		6:1	The Temple was begun in the 4th year of Solomon's reign...
			Exodus + "480"[510] ≏ 252 ......
949	[2303]	6:38	The Temple was "seven years in building"... so both completed in
		7:1	The house took [13] ≏ 10 years to build .....
948	c.[2304]	9:15f	Solomon rebuilt Gezer for his wife, Pharaoh's daughter
		11:42	Solomon's [40]th year ≏ 28th year
931	[2330]	:43	Rehoboam became king of Judah, for "17"[20] ≏ 14 years (14:21) beginning in
930	[2331]	12:20	Jeroboam became king of Israel, for [22] ≏ 16 years (14:20) beginning in
926	[2335]	14:25	Shishak (Sheshonk) sacked Jerusalem the 5th year of Rehoboam (Egyptian stele)
916	[2351]	15:1,2	Abijah king of Judah [3]+[10] (II Chron. 14:1) = [13] ≏ 10 years, from
914	[2353]	:25	Nadab king of Israel "2"[12] ≏ 9 years, from
906	[2364]	:10	Asa king of Judah [41] ≏ 29 years, from
905	[2365]	:27,33	Baasha killed Nadab, was king of Israel [24] ≏ 18 years, from
		:16f	Ben-hadad I of Syria defeated Baasha in
888	[2421]	16:8	Elah ben-Baasha king of Israel 2 years, from
887	[2422]	:10	Zimri killed Elah, was king for the last 7 days of
886	[2423]	:15f	Omri defeated Zimri, and Tibni, ruled Israel [12] ≏ 9 years, from
885	[2424]	:23	Omri made Samaria his capital city in
879	[2433]	22:41f	Jehoshaphat king of Judah [25] ≏ 16 years, from
877	[2435]	16:29	Ahab ben-Omri king of Israel [22] ≏ 16 years, from
876	[2436]	20:1f	Ahab defeated Ben-hadad I (?)
866	[2452]		Ahab defeated Ben-hadad II
865	[2453]		

Reference	Gregorian	Hebrew	Event
I K.22:1	-864/3/2	[2454,5,6]	Three years without war between Syria and Israel
:2f	861	[2460]	Ahab allied with Jehoshaphat fought Ben-hadad II at Ramoth-gilead, Ahab killed
:51	860	[2461]	Ahaziah ben-Ahab king of Israel 2 years, from
II K.3:4f			Jehoshaphat and *Ahaziah fought Mesha of Moab
I K.22:48f	859	[2462]	Jehoshaphat built ships at Ezion-geber; refused to have Ahaziah share an expedition to Ophir; the ships were broken. Both kings died in
II K. 8:16f	858	[2463]	Jehoram ben-Jehoshaphat king of Judah "8"[11]⇌ 8 years, from...
3:1	854	[2500]	Jehoram ben-Ahab king of Israel [12]⇌ 9 years, from... *Battle at Karkar against Shalmaneser III of Assyria (Monolith inscription)
8:25f	850	[2504]	Ahaziah king of Judah 1 year; with Jehoram of Israel he fought Syria at Ramoth-gilead; (4:36; 8:1)*Elisha warned the Shunammite woman of "seven-year famine"; (9:6) had Jehu anointed king of Israel; (9:24ff) Jehu killed Ahaziah of Judah, Jehoram of Israel, Jezebel...
10:36	849	[2505]	Jehu king of Israel "28"[31]⇌ 22 years, from.............
11:1-3			Athaliah, mother of Ahaziah, killed her grandsons (but Joash survived), made herself queen of Judah for 6 years, from...
:4ff			Athaliah assassinated; Joash king of Judah [40]⇌ 28 years, from...
6:24	843	[2514]	Ben-hadad II besieged Samaria *the 7th year of Jehu...
7:6			The "noise" of a conqueror routed the Syrians...
8:5	842	[2515]	The Shunammite Elisha had warned returned after "7" years...
:15			Hazael assassinated Ben-hadad II at Elisha's suggestion...... *Shalmaneser III put Hazael to tribute, and received tribute from Jehu of Samaria (Black Obelisk)......
13:1	841	[2516]	Jehoahaz ben-Jehu king of Israel "17"[14]⇌ 11 years, from
:3	827	[2536]	Hazael king of Syria dominated Israel throughout the reign of Jehoahaz.
:10	816	[2553]	Jehoash ben-Jehoahaz king of Israel [16]⇌ 13 years, from
12:18f			Joash of Judah paid tribute to Hazael and was assassinated in......
14:1,2	815	[2554]	Amaziah ben-Joash king of Judah "29"[33]⇌ 24 years from......

199

Detailed Chronology
Judah & Israel

Reference	Event	Year: Hebrew base-7	base-10	Gregorian
II K.13:14f	Elisha died	c.[2561]		-811
:24	Ben-hadad III succeeded Hazael (Syrian records)	[2562]		810
:25	Jehoash of Israel defeated the Syrians three times, probably	[2562]/[2564]		810/808
14:8f	Amaziah challenged Jehoash and lost; Jehoash plundered Jerusalem, but died soon after, in	[2601]		804
:23	Jeroboam II king of Israel [41] ≑ 29 years, from	[2602]		803
:17	Amaziah lived for [15] ≑ 12 years after Jehoash died, until	[2616]		792
15:1,2	Azariah king of Judah [52] ≑ 37 years, from	[2620]		791
14:29	Zachariah succeeded Jeroboam II as king of Israel	[2643]		774
15:8	Zachariah's reign —*11 years 6 months— included the first 6 months of	[2660]		763
:10f	Shallum killed Zachariah, ruled *7 months, including the first month of	[2661]		762
:14	Menahem killed Shallum, ruled "40" 4 years 11 months, from the 2nd month of			
:23	Pekahiah (*coregent under Menahem) for 2 years, from	[2666]		757
:25f	Pekah (*coregent under Menahem) for [20] ≑ 14 years, from	[3001]		755
:32f	Jotham king of Judah [16] ≑ 13 years, from	[3002]		754
16:1,2	Ahaz ben-Jotham king of Judah 16 years, from......			
	Siege of Jerusalem by Rezin of Syria and Pekah of Israel broken by Tiglath-pileser's attack on Damascus, to assist Ahaz ...	[3021]		741
15:19	Menahem paid "Pul" tribute to keep control of Israel			
:30	Hoshea ben-Elah killed Pekah, became king of Israel in........			
16:10	Ahaz met Tiglath-pileser in Damascus in year [3033] which was changed to when base-10 counting was made retroactive to his first year of reign.		3030	732
17:1	Hoshea, in '12 Ahaz', began again with "1" in the base-10 system		3032	730
16:20	Hezekiah ben-Ahaz king of Judah 29 years (18:2), from		3037	725
18:9	Shalmaneser V besieged Samaria 3 years		3037/3039	725/723
:10	Samaria fell to Assyria (king Sargon II) in '9 Hoshea' (*actually '20 Hoshea')		3040	722

J U D A H

Reference	Event	Year: Hebrew	Gregorian
II K. 18:13f	Hezekiah paid tribute in his 14th year to *Sargon II (see Isaiah 20:1)	3050	-712
20:12ff	He received the ambassador of Merodach-baladan *who organized a coalition to revolt when Sargon died and Sennacherib became king of Assyria	3057/8	705/4
:20	He cut a conduit to safeguard the water supply, and strengthened the city to stand a siege (II Chron. 32:3-5, 30)		
19:—	Hezekiah held out under siege by Sennacherib, *in his 24th year.	3061	701
21:1	Manasseh king of Judah 55 years, from	3066	696
19:37	Sennacherib assassinated by two sons; a third son, Esarhaddon became king	3082/3	681/0
	He required Manasseh to visit Ninevah (Assyrian annals;cf. II Chron.33:11ff) in	3085	678
21:19	Amon king of Judah 2 years, from	3121	641
22:1	Josiah ben-Amon king of Judah 31 years, from	3123	639
:3	The "book of the Law of Moses"(Deut. ?) found by Hilkiah the priest in '18 Josiah'	3140	622
23:29	*Cyaxares the Mede and Nabopolassar of Babylon destroyed Assyria, finally in	3152	610
	Pharaoh Necho, going "against the king of Assyria" (Ashur-uballit leading a remnant south of Euphrates?) challenged by Josiah who died at Megiddo	3153	609
:31f	Jehoahaz king 3 months, captured by Necho, replaced by Jehoiakim, 11 years f.	3154	608
24:1	Jehoiakim submitted to Nebuchadnezzar of Babylon who defeated Necho in	3157	605
	Later, Jehoiakim rebelled; there was war with Babylon;		
:8	Jehoiachin became king; after 3 months he surrendered and was taken captive to Babylon in the 8th year of Nebuchadnezzar	3164	598
24:17	Zedekiah king of Judah 11 years, from	3165	597
25:8	Zedekiah rebelled; Nebuchadnezzar destroyed Jerusalem;		
:11	took the people captive to Babylon in his 19th year	3175	587
:27	Evilmerodach released Jehoiachin from prison in the 37th year of his captivity	3201	561
II Chron. 36:21f	Cyrus of Persia in his first year as king of Babylon released the captives	3225	-537
	Captivity lasted "seventy" (actually 49) years.		

Adding: 536 — 536

3761 = -1

3762 = +1

*interpolated

Since there is no "zero" year in the Gregorian calendar

PATRIARCHS	Hebrew	Gregorian	EGYPT	MESOPOTAMIA
		−3000	4th Dynasty / Khufu, Great Pyramid	Sumer & Akkad / 1st Dynasty of Ur / Akkadian Empire / 3rd Dynasty of Ur / Isin & Larsa / Babylon / Hammurabi
		−2000	11th Dynasty / 12th Dynasty / 13th Dynasty	
Shem	0	1785		
Arphaxad	[100]	1736		
Salah	[135]	1710		
Eber	[165]	1689	HYKSOS	
Peleg	[232]	1664		
Reu	[262]	1643		
Serug	[324]	1620	18th Dynasty	
Nahor	[354]	1599	Ahmose I (1580)	
Terah	[416]	1576	Amenhotep I (1557)	KASSITES
			Thutmose I (1545)	
Abraham	[516]	1527	Hatshepsut (1501)	
to Canaan	[561]	1497		
Ishmael	[602]	1489		
Circumcision	[615]	1479	Thutmose III (1480)	
Isaac	[616]	1478	Conquest of Canaan	
Jacob, Esau	[1006]	1436	Amenhotep II (1448)	

Event	Hebrew	Gregorian	EGYPT	MESOPOTAMIA (Kassites)
SOJOURN				
Abraham died	[1024]	-1424		
Joseph	[1064]	1396	Thutmose IV (1420)	
sold in Egypt	[1114]	1382	Amenhotep III (1411)	
promoted	[1124]	1375		
Jacob to Egypt	[1136]	1366	Akhenaton (1375)	
Jacob died	[1156]	1352	Amarna Letters	
			Tutenkhamen (1358)	
	[1161]	1350	19th Dynasty	
Joseph died	[1204]	1340	Horemhab	
or possibly	[1240]	1316		
	[1241]	1315	Rameses I	
	[1243]	1313	Seti I	
	[1303]	1292	Rameses II	
Moses	[1404]	1242		
	[1430]	1225	Merneptah	
Moses fled	[1434]	1221		
	[1435]	1220	Victory stele	
	[1443]	1215	Amenmeses	
returned c.	[1444]	1214	Merneptah–Siptah	
	[1452]	1209	Seti II	
EXODUS	[1454]	1207	Period of Anarchy	
			20th Dynasty	
	[1464]	1200	Setnakht	
	[1466]	1198	Rameses III	
Moses died	[1510]	1190	"Peoples of the Sea" invade Canaan	
	[1524]	1179		

Egypt's ancient chroniclers credited this whole period to Horemhab.

	Hebrew	Gregorian	EGYPT (Rameses III)	MESOPOTAMIA (Kassites)
JOSHUA, JUDGES				
Jericho fell	[1525]	-1178		
Joshua died	[1534]	1172		Kassites overthrown by
Chushan-rishʾm	[1535]	1171		Elamites c. 1168
Othniel	[1546]	1163		4th Dynasty of Babylon c.1162
Eglon of Moab	[1616]	1135	Rameses IV (1167)	Nebuchadnezzar I (1124/1103)
Jabin of Canaan	[1640]	1120	Rameses V (1161)	ASSYRIA
Midianites	[1660]	1106	Rameses IX (1142)	Tiglath-pileser I (1115/1077)
Gideon	[2000]	1099	Rameses XII (1118)	conquered Syria
Abimelech king	[2040]	1071	Egypt divided (1090)	
Tola	[2042]	1068	Priests rule at Thebes	
Jair	[2066]	1051	21st Dynasty at Tanis	2 kings
Jephthah	[2121]	1035	*Ammon dominates Gilead)*	
Ibzan	[2130]	1029	4 kings	Shalmaneser II (1030/1019)
Elon & Eli	[2140]	1022	Amenemopet (1026)	
Abdon	[2150]	1015		Ashur-rabi II (1010/970)
Philistine Domination (1007/980)		(1007/980)		
Samson	[2161]	1007		
K Samuel, Saul	[2211]	993		
I David JUDAH	[2221]	986		Hiram of Tyre (980/936)
N ISRAEL	[2224]	983		
G Jerusalem	[2231]	979	Siamon	
D Solomon born?	[2234]	976	Pesibkhenno II	Tiglath-pileser II (966/935)
O Solomon king	[2261]	958	22nd Dynasty	
M Temple begun	[2264]	955	Sheshonk I (945)	

JUDAH	Hebrew	Gregorian	ISRAEL	EGYPT	SYRIA	ASSYRIA
Rehoboam	[2331]	-930	Jeroboam			Ashur-dan II (934/912)
5th year	[2335]	926		(Sheshonk I) plundered Judah & Israel		
Abijah	[2351]	916		Osorkon I (924/895)		
	[2353]	914	Nadab			Adad-nirari II (911/891)
Asa	[2364]	906				
	[2365]	905	Baasha			
	[2422]	887	Elah			Tukulti-Ninurta II (890/884)
	[2424]	885	Omri			
Jehoshaphat	[2435]	877			Ben-hadad I c. 900	Ashurnasirpal II (883/859)
	[2436]	876	Ahab			
	[2452]	866	defeated –		Ben-hadad I (or II)	
	[2453]	865	defeated –		Ben-hadad II	
	[2460]	861	killed at Ramoth-gilead			
	[2461]	860	Ahaziah ben-Ahab			
	[2463]	858	Jehoram ben-Ahab			Shalmaneser III (858/824)
fought Moab	[2500]	854	wounded at Ramoth-gilead		battle at Karkar	Monolith Inscription
Jehoram ben-J.	[2504]	850	Jehu			
5th year	[2505]	849				(Black Obelisk)
Ahaziah	[2514]	843	"noise" defeats Ben-hadad		Hazael	Jehu paid tribute –841
Athaliah	[2515]	842				
Joash	[2536]	827	Jehoahaz			Shamshi-adad V (823/811)
	[2553]	816	Jehoash			
	[2554]	815	defeated			
Amaziah	[2600]	805			Ben-hadad III (810)	Adad-nirari III (810/783)
	[2602]	803	Jeroboam II			Jehoash paid tribute 805 (stele)

JUDAH	Hebrew	Gregorian	ISRAEL	SYRIA	ASSYRIA
Azariah	[2620]	-791			Shalmaneser IV (782/772)
	[2643]	774	Zachariah	Tabeel (772)	Ashur-dan III (771/754)
	[2660]	763	Shallum		
	[2661]	762	Menahem		
	[2666]	757	Pekahiah		
	[3001]	755	Pekah		
Jotham	[3002]	754		Rezin (752)	Ashur-nirari V (753/746)
					Tiglath-pileser III (745/727)
Ahaz	[3021]	741	Hoshea	Rezin & Pekah allied against Ahaz; Tiglath-pileser saved Ahaz by attacking Damascus; He took tribute from Menahem, approved accession of Hoshea.	
changed counting after trip to Damascus in	3030	732		Damascus taken; Ahaz paid tribute.	
12th year	3032	730	1 Hoshea base-10		
	3036	726	5 "		Shalmaneser V (726/722)
Hezekiah	3037	725	6 "		began 3-year siege of Samaria
	3038	724	7 "		
	3039	723	8 "		
	3040	722	9 "		Samaria fell
			Israel taken into captivity		Sargon II (721/705)

Hebrew	Gregorian	JUDAH (Hezekiah)	EGYPT	ASSYRIA	BABYLONIA
					Marduk-apal-iddina (Merodach-baladan) king 721/711 vice-regent with Sargon to 705
3050	712	14th year paid tribute to Assyria	24th Dynasty Bocchoris (718) 25th Dynasty (Nubian) Shabaka released Iamani of Ashdod to Sargon	(Sargon II) threatened Egypt and Judah	instigated revolt among Assyrian tributaries
3058	704	saw Merodach's ambassador built water conduit strengthened city		Sennacherib (704) drove off Merodach-Baladan(703), installed – besieged Egypt and Judah but withdrew	Bel-ibni (702) deposed in favor of
3061	701	stood siege	Taharka Shabataka (700)	Sennacherib's son,	Ashur-nadin-shum (699) captured by Elamites who installed
					Mushezib-Marduk (693)
3066	696	Manasseh	Taharka (688)	Sennacherib retaliated with thorough destruction of Babylon (689)	– rebuilt Babylon
		That he spilled "innocent blood" (II K. 21:16) suggests he supplied conscript troops to Assyria. He was evidently a faithful vassal after Esarhaddon had him in Ninevah (II Chron.33:11 "Babylon") c. 678	From 674 to 664 he and his son-in-law Tanutamon fought Assyria for control of Egypt, until – destroyed Thebes, then installed Psamtik (663)(26th Dyn.) rebelled and drove out Assyrians c. 652.	assassinated in 681 Esarhaddon (680) Ashurbanipal (668) defeated his brother installed the Chaldean noble	Shamash-shum-ukin (668) installed the Chaldean noble Kandalanu (647) as viceroy
3121	641	Amon			

JUDAH	Hebrew	Gregorian	EGYPT	ASSYRIA	BABYLONIA
Josiah	3123	639	(Psamtik I)	(Ashurbanipal)	CHALDEANS
				Ashur–etil–ilani (629)	Nabopolassar (626)
				Sin–shar–ishkun (622?)	

Cyaxares the Mede attacked Assyria c. 612; was joined by Nabopolassar. Ashur and Ninevah were destroyed. For three years Ashur–uballit II held out at Harran. He was defeated and the empire divided in 609.

JUDAH	Hebrew	Gregorian	EGYPT	ASSYRIA	BABYLONIA
killed in battle at Megiddo	3153	609	Necho (609)		
Jehoahaz, after 3 months, taken captive to Egypt;					
Jehoiakim	3154	608	- installed		
	3157	605	Necho lost Canaan & Syria to		Nebuchadnezzar (605) attacked Jerusalem; installed
rebelled	3164	598			
Jehoiachin, after 3 months, surrendered; was taken captive to Babylon;	3165	597			
Zedekiah			Psamtik II (593)		
			Hophra (588)		
rebelled					
Jerusalem fell	3175	587			destroyed Jerusalem
	3176	586	captives taken to Babylon		
	3201	561	Jehoiachin "lifted up" by		Amel–Marduk (Evil–merodach)(561)

Cyrus of Persia (c. 552/530) became king of Babylon (538)

JUDAH	Hebrew	Gregorian	EGYPT	ASSYRIA	BABYLONIA
captives return	3225	537			

The notes are numbered in sequence on each page. They are arranged here by page number and note number in a decimal system. For instance: the second note on page 74 is numbered 74.2. It is hoped the reader will find this system facilitates locating the notes as he is reading, and locating the passage to which a note applies.

2.1 Edwin R. Thiele, *The Mysterious Numbers of the Hebrew Kings* rev. ed. (Grand Rapids, 1965) p.12. Dr. Thiele's first chapter supplies an excellent concise treatment of its title topic, "The Problems of Old Testament Chronology."

3.1 Mary Ellen Chase, *Life and Language in the Old Testament* (N.Y., 1955) pp.34-35.

3.2 James Henry Breasted, *A History of Egypt* (N.Y., 1905) Bantam ed. 1967, pp.297, 326-27. This book has enjoyed more than thirty reprintings. Breasted's "Chronological Table of Kings" has been relied upon for Egyptian dates.

3.3 R. K. Harrison, *The Archeology of the Old Testament* (N.Y., 1963) Harper Chapelbook 1966, p. 42; J. B. Pritchard (ed.)*Ancient Near Eastern Texts Relating to the Old Testament* (1950) p.378.

3.4 Breasted, p.391.

4.1 T. Eric Peet, *Egypt and the Old Testament* (Boston, 1923)

4.2 Elmer W. K. Mould, *Essentials of Bible History* (N.Y., 1939) p.42.

4.3 Harrison, p.42.

4.4 Harrison, note 55, Chap. III.

5.1 Harrison, p.75; Daniel David Luckenbill, *Ancient Records of Assyria and Babylon*, I (Chicago, 1926) sec. 611.

5.2 Harrison, p.76; Pritchard, p.281.

6.1 Werner Keller, *The Bible As History*, trans. William Neill (N.Y., 1956) pp. 235 ff.

7.1 Breasted, pp. 440 ff.

7.2 Breasted, p. 443.

7.3 *Bible & Spade*, I, 1 (Winter 1972); *IRAQ* XXX, part 2 (Autumn 1968); *The Catholic Biblical Quarterly*, XXXII, 3 (July 1970).

9.1 *Bulletin of the American Schools of Oriental Research*, No. 100 (December 1945) pp. 16-22.

9.2 W. F. Albright, *The Biblical Period from Abraham to Ezra*, Harper Torchbooks ed. (N.Y., 1963) pp. 116, 117.

9.3 Thiele, p.60, note 2.

9.4 Albright, ...*Abraham to Ezra*, p. 117

10.1 *ibid.* p.183.

12.1 *ibid.* note 110.

12.2 Thiele, p.60, note 2.

13.1 *ibid.* p. 183.

14.1 I am indebted to Thiele for this, also. See Thiele, p.12, for the translations, p.11 for the Latin, from Hieronymus, *Traditio catholica*, ed. J. P. Migne (Paris, 1864) Vol. I, Ep. 72, *Ad Vitalem* (Patrologia Latina, Vol.XXII, co. 676).

16.1 *Joshua and Judges*, Soncino Books of the Bible (London, 1950) p. 152.

16.2 *Samuel*, Soncino Books of the Bible (London, 1951) p. xiii.

16.3 Josephus, *Complete Works*, trans. Wm. Whiston (1737), currently available in both hardcover and paperback with foreword by William Sanford LaSor (Grand Rapids, 1960). The quotation is from "Dissertation V" section 31.

17.1 S. Goldman, p.68.

19.1 Harrison, p. 90; R. W. Rogers, *Cuneiform Parallels to the Old Testament* (1912), p. 383.

20.1 included in Josephus, *Works*, edition cited.

20.2 Josephus, *Against Apion*, I,21.

20.3 Josephus, *Antiquities*, II,xv,2.

21.1 see *Against Apion*, I,26.32.34; II,2.

23.1 *Antiq.* I,vi,5.

23.2 *Antiq.* VIII,iii,1.

23.3 see Whiston, *Dissertation V*, sect.11.

24.1 from 'table of intervals' items 8,9,10, *ibid.*, sect. 9.

32.1 Isidore Epstein, *Judaism* (Baltimore, Md., 1966) p. 18, note 6, Chapter 1.

33.1 *Against Apion*, I, 14. Portions, set by Whiston as direct quotations of Manetho, seem actually to be paraphrase; I have retained Whiston's punctuation.

33.2 *Against Apion*, I, 26 ff.

34.1 *Antiq.* II, xv, 2.

34.2 Breasted, p. 184.

34.3 *loc. cit.*

34.4 *Against Apion*, I, 15.

34.5 *ibid.* I, 16.

35.1 Breasted, pp. 181 f.

40.1 Samuel Noah Kramer, *Cradle of Civilization*, Time-Life series Great Ages of Man (N.Y., 1967) p. 124.

40.2 *loc. cit.*

40.3 These views I was pleased to find shared by P.R. Ackroyd and C.F.Evans (eds.) *Cambridge History of the Bible*, (London, 1970) I, 35 ff.

41.1 Hugh J. Schonfield, *A History of Biblical Literature*, (N.Y., 1962) p.78.

41.2 Fred Gladstone Bratton writes, "Between the time of the original composition and the earliest manuscripts, as well as during the successive manuscript stages, numerous changes were made, both deliberate and accidental." *A History of the Bible* (Beacon Paperback, 1967) p.2.

42.1 Rudolf Kittel, *A History of the Hebrews*, trans. Hope W. Hogg & E.B.Speirs (London, 1896) II, 235-6.

42.2 *Mathematics for the Million* (N.Y., 1937) rev. ed. 1943 p. 292.

43.1 *ibid.*, p. 290.

45.1 see O. Neugebauer, *The Exact Sciences in Antiquity* (Rhode Island, 1967) p. 10 f.

45.2 *They Wrote On Clay*, ed. George G. Cameron (Chicago, 1938) Phoenix ed., 1955, p. 156.

46.1 *The Beginnings of Civilization* (N.Y., 1965) Mentor ed. p. 143.

46.2 Neugebauer, p.19.

48.1 (N.Y., 1918)

52.1 Woolley, pp. 69 f.

52.2 George Sarton, *A History of Science* (Harvard, 1966).

57.1 Neugebauer, p.25.

59.1 When the tile pattern was first published several readers noted that on a mathematical basis there would be room for more tiles in later rows than the number in the pattern. It is true that more tiles can be squeezed in, but only by eliminating, or at least seriously reducing space between tiles - grout space.

One who raised the question was Paul B. Johnson, Dept. of Mathematics, U.C.L.A., who later wrote:

"Circumference for 60° arc, $C = 2\pi r/6 = 3.1416 r/3 = 1.0472 r$, $\therefore$ to maintain the nice pattern you suggest the arc-wise spacing of the tiles must be 1.0472 times the radial spacing. This agrees with your figure."

(I had found the same answer but less succinctly.)

This means the grout space in the circumference must be greater than in the radial. The necessary difference is established in the first few rows. Maintaining this spacing uniformly thereafter precludes the introduction of an extra tile.

59.2 The number (A) of tiles in a pattern of R rows may be found by $A = 3R(R+1)$, roughly comparable to $A = \pi R^2$, the area of a circle.

62.1 Hogben, p. 301.

64.1 Precession of the equinox makes the solar year shorter than the sidereal year. Until the Gregorian correction no calendar was adjusted to take account of this anomaly.

65.1 One such die is displayed in the University Museum, University of Pennsylvania, Philadelphia, Penn.

65.2 Herodotus, *History*, transl. George Rawlinson (Tudor, 1956) p. 137.

66.1 "The Sword and the Sermon," *National Geographic*, July, 1972, pp. 2-45.

67.1 *cast* v. transitive 11, intransitive 5, Webster's New International, 2nd ed. 1950. Note also, intr. 4, "to calculate, to add figures."

70.1 Geza Vermes, *The Dead Sea Scrolls in English* (Great Britain, 1962) rev. ed. 1965, p. 43.

70.2 *loc. cit.*

71.1 Aaron Bakst, *Mathematics: Its Magic and Mystery* (Princeton, 1967) pp. 5, 6, discusses the matchstick numerals.

73.1 *New Larousse Encyclopedia of Mythology*, trans. Richard Aldington and Delano Ames (1968) p. 27.

74.1 *Against Apion* I, 22.

74.2 see note of H. St. J. Thackeray to *Against Apion* I, 22, in his translation of Josephus (London, 1926, 1961).

74.3 *loc. cit.*

75.1 P. H. Newby, "Introduction" p. viii, *Tales From the Arabian Nights*, a selection by P. H. Newby from *The Arabian Nights' Entertainment*, transl. Sir Richard Burton, (N. Y., 1951, 1967).

75.2 *loc. cit.*

76.1 Herodotus, p. 154.

89.1 Breasted, p. 398.

90.1 *loc. cit.*

91.1 John Patterson, based on a study of 15th and 13th century B.C. Egyptian sculpture depicting "Philistines," concludes they came from the "coast of Illyria or in the region of the Danube" rather than Crete. — see "The Old Testament World," *The Bible and History*, ed. William Barclay (England, 1968).

95.1 A.V. says (Gen. 33:18), "Jacob came to Shalem, a city of Shechem," agreeing with the Septuagint rendering, "Jacob came to Salem, a city of Secimon." But J.P.S.A. translates the Hebrew more correctly, "Jacob came in peace to the city of Shechem." N.A.B. reads, "Jacob arrived safely..." and N.W.T., "Jacob came safe and sound to the city of Shechem." It is worth noting that Josephus says only, "he went to Shechem." (*Antiq*. I, xxi, 1) in accord with the Hebrew text but not the Septuagint. Clearly, Jacob did not go to Jerusalem as LXX and A.V. suggest.

96.1 Joseph was 2 when the family returned from Haran. He was taken to Egypt [15] years later. The "17" may be the base-10 sum of these figures, though they no longer appear in the text.

96.2   Hebron, or more properly *chebron*, might be translated "Union"; cf. *chaber* "joined, united," *cheber* "community," *chebrah* "society, company."

96.3   Rabbi Solomon ben Isaac (1040/1105).

96.4   This "17" may derive from subtracting by base-10 rules Jacob's age of [130] upon arrival in Egypt from "147" as his terminal age was wrongly understood.

98.1   see Breasted, pp. 312-318, Ikhnaton.

99.1   notably Cyrus Gordon and H. H. Rowley.

99.2   John Bright, *A History of Israel* (Philadelphia, 1959) pp. 84 f.

101.1 Charles F. Cooper, "The Ecology of Fire," *Scientific American* Vol. 204, No. 4 (April 1961) 150-151.

101.2 *Larousse*, p. 83.

101.3 Others suppose "pirate" comes from Greek *peiran* which they translate "to attempt, attack." But this distorts the sense of the Greek which means "to try, attempt, undertake: to test: to know by experience," and does not connote "attack" in a violent sense.

101.4 Breasted, p. 327.

102.1 Breasted, pp. 334 ff.

103.1 Cyril Aldred, *Akhenaten, Pharaoh of Egypt - a new study*, (N.Y., 1968) New Aspects of Archeology Series, ed. Sir Mortimer Wheeler, p. 134. See also, Plate 2.

105.1 *Genesis*, translation, introduction and notes by Ephraim A. Speiser, The Anchor Bible (N.Y., 1964).

110.1 see Breasted, p. 339.

118.1 Breasted, p. 371.

118.2 G. Ernest Wright, *Biblical Archeology* (Phila., 1957) p. 57; see also R. K. Harrison, *Old Testament Times* (Grand Rapids, 1970) pp. 113, 122; John D. Davis & Henry S. Gehman, *Westminster Dictionary of the Bible* (Phila., 1944); Pierre Montet, *Le Drame d'Avaris* (1940) pp. 18 ff, *Les Nouvelles fouilles de Tanis* (1929-33), "Avaris, Pi-Ramses, Tanis," *Syria* XVII (1936).

118.3 Wright, p. 57.

118.4 Davis & Gehman, "Rameses".

118.5 Breasted, pp. 157, 165, 169.

118.6 Wright, p. 57.

118.7 Bright, p. 111.

121.1 Breasted, p. 388.

121.2 "A bowl that was salvaged from the ruins (of Lachish) bears an inscription giving its date as the fourth year of Merenptah (*sic*)." Keller, p. 157.

122.1 Breasted, p. 150.

131.1 see Soncino Books of the Bible in Bibliography.

131.2 Goldman credits Ralbag for this interpretation.

131.3 "Dissertation V" sec. 18, item 5.

131.4 For maps see Nelson Beecher Keyes, *Story of the Bible World* (C.S. Hammond & Co., 1959) or other books by the same publisher.

135.1 see Dr. Goldman's most informative note to this passage in *Samuel*, Soncino Books of the Bible.

139.1 *Samuel*, I, viii, 1, Soncino.

143.1 Slotki so notes, Judges 10:8, Soncino.

146.1 Joshua, Judges, I & II Samuel, I & II Kings (the Former Prophets) are believed to have been canonized about -200; see Bratton, p. 117.

146.2 Bratton, p. 122, who notes Driver has reservations.

165.1 Thiele, p. 66 n.7.

166.1 Luckenbill, II, sect. 611.

166.2 NAB recognizes the problem but seeks to solve it by suppressing the name of Jehoshaphat; see its note to 2K.3:1.

171.1 Albright, *Bib. Per....to Ezra*, n.145.

174.1 Israel W. Slotki, note to II Kings 6:32, Soncino.

174.2 cf. note to II K. 8:4, I.W.Slotki, Soncino.

174.3 I.W. Slotki, note to II K. 8:8, concurs.

176.1 Georges Roux, *Ancient Iraq* (England, 1964) Pelican ed. 1969, pp. 270 ff.

177.1 Roux, p.274.

177.2 see Thiele, pp. 91-93.

177.3 Harrison, *Arch...O.T.*, p.78; Luckenbill, I, sect. 816.

178.1 Luckenbill, I, sec. 772. See Roux, p.279.

178.2 Luckenbill, I, sec. 801.

179.1 Luckenbill, I, sec. 770.

179.2 A.T.Olmstead, *History of Assyria* (N.Y., 1923) p. 184.

179.3 Thiele, p.94.

179.4 Luckenbill, I, sec. 770.

180.1 Luckenbill, I, sec. 816.

181.1 Luckenbill, I, sec. 240.

181.2 Thiele includes a copy; also found in Luckenbill.

181.3 Harrison, p.78; Luckenbill, II, sec. 240.

181.4 H.W.F.Saggs, *The Greatness That Was Babylon* (N.Y., 1962) Mentor ed. 1968, p. 121.

182.1 Roux, p. 282; see Luckenbill, II, Secs. 30, 62.

182.2 Harrison, p. 79.

183.1 Harrison, p. 79; Luckenbill, II, sec. 240.

185.1 Harrison, p. 80; Luckenbill, II, sec. 690.

190.1 Speiser, comment to his section 13; NAB note Gen.11: 28.

190.2 *loc. cit.*

191.1 *International Atlas* (Rand McNally, 1969) p. 122.

191.2 *ibid.*, p. 130, 31°N, 38°E.

191.3 Kramer, *Cradle of Civilization*, p. 104; —— *Sumerian Mythology*, rev. ed. (Harper Torchbooks, 1961) pp. 97, 98; Pritchard; Bratton, pp. 26-29.

191.4 Josephus, *Antiq.* I, iii, 5-6; XX, ii, 2; and Whiston's note equating "Xisuthrus" (Ziusudra) with Noah.

191.5 The past well-watered state of **Arabia** is seen in *Earth Photographs from Gemeni III, IV, V* (N.A.S.A. SP 129, 1967) pp. 19, 20, 21, 26, 46, 47, 238, 239; of Algeria pp. 98, 99, 102. In connection with man's habitation see Geoffrey Bibby, *Looking for Dilmun* (N.Y., 1969) especially regarding Thaj, p. 316.

Abercrombie, Thomas J. "The Sword and the Sermon," *National Geographic*, (July 1972) pp. 2-45.

Ackroyd, P.R. and C.F. Evans (eds.). *Cambridge History of the Bible*. London, 1970.

Albright, W.F. *The Biblical Period from Abraham to Ezra*. N.Y., 1949; rev. ed. Harper Torchbooks, 1963.

——. *Bulletin of the American School of Oriental Research*. No. 100 (December 1945) 16-22.

Aldred, Cyril. *Akhenaten, Pharaoh of Egypt: a new study*. New Aspects of Archeology Series, ed. Sir Mortimer Wheeler. N.Y., 1968.

Bakst, Aaron. *Mathematics: Its Magic and Mystery*. Princeton, 1967.

Bibby, Geoffrey. *Looking for Dilmun*. N.Y., 1969.

Bible and Spade, I (Winter 1972) 20.

Bratton, Fred Gladstone. *A History of the Bible*. Boston, 1967.

Breasted, James Henry. *A History of Egypt*. N.Y., 1905; Bantam ed., 1967.

Bright, John. *A History of Israel*. Philadelphia, 1959.

Chase, Mary Ellen. *Life and Language in the Old Testament*. N.Y., 1955.

Chiera, Edward. *They Wrote on Clay*. ed. George G. Cameron. Chicago, 1938; Phoenix ed., 1955.

Cooper, Charles F. "The Ecology of Fire," *Scientific American* CCIV (April 1961) 150-160.

Davis, John D. and Henry S. Gehman. *Westminster Dictionary of the Bible*. Philadelphia, 1944.

Earle, Arthur. "Tile Pattern - New Math Discovery?" *Popular Science Monthly*, CXCV (July 1969) 150-1, 170-2.

Epstein, Isidore. *Judaism*. Baltimore, 1966.

Goldman, S. "Introduction" and commentary to *Samuel*. See 'Soncino'.

Harrison, R.K. *The Archeology of the Old Testament*. N.Y., 1963; Harper Chapelbook ed., 1966.

——. *Old Testament Times*. Grand Rapids, 1970.

Herodotus. *History*. trans. George Rawlinson. ed. Manuel Komroff. Tudor Publ. Co., 1956.

Hogben, Lancelot. *Mathematics for the Million*. rev. ed. N.Y., 1943.

International Atlas. Rand McNally, 1969.

Josephus. *Complete Works*. trans. William Whiston (1737), "Foreword", W.S. LaSor. Grand Rapids, 1960.

——. *Against Apion*. trans. H. St. J. Thackeray. London, 1926, 1961.

Keller, Werner. *The Bible as History*. trans. Wm. Neill. N.Y., 1956.

Keyes, Nelson Beecher. *Story of the Bible World*. C.S. Hammond & Co., 1959.

Kittel, Rudolf. *A History of the Hebrews*. trans. Hope W. Hogg, and E.B. Speirs. II, London, 1896.

Kramer, Samuel Noah. *Cradle of Civilization*. Great Ages of Man Series, Time-Life, 1967.

——. *Sumerian Mythology*. rev. ed., Harper Torchbooks, 1961.

Luckenbill, Daniel David. *Ancient Records of Assyria and Babylon*. 2 vols., Chicago, 1926-27.

Mercer, Samuel A.B. *A Sumero-Babylonian Sign List*. N.Y., 1918.

Montet, Pierre. *Eternal Egypt*. trans. D. Weightman. N.Y., 1968.

——. *Le Drame d'Avaris*. 1940.

——. "Avaris, Pi-Ramses, Tanis," *Syria*. XVII, 1936.

——. *Les Nouvelles fouilles de Tanis*. 1929-33.

Mould, E.W.K. *Essentials of Bible History*. N.Y., 1939.

NASA SP 129. *Earth Photographs From Gemini III, IV, V*. 1967.

Neugebauer, O. *The Exact Sciences in Antiquity*. R.I., 1957.

New Larousse Encyclopedia of Mythology. trans. Richard Aldington and Delano Ames. 1968.

Newby, P.H. "Introduction," *Tales From the Arabian Nights*. a selection by P.H. Newby from *The Arabian Nights' Entertainments*. trans. Sir Richard Burton. N.Y., 1951, 1967.

Olmstead, A.T. *History of Assyria*. N.Y., 1923.

Patterson, John. "The Old Testament World," *The Bible and History*. ed. William Barclay. England, 1968.

Peet, T. Eric. *Egypt and the Old Testament*. Boston, 1923.

Pritchard, James B. (ed.). *Ancient Near Eastern Texts Relating to the Old Testament*. Princeton, 1950-55.

Roux, Georges. *Ancient Iraq*. England, 1964; Pelican ed., 1969.

Saggs, H.W.F. *The Greatness That Was Babylon*. N.Y., 1962; Mentor ed., 1968.

Sarton, George. *A History of Science*. Harvard, 1966.

Schonfield, Hugh J. *A History of Biblical Literature*. N.Y., 1962.

Soncino Books of the Bible. Hebrew text and J.P.S.A. English translation. ed. Rev. Dr. A. Cohen. London: *Chumash*, 1947; *Joshua - Judges*, 1950; *Samuel*, 1951; *Kings I & II*, 1950; *Chronicles I & II*, 1952.

Slotki, Israel W. "Introduction" and comments, *Kings I & II*. see 'Soncino'.

Slotki, Judah J. "Introduction" and comments, *Judges*. see 'Soncino'.

Speiser, E. A. *Genesis.* trans., notes and comments. The Anchor Bible. N.Y., 1964.

Thiele, Edwin R. *The Mysterious Numbers of the Hebrew Kings.* rev. ed., Grand Rapids, 1965.

Vermes, Geza. *The Dead Sea Scrolls in English.* rev. ed., Great Britain, 1965.

Whiston, William. "Dissertation V; Upon the Chronology of Josephus," included in *Complete Works.* see 'Josephus'.

Woolley, Leonard. *The Beginnings of Civilization.* Vol. One, Part II, History of Mankind; Cultural and Scientific Development. UNESCO. Mentor Books, 1965.

Wright, G. Ernest. *Biblical Archeology.* Philadelphia, 1957.

Abbreviations used for translations consulted:

A.V.	Authorized Version (King James).
J.P.S.A.	Jewish Publication Society of America.
LXX	Septuagint.
N.A.B.	New American Bible.
N.W.T.	New World Translation.
R.S.V.	Revised Standard Version.

INDEX of MODERN AUTHORS

INDEX of GREEK WORDS